The Last of the Racetrack Touts

This book is dedicated to the memory of the men who worked in the tip sheet industry on the New Jersey–Florida racing circuit from 1946-1998.

ACKNOWLEDGMENTS

A heartfelt thank you to my wife, Joan, whose love and encouragement throughout the decades have made all of my accomplishments possible.

A special thank you to my editor, Stephanie Darby, whose advice was invaluable in the completion of this work.

Posthumous acknowledgments to Bernard "Rip" McKenna, Israel "Issy" Bornstein, and Robert "Jigger" Higgins, each of whom provided me with anecdotes which are recounted in this story.

CHAPTER 1 – Opening Day, June 11, 1957

The road leading to Monmouth Park was jammed with traffic. As young Billy Mulray awaited the track-bound bus he became anxious, fueled by the knowledge that he would never be able to make his appointment on time. Billy had been promised a summer job selling mutuel tickets at the track, but had been told to be there by 11:30 a.m. It was already quarter after, and the traffic was moving so slowly that Billy wondered if the bus was ever going to come.

Finally, he spotted it inching its way up Oceanport Avenue toward the bus stop. Billy nervously boarded, along with a dozen or so other impatient race goers who desperately wanted to get to the track. The bus was already packed to capacity, so Billy and the others who boarded at his stop had to stand in the aisle.

The atmosphere on board the bus was that of a carnival. The riders, mostly people in their twenties and thirties, laughed and joked as the overloaded bus crawled toward its destination. The air was thick with anticipation, and a sort of electricity—a certain camaraderie—made the trip exhilarating.

At 11:52 the bus finally pulled up in front of the racetrack. The riders poured out of the bus and joined the rush of the racing fans making their way toward the entrance. There were people everywhere, all excited and trying to get into the track.

Billy located the employee gate and went inside to find the head of mutuels. He had to battle throngs of people at every step, but finally reached the counter and asked to see the manager. After a few minutes, a heavy, middle aged, balding man who seemed flustered and in a rush, appeared across the counter in front of Billy.

Billy had to speak up so he could be heard above the hum of the crowd.

"Mr. James? I'm Billy Mulray. My dad told me to report to you for a job selling tickets."

The man called out across the counter, "I'm sorry son, but it's too late for me to do anything for ya today. You're gonna have to get here earlier. Come back tomorrow before 11:30 and I'll see what I can do." Without waiting for a response, Mr. James turned and briskly walked off in the opposite direction.

A couple of windows down, a man had been getting several rolls of coins from a cashier and had heard the exchange between Billy and the mutuel manager. The man, who was slim, short, in his mid fifties and well dressed with a black and white Houndstooth jacket and a grey wool fedora, approached Billy as he stood pondering his next move.

"You lookin' for a job, kid?"

"Well, I have one, I think. I'm supposed to sell tickets but I got here too late today. I guess I'll have to start tomorrow."

The man chuckled. "Punchin' tickets pays about ten bucks a day. I can give ya a job that pays five, sometimes ten times that. Ya interested?"

Billy immediately thought that his offer was too good to be true.

"What's the catch?" he asked suspiciously.

"Well," the man said, pointing at Billy, "the catch is that you have to be thick skinned. You have to be bold and you have to be capable of competin' against some of the best in the business. If you can do all that, you can make money in my game."

"And which game is that?"

"Tip sheets!" the man said with a broad smile, his eyes twinkling. "I'm a tout!"

Billy had no idea what the man was talking about. He had never been to a racetrack before today and didn't have the slightest inkling what a tip sheet—or a tout—was.

"Okay, okay," Billy said. "I don't know what you mean by 'tip sheets' or 'touts' or anything. Tell me what I'd have to do."

The man hadn't realized that he was dealing with such a total novice. "Look, kid. I'm short handed. I need a man to put on the stand to sell my sheets. I really don't have the time to explain everything right now."

Billy, thoroughly confused and still skeptical, shook his head and began to walk away. The man placed his hand on Billy's arm to halt his retreat, then reached into the top pocket of his Houndstooth jacket and produced a $20 bill, holding it up in front of Billy's face.

"Just give it a try. If you don't like it, keep the twenty. No questions asked."

Billy stared at the bill for a moment, then took the money out of the man's hand.

"Great!" the man said. "My name is Issy. I run the *Lawton* sheet here."

Issy extended his hand and Billy, still not certain of what he had agreed to, shook it tentatively.

"I'm Billy. Billy Mulray."

"Oh, an Irishman, huh? Well, you'll fit in with a lot of the guys on the line!" Issy said.

"The line?"

"Yeah. It's where we sell the tip sheets. C'mon, follow me!"

Issy started across the crowded floor of the clubhouse with Billy following closely behind. They bumped into a number of the fans as they made their way outside and around the red brick wall that led to the grandstand side of the racetrack. Although Billy was tall, lean, and possessed an athlete's physique, he had difficulty keeping up with Issy, who walked quickly despite having a noticeable limp in his right leg.

Billy had never seen so many people in one place at the same time. Everywhere he looked there were fans of all ages. Men in suits sporting carnations in their lapels and women wearing colorful dresses and wide, ornate hats filled the clubhouse.

Issy and Billy maneuvered through the crowd and toward the grandstand. As they drew nearer, Billy could make out some sort of commotion coming from a small building near the steps that led into the racetrack. There was shouting coming from the spot, and there appeared to be a horde of people gathering. Billy, still confused about the whole situation, continued to follow Issy as he led him directly for it.

The small building became clearer to Billy as he got closer. It looked like a long booth, with a roof but open sides and an open front and back. There was a row of men standing behind a counter inside it, and all of them were shouting and waving colored sheets of paper.

"I got the day-leeeee double!" one man barked, waving a red, white, and blue sheet.

Another, brandishing a narrow, white card with red printing, shouted, "A winning card, a winning day! *Longshot Riley* heah!"

Yet another asked, "What do you want? Winnahs, or po-ropaganda!?" as he furiously flagged a gold sheet in front of him.

"Another big day, the old, reliable *Jack*!" was the pitch of a man holding up a folded green sheet.

The men were loud and animated, and the crowd pushed close to the stand and snapped up the sheets almost as fast as they could dispense them. It seemed to Billy as if everyone entering the track bought at least one of the sheets, and some bought two or three. The men had fistfuls of bills and huge piles of coins on the stand in front of them, and it occurred to Billy that perhaps Issy had been telling him the truth. Maybe he could earn $50 a day if he could duplicate the business that the men on the stand were generating.

Issy worked his way around the rear of the stand as Billy followed. There was an empty space in the line, and a huge stack of orange sheets lay on the counter.

"Okay," Issy shouted to Billy so he could be heard over the roar of activity. "Get in there and hustle. The sheets are half a smash apiece. You get twenty cents for every copy you sell."

"Umm, what's a 'half a smash'?" Billy asked sheepishly.

One of the men in the stand, a tall fellow with bushy brown hair, turned and barked, "Jesus Christ, Issy! What are you doin' bringin' some greenhorn around here? This ain't no place for some fuckin' schoolboy!"

Issy ignored the man and answered Billy. "That's half a buck. Fifty cents." Then Issy leaned toward Billy and lowered his voice. "Don't let that guy bother you. He's not all that bad once you get to know him."

Billy was having second thoughts about the whole endeavor. Having come from a well-heeled, educated family, he had never done anything like this before. The men on the line seemed like carnival barkers or snake oil salesman, and he was certain that his parents would disapprove if they ever found out.

There were nearly a dozen of them, all in their thirties, with the exception of a tall, hulking young man on the end who appeared to be in his early twenties. They were a loud and boisterous crew, and they prodded each other with verbal barbs as they went about vending the sheets.

Issy motioned toward the orange sheets on the stand. "Go on, kid, give it a try. You'll never know if you can do it or not unless you try it."

Issy's suggestion sounded an awful lot like a challenge. Billy peered at the stack of sheets, looked at Issy, then squeezed his way between the vendors on either side and up to the counter. He glanced over his shoulder but Issy had already departed, limping toward the far end of the racetrack at a rapid pace.

Billy looked at the sea of people that were collected at the front of the booth and nearly panicked. He really had no idea of what he was supposed to be doing except selling the orange sheets for fifty cents apiece. Observing the other men and trying to get a feel for what they were doing, he quickly realized that they all held the sheet in one hand where people could see it, then delivered a pitch.

Billy took one of the orange sheets from the stack, held it up high, and shook it.

"Over here, over here," he said half-heartedly.

The men on either side of him, a rotund man with a crewcut on his right and the tall fellow with shaggy hair on his left, stopped in unison, looked at each other and howled with laughter.

"Holy shit!" the tall man chortled. "Welcome to Ted Mack's amateur hour!"

Billy was appalled. The rudeness of the men was something he had never before encountered to that degree. His instinct was to walk off the stand immediately but his competitive spirit, and pride, would not let him. He was now determined to show these boors that he was up to the task.

The next couple of hours were the longest Billy had ever experienced. Time and time again, customers would step up to Billy, but invariably one of the other hustlers would lure them away and sell them their sheet.

"You don't want that orange sheet. C'mere and let me mark you a winner," was the usual yarn.

The men on the line were cold and indifferent to Billy, ignoring him while fraternizing amongst themselves. They joked with each other while hustling the sheets, and most of them would occasionally sneak a sip of beer from cans they hid beneath the counter.

Check out time arrived at 2:15 p.m. One by one, the vendors were visited by men who collected huge sums of cash. Some used money bags, others pillow cases, and most of them had a nearly full sack when they left.

Finally, Issy came by to collect from Billy. Despite his best efforts, Billy had only been able to sell 34 sheets.

"Oh, my," Issy said. "They really did a number on ya, didn't they?"

Billy looked down and slowly nodded.

"Well, tomorrow's another day!" Issy chirped. "Come back and get 'em tomorrow!"

Billy held out the money for Issy.

"Keep it, I insist," Issy said with a smile.

Billy felt worse than ever. Not because of how he had been treated by the others, but because he felt like he had let Issy down. He thanked Issy and put the money in his pants pocket.

"Now come on over here with me and we'll talk," Issy said.

Billy left the stand and walked around the front to join Issy. The crowd had dissipated considerably by then, and the two were able to find a spot on the bench under a tree that faced the tip sheet stand.

Issy put his hand on Billy's shoulder. "Don't let it get ya down. This was only the first day and it was kinda rough. It should've been expected."

Billy lowered his head and listened as Issy continued, "You're gonna get better with each day. Just don't let those fellas over there run all over ya. Show 'em that you can dish it out as good as the next guy."

Billy looked at the men on the stand.

Issy leaned back against the bench and glanced in the direction of the stand as he began to mentor Billy. "You have to fight fire with fire," Issy instructed. "Those guys are pros. They know all the angles. You have to figure out how they do it, then do 'em one better." Then Issy turned to Billy and said, "Don't be afraid to use your pencil, boy. Call the people over and tell 'em you're gonna give 'em somethin' good. Then, mark a couple of the top horses on the sheet and stuff it in their hand before they know what hit 'em. Nine times out of ten they'll throw a couple of quarters at ya and be on their way."

"Well, that's the thing, Issy. I'm not even sure what it is I'm supposed to be selling over there."

Issy chuckled at the newcomer's naiveté. "The sheets are just the picks for the day. They have the horses that we recommend people bet on," Issy said. "The guys—like me—who pick the horses are called handicappers. Our sheets are called tip sheets, or tip cards. They give the average fella who comes in here a fightin' chance at cashin' some tickets. The guys who sell—like you—are known as hustlers. Some people refer to the lot of us as 'touts'."

Billy felt relieved. At least now he finally knew what it was he was selling on that orange piece of paper.

Issy and Billy sat surveying the men on the stand across from them. They were close enough to see them, but far enough away that nobody on the stand could hear their conversation.

Issy reached into a side pocket of his jacket and took out a shiny red apple. He took a pen knife out of the other pocket and began to peel the fruit.

"I'm gonna fill ya in on the guys on the line," Issy said. "The fat guy on the end with the crew cut, the one that was on your right today, that's Curly. Some of the guys here gave him that nickname on account of his resemblance to Curly from the Three Stooges. Anyway, best as anyone can tell, he came here from California a few years ago when things must've gotten too hot for him out there. Nobody knows exactly what he did, but the rumor I heard is that he was fond of goin' to Tijuana for the young girls, you know, the 14 or 15 year-old kind. I was told he made the mistake of bringin' one back over the border. That kinda stuff may fly in Mexico, but it sure don't here in the states. Anyway, the general feelin' is that he was in trouble with the law and had to flee."

Billy listened intently as Issy spoke.

"Now, the guy next to him—that was the guy on your left today—he's Rip McKenna," Issy said. "He's a sharpie from Philadelphia. He got here years ago when the bookie joint he worked for on Market Street got raided. Story is that he grabbed a couple thou' when the cops broke in, ran out the back door and skipped town on the double. The guys he worked for must've never figured out he got away with the dough, 'cause they'd have tracked him down and, well, let's just say they're not the kind of guys you steal from."

Young Billy was intrigued. "What about the others?" he asked.

"Okay. The little bald guy next to Rip is Onion Joe," Issy continued. "He was an onion farmer in upstate New York. Scoop on him is that he woke up one mornin', left the farm and drove to Saratoga, and never went back. Never called, never wrote, never went back. Left a wife and four kids. He's a little on the loony side, if ya ask me."

"Then ya have the Alligator. What a piece of work," Issy chuckled. "He's an ex-jockey. Never had any success to speak of, and quit a few years ago. There ain't no scam too big or too bold for him to try. Be careful of him. Even as hustlers go, he's a bad egg."

9

Billy studied the Alligator from afar. He was a short, thin man with a deep tan, and wore a white panama hat with a wide black band. He constantly had a cigar clenched in his teeth, which seemed like a prop because no smoke ever seemed to emanate from it.

"Why do they call him 'the Alligator'?" Billy asked.

"Ever see the teeth on an alligator? That guy has chewed up and spit out so many people that the comparison is a natural."

"Let's see," Issy continued. "The guy with the beer gut and red face next to the Alligator is Jigger Higgins. He was a bartender in Providence and somehow landed a job tendin' bar in the Republican Club in Washington. He served all sorts of senators, congressmen, you name it. He got to see some of the most powerful men in the world paralyzed drunk, sayin' all sorts of things. Problem was, everybody in Jigger's whole family are Democrats. Once they found out that he was a registered donkey, out he went a'flyin'!"

Issy finished peeling the apple, cut a slice and offered it to Billy. He declined.

"That tall, thin guy with slicked back hair next to Jigger is Bernardo." Issy said. "Most of the guys on the line are either Jews or Irish. Bernardo is our only Italiano," Issy chuckled. "He got here by way of college, believe it or not. He graduated but couldn't find a job. Well, Burke—the guy who owns the red, white, and blue sheet—needed help and went into the unemployment office where Bernardo was in line to get a check. Burke calls out, 'anybody here know how to type?' Bernardo is the only one who raises his hand. So Burke says to Bernardo, 'Come with me. You got a job.' And that's how Bernardo wound up hustlin' sheets. He's a cultured kinda guy. Likes Broadway plays and such. Reads novels. Just last week he went up to New York to do some Italian stuff—see Rigoletto at the opera and have dinner at Grotta Azzurra in Little Italy. Not a bad guy, just a little too refined for this crowd."

"Cockeye Sol is next to Bernardo. He's originally from Brooklyn. Used to hang around at Belmont and Jamaica bettin' horses until one day somebody gave him a job hustlin'. They needed some guys to come here when this place opened years back, and Sol was one of 'em. Been comin' here every summer since. He's one of the cheapest buggers I've ever come across. He wouldn't give ya ice in the winter or the sweat off his balls in the summer."

"Bullet Bob comes after Cockeye," Issy said. "The word on him is that he was in the Army in Korea and got discharged when he got shot in the rear end by one of his own men. That's how he got the nickname 'Bullet'."

"The wild-haired guy next to Bullet Bob is called Crazy Tommy. He's a real kookamoola. No joke, kid. He's been in and out of the nut house and even gets a check from the government every month for bein' a lunatic."

Billy continued to absorb the information with great interest, and tried not to stare as Issy continued down the line.

"Next to Crazy Tommy, the guy with half his left arm missin', is Wingy. He's another veteran, but from World War II, not Korea. Durin' the D-day invasion, a mortar round went off near where he was in a foxhole and the shrapnel mangled his arm so bad that the doctors had to take it off a little above the elbow. The blast killed the guy next to him, so, all things considered, he's lucky."

"Last, but not least," Issy said, "we have Big Mike on the end. He's probably only a couple o' years older than you. Another Irish guy from Providence. He's a real operator. Used to deal with gaff up around Boston 'til things went sour."

"What's gaff?" Billy asked.

"Fake watches, fake jewelry, that sort of thing. You can only do that for so long before ya have a lotta people lookin' for ya."

Billy looked across and studied Big Mike. He thought to himself that whoever had given him the moniker "Big Mike" had been right on the money. Mike was about 6'4" and probably 250 pounds if he weighed an ounce. He projected an intimidating presence which was augmented by a deep, gravelly voice that seemed to send shock waves when he bellowed his tip sheet pitch. Big Mike was a chain smoker, and Billy watched him take one huge drag after another, exhaling a series of billowing clouds of smoke.

Issy broke Billy's concentration. "Well, I'm off," he said. "Come on back tomorrow and give 'em hell! Okay?"

Billy had already made up his mind. "Sure will. Where do you want me to meet you?"

"The other side of Oceanport Ave. is where we all print the sheets. Right past the railroad tracks. You'll see the trucks in the back yards along there. Come by about ten o'clock or so."

"'kay, Issy," Billy said. "And thanks for everything today."

Issy slapped Billy on the shoulder and grinned. "Don't mention it. You don't realize it now, but you've stumbled onto paradise. See ya tomorrow!"

Billy continued to sit under the tree as Issy limped toward the tip sheet stand. The old man stopped in front of Rip and chatted with him for a couple of minutes before hobbling off toward the end of the grandstand.

Rip pushed his remaining sheets to Onion Joe. He reached under the counter for a beer, then walked around the stand and toward Billy.

"So, Issy tells me you're Irish," Rip said, drawing closer.

"Yeah. My dad and mom are both Irish."

Rip took a long drink from the can of beer, then continued to interrogate Billy.

"Where did your people come from?"

"County Cork, I think."

"You think!" Rip shouted. "What kinda Irishman worth his salt doesn't know where his people came from?"

Billy shrugged.

"Are you a pape?" Rip asked.

Billy stared quizzically at Rip. "A pape? What's a pape?"

"A Catholic, A CATHOLIC!" Rip roared.

Billy was becoming annoyed at Rip's grilling. He barely knew this man, and already Rip was asking questions that Billy thought to be quite personal.

"Yes. Does it make a difference?"

"Of course!" Rip said. "Nothin' worse than a damned blackleg Irishman! Half the guys around this place are Irish. Not a blackleg in the bunch."

Billy scowled and asked, "What's a blackleg?"

"A protestant! Haven't you ever heard of William of Orange? Jesus Christ! Do you know anything?" Rip barked.

"Well, I know that asking a stranger these sorts of questions is bad manners!"

Rip smiled and extended his hand for Billy to shake.

"Don't get excited," Rip said. "I don't mean anything by it. Besides, us Irish have to stick together."

Billy half-heartedly shook Rip's hand, not sure yet whether this guy could be trusted or even if he should be talking to him.

Rip finished his beer and tossed the empty in a nearby trash can. "C'mon. Let's go inside and I'll introduce ya to some of the people around here."

Reasoning that he could make a hasty retreat if need be, Billy agreed to accompany him. "Okay, but I can't stay long," he said.

Rip led Billy through the passage to the clubhouse bar and entered with the newcomer close behind. Everywhere there were racing fans, drinking, laughing, chatting with one another, and that spirit of camaraderie—the kind he had observed on the bus that morning—charged the atmosphere of the barroom.

Rip forced his way through the crowd and got his arm onto the bar where the barmaid, a tall, shapely, attractive blonde in her late twenties, was trying to keep up with the orders. She glanced up and saw Rip working his way to the forefront.

"Rip!" she shouted, displaying a broad, dazzling smile. "I was wondering when you'd finally show up!"

Rip squeezed past the fans surrounding the bar, and the barmaid temporarily stopped pouring drinks and leaned over to embrace and kiss him.

"My god, I've missed you!" the barmaid said, holding Rip's smiling face in her hands.

"Reenie, honey, there's barely a day that went by that I didn't think of you."

"Ha!" Reenie said. "You tell that to a different girl at every track you go to, I'm sure. But I still love ya!"

Rip reached back, grabbed Billy's shirt and pulled him through the crowd to the bar.

"Meet Billy Mulray," Rip said. "He's the new kid on the block. A good Irish lad! Sellin' sheets for Issy."

"Hi, Billy. Nice to meet ya," Reenie said as she drew a beer from the tap at the bar.

"Same here, ma'am," Billy said, returning Reenie's smile.

"Oh, lord, just call me Reenie. You're making me out to be an old maid or something, calling me ma'am!"

Rip held up two fingers and within seconds, Reenie put two large cups of beer on the bar in front of Rip. He handed one to Billy.

"Um, I'm not old enough to... to drink yet," Billy said. "I'm only twenty."

"Well, I'd have gotten ya chocolate milk, but they just ran out," Rip chuckled. "Go on. Take it!"

Billy took the cup of beer and stood awkwardly as Rip took a long drink from his.

"C'mon, kid," Rip chided Billy. "Ya can't have another until ya finish that one!"

Billy slowly raised the cup to his lips and took a short sip. The beer was ice cold and actually tasted good after being on the stand for the past couple of hours with nothing to drink.

"So," Rip said as he finished his beer and pushed the empty cup in Reenie's direction, "what brings a young guy like you to the racetrack?"

"Well, my need for a summer job," Billy replied, taking another sip of the cold brew. "I recently finished my second year in college, and I need to make some money for expenses. I was supposed to sell tickets, but got here too late today. That's when I met Issy."

"Oh, a college boy, huh? Which school?" Rip asked.

"I go to Rutgers," Billy said. "It's our state college in New Brunswick."

"How are your grades? Any good?"

"Well, fairly good. I have a little better than B average so far."

"You have a major? What do ya want to do when you get out?"

"Yeah. I'm a history major," Billy said. "I'm not really sure what I want to be. I guess I'd like to teach, eventually. Or, I was thinking of maybe going to law school when I graduate."

"A lawyer, huh?" Rip laughed. "Good. Most of the hustlers around here can use a mouthpiece from time to time! I'm sure ya can meet a lot of future clients around this place! Just make sure you get paid in advance!"

Reenie placed Rip's refill on the bar in front of him and, without hesitation, he picked up the cup and took a gulp.

"You look like a ballplayer," Rip said. "Play any sports?"

"Yes. I'm on the varsity baseball team. I catch most of the time, but play the outfield once in a while, too," Billy said.

"Can ya hit?"

"Pretty good. I batted .311 this season—my first on varsity."

Rip and Billy continued to chat. Before long, several races had passed, and Rip had poured down three beers before Billy was able to finish his first. Reenie placed yet another beer on the bar in front of Rip, and as he lifted it to his lips, his eyes caught a man who was getting a drink at the other end of the bar. Rip crouched somewhat, hiding behind Billy and peering over his shoulder at the man. He quickly glanced at the racing program, as if looking for some sort of clue.

"Just look at me!" Rip instructed Billy in a voice barely above a whisper. "Now turn around slow, and look at the end of the bar. See that guy with the white jacket gettin' a drink?"

Billy looked over his shoulder at the man. "Yeah. What about him?"

Rip pulled out his wallet, removed ten $100 bills and shoved the wad into Billy's hand. "Now that guy is gonna go to the $50 window," Rip said. "He's gonna bet either the six or the seven. I want you to follow him and find out what he bets. Whatever he bets, you bet a grand on it, too. Whatever ya do, don't let him know you're followin' him!"

Billy began to tremble as he realized he held $1,000 in his hand. He had never been in control of $100 in his life, let alone $1,000. "But, I don't know how to bet," he said.

"Find out what number he bets, then tell the clerk you want $1,000 to win on it! Give him the money, and he'll give you twenty $50 win tickets! There he goes! Now, follow him!"

Billy's heart was pounding and his palms were sweating as he held the money in his hand like a vise. He tried to inconspicuously follow the man as he made his way toward the betting window.

Billy got in line behind the man and tried to stay close as he leaned into the window to make his bet. He strained to hear the number the man asked for, but could not make it out above the hum of the crowd.

"One minute to post!" the track announcer called out.

The man scooped up his tickets, brushed past Billy and disappeared into the crowd. Billy was in a bind now; he had not heard the number the stranger had bet, and it was nearly post time.

Billy stepped up to the window and asked the clerk, "What number did the man in the white jacket bet?"

15

"I don't remember," the ticket seller smirked.

Billy could see the horses approaching the starting gate. In a few seconds, it would be too late to make the bet for Rip.

Billy reached inside his shirt pocket and pulled out the $20 bill that Issy had given him earlier. He held it up in front of the clerk and asked, "How about now? Does this do anything to improve your memory?"

"Sure does," the clerk grinned as he grabbed the bill. "He bet the seven horse. All win tickets. No place or show."

Billy tossed Rip's money on the counter in front of the clerk. "Give me $1,000 to win on the seven! Hurry up!"

The clerk began to punch the tickets and as the last one shot out of the mutuel machine, the bell rang.

"And they're off!" shouted the announcer.

Billy ran back into the bar and pushed the tickets into Rip's hand. "Okay, good job!" Rip said. "Now let's go on outside and see if this rodent can get the money!"

Rip and Billy shoved their way through the crowd and out to the front of the racetrack. The field had already entered the first turn by the time they got into position to watch the race.

"What's the name of your horse," Billy asked excitedly.

Rip glanced at his program. "Romantic Blonde."

"C'mon, Romantic Blonde!" Billy shouted. "Run!"

Rip chuckled. "Save your breath. They have a long way to go and she hasn't even started to make her move yet!"

The horses raced down the far side of the track and into the final turn, and Romantic Blonde had hardly been mentioned by the announcer. Billy was sure that Rip had made a big mistake by betting the same horse as the man in the white jacket.

But, just as Billy became convinced that it was a lost cause, the announcer roared, "And on the far outside, here comes Romantic Blonde with a rush!"

Rip grabbed Billy by the shoulder and began to shake him as his eyes remained glued to the horses racing down the homestretch.

"Now!" Rip yelled as he shook Billy. "Root for her now!"

"C'mon, Romantic Blonde! You can do it! Don't quit now, girl!" the two shouted as the horses hit the wire for the finish.

"Oh! That's far too close to call!" the announcer bellowed. "We're going to need a photo to separate them!"

Rip coolly counted his tickets as the photo finish was being developed.

"I hope she got there. I saved up a grand for a car. But I saw a brand new Corvette in the showroom this mornin'. A beaut, but it cost $4,600. I knew I'd have to make a big bet or I'd never get the cash to buy it. This photo means the difference between havin' to walk and ridin' in style."

After what seemed like an eternity, the photo finish light on the odds board was removed, and the numbers posted.

"And the winner in a tight photo, number seven, Romantic Blonde!" the announcer chimed.

"YEEEES!" Rip shouted.

"Way to go, Rip!" Billy smiled, shaking Rip's hand.

"Let's go collect!"

Rip and Billy went back inside the track and walked up to the $50 win, place, and show cashier. Rip surrendered his tickets and calmly stood at the window as the man dealt him a stack of forty eight crisp $100 bills.

"She paid $9.60," Rip said. "That gives me $200 more than I need for the car. Here."

He handed two of the $100 bills to Billy.

"Oh, I couldn't take that," Billy said.

"Don't be a sap. I just made a big score. The $200 is your share for gettin' the tickets for me."

Billy, still shaking from the excitement of the race, took the bills from Rip's hand.

"Thank you," Billy whispered. "This is the most money I've ever had in my life."

"No, problem," Rip chuckled. "There's plenty more to be made around this place, you'll see!"

In unison, Rip and Billy took their wallets out and tucked away their bounty. Rip nodded his head in the direction of the bar and Billy followed him as he returned to the spot in front of Reenie.

"How'd ya make out, Rip?" Reenie asked as she poured two fresh beers.

Rip winked at Reenie and smiled. "Real good, honey, real good. Made a major score. That gives me an idea."

Rip reached inside his pocket and produced a big wad of cash. He peeled off a pair of $20 dollar bills and laid them on the bar in front of Reenie.

"You know what tonight is, right?" Rip asked.

Reenie finished pouring the beers and placed them on the bar in front of Rip. "I think so. You guys having your regular opening day bash tonight?"

"Of course, of course!" Rip said. "What would openin' day be without a party at our place? Ya comin'?"

"You know I'll be there!" Reenie smiled.

"'Atta girl!" Rip said. "I want ya to take these Jacksons and buy a new outfit for tonight. Somethin' that's gonna make the guys go crazy and the girls green with envy."

"Will do," Reenie giggled as she stuffed the bills inside her bra.

Now that the episode was over, Billy was curious how it had all come to pass.

"How did you know to bet the same horse as the guy in the white jacket?" Billy asked.

Rip took a long drink from his beer then whispered, "I've been tailin' that guy for years. He's a jockey agent—a guy who books mounts for riders. He has two that he represents, that's how I knew he was either gonna bet the six or the seven. His jockeys were ridin' those two horses. He's a big bettor when he thinks he has an edge, and he usually wins."

The barroom door opened and several of the tip sheet hustlers shuffled in. They were led by Bernardo, who was carrying a bottle of wine in his hand.

Rip reached into his pocket, peeled off more bills from his wad of cash and threw them on the bar. "Give these beggars a drink on me," he instructed, and Reenie immediately began to pour drinks for the group.

Bernardo placed the bottle of wine on the bar next to Rip.

"What are ya doin' now, Bernardo? Sellin' dago wine door to door?" Rip laughed.

"Very funny," Bernardo said. "No, actually I came to see if you want in on a little side wager, of sorts. I was reading in a magazine about a platoon of doughboys from World War I who made a pact when they were in France. Seems they got ahold of a bottle of wine and vowed that it would go to the last man left alive. Those who are still living meet every year in the same place and will continue until there is only one left. The last man standing gets to open the wine. We're going to do the same."

"Is that right?" Rip said. "I'll bet half of the poor bastards died of syph from those French whores before they were even able to get out of the place! I hope the same doesn't happen to us!"

The barroom erupted with laughter.

Rip picked up the bottle and began to read the label. "Who's in?"

Bernardo pointed at the men as he called out their names. "Big Mike, Jigger, the Alligator, Wingy, and me. Want in?"

"Sure, why not?" Rip said. "How much?"

"Five bucks a man. I already asked the young assistant in admissions, Ronek, to hold the bottle for us. He's likely to be around for a while."

Rip once again reached into his pocket for money. He rifled through the cash and flung a $10 bill at Bernardo. "That's for the two of us," Rip said. "Me and the kid here. We're in."

Bernardo collected the bill and placed it in his shirt pocket. "Okay, we're all set then."

Bernardo then lifted his beer high, and the hustlers at the bar did the same. "To the last man standing!" he toasted. The salutation was followed by a chorus of "hear, hear," from the men, who chugged the cold beer in affirmation.

After a few minutes, the group of hustlers began to disperse, until only Rip and Billy remained at the bar. Rip downed the rest of his beer and turned to Billy. "Well, let's go. Time to pick up those wheels I was talkin' about!"

Rip led Billy down the steps of the clubhouse to the valet area where they hailed a cab. Within minutes, the cab delivered them to the nearest Chevrolet dealership, where Rip had inspected the Corvette that very morning. Rip tossed the cabbie a $5 bill for the seventy five cent fare, saluted the man and said, "Keep the change, general."

Rip and Billy entered the building and, after a short discussion with a salesman, Rip handed over $4,600 cash, then signed a couple of documents. Following a quick wash and installation of temporary plates, the shiny, two-tone Venetian Red and white Corvette convertible was ready to go.

"Hop in, kid," Rip said with a big smile. "Let's see what this jalopy can do!"

Billy had never been close to, let alone ridden in, such a magnificent automobile. He stood awestruck for a moment, then slid into the bucket seat on the passenger's side.

"What a machine *this* is!" Rip said, as he turned the ignition and the engine sprang to life. "Ever rode in one of these?"

"Heck no," Billy replied as he quickly glanced about the interior of the car. "I mean, I've seen them on the road every once in a while, but I sure have never been inside one!"

"Well, then you're in for a treat!" Rip said as he drove the Corvette out of the lot and roared down the roadway.

Rip began to fill Billy in on the details of the car as he seamlessly shifted gears and the Corvette picked up speed.

"This baby is *loaded*. Ya know, you don't just find one on the lot everyday. Most 'vettes are custom ordered, and the few that dealers have in inventory have all the options."

Rip had to raise his voice to be heard above the engine's roar as the Corvette accelerated. "Four on the floor with a 283 cubic inch, 283 horse V-8 under the hood! Heater, radio, power windows, power foldin' top and whitewall tires! Man, nothin' can top this honey!"

The cool breeze riffled through Rip's and Billy's hair as they drove across town and down along Ocean Avenue. Billy had never experienced the exhilaration that he felt as they soared along the coastline, inhaling the clean salt air and watching the waves break along the shore.

Finally, Rip pulled into the parking lot of a big seashore restaurant and drove up to the valet parking entrance. "Time for dinner. This is one of the best seafood joints on the shore. I eat here all the time when I'm in town."

Rip and Billy entered through the huge, ornate, wooden doors that led to the restaurant and walked up to the podium where the maître d' awaited.

"Mr. McKenna, how nice to see you again!" the maître d' smiled as he greeted Rip. "The usual accommodations will be satisfactory, I trust?"

Rip covertly pulled out his stash of bills, peeled off a $10 note, and pushed it in the maître d''s palm. "Nice to see you again, too, Henry. Yes, you know what I'm lookin' for."

Henry led them through the dining room to a table near a window that overlooked the ocean. "Enjoy your dinner, gentlemen. If you need anything, do not hesitate to ask."

"Well, there is one thing, Henry," Rip grinned.

"Yes, Mr. McKenna," Henry said. "I will make certain that she is your server for the evening."

Rip winked at Henry, then turned toward Billy. "Ya like shrimp?"

"Well, yes, why?"

"'cause they make the best shrimp cocktail in the world right here. We'll get us a couple of those as an appetizer. Half a dozen of the biggest prawns you ever saw, in a special cocktail sauce. Absolutely delicious!"

"Um, I don't know, Rip," Billy said nervously.

"Hey, don't worry about the tab. Get whatever ya want. I made a score today and you helped, don't ya remember? Someday you'll make a score and you can treat me. That's the way it works here."

Billy was impressed by Rip's generosity. "Okay, thanks. Hopefully, I'll be able to return the favor someday."

Rip glared into Billy's eyes and said, "You bet your ass you will, boy. One thing that nobody likes is a deadbeat. You're not a goddam deadbeat, are ya?"

Billy was taken aback by Rip's question. "Uh, no, of course not!" Billy blurted out in his most serious tone.

Rip reached across the table, grabbed Billy's shoulder and shook him as he roared with laughter. "Take it easy, kid. I'm only yankin' your chain. Where's your Irish sense of humor?"

Billy, realizing that he had simply become the brunt of one of Rip's jokes, chuckled in relief.

As their laughter subsided, the server appeared at the table. The young lady was stunningly beautiful—a tall, voluptuous woman in her mid-twenties with long, jet black hair and olive skin—and Rip's attention immediately turned to her.

"Hello, Kerra. My goodness, you're more lovely than ever," Rip said as he lifted her hand and kissed it.

"Oh, Mr. McKenna," Kerra replied with a soft smile. "You're sweet. How have you been?"

21

"Fine, sweetheart. And please, call me Rip. After all this time, you shouldn't be so formal. Billy, Kerra... Kerra, Billy."

Kerra turned to Billy and smiled. "So nice to meet you, Billy. Do you work with Mr. McKenna?"

Billy was intimidated by Kerra's beauty and paused prior to responding. "Um... yes... well, not exactly," he stammered.

Rip, upon seeing how flustered Billy had become, came to his aid. "He just started today, Kerra. He's gonna be workin' with Issy this summer."

"Excellent," Kerra said. "Mr. Bornstein is a very nice man."

Rip ordered the shrimp cocktails and a double Beefeater martini, and studied Kerra's form as she walked away. "That is one special woman," he sighed, as she disappeared into the kitchen. "If a guy was ever gonna settle down, she would be everything a man could want."

Rip snapped out of his fog and changed the subject abruptly. "So, Issy told you about all of us. What do you know about Issy?" Rip asked.

"Well, nothing really."

"Okay, then I'll fill ya in," Rip said. "Issy... well, Issy is a real sweetheart. He'd give ya the shirt off his back. There's barely a person who's met him that doesn't love him."

"Yes, I just met him and he's been really nice to me. He seems to like me, too."

"Oh, no doubt," Rip said. "Issy likes almost everybody. If Issy doesn't like you, then ya have to be a really lousy human bein'."

Kerra returned to the table and placed the martini in front of Rip. "Why, thank you, dear," he said, exchanging smiles with her.

Rip waited for Kerra to leave and, once she was out of earshot, he pointed to the mixture and said, "See this drink?"

"Yes. What about it?"

"If you can ever get a broad to drink three of these, you're home free, my boy! These things are pure booze... gin, vermouth, that's *all*."

Billy watched as Rip lifted the glass and took a long gulp. It had already become evident that he was very fond of alcohol, and Billy couldn't help but wonder to himself when, or if, Rip's consumption was going to slow down.

Rip lowered the glass and resumed the conversation. "Okay, where were we? Oh yeah, Issy. Not only one of the best people you're ever gonna meet, but one of the best handicappers in the game. That orange sheet you're sellin' wouldn't be worth a bagful of assholes if it wasn't for Issy. He's been pickin' winners here for years. Single handedly turned *Lawton* into the biggest seller at Monmouth."

Billy was still trying to grasp the intricacies of the tip sheet business, but he was certain that Issy's track record would come in handy as a selling point.

Rip took another gulp of his drink, then continued. "But, you shouldn't think Issy was born a tout. Nope. He's no different from the rest of us. He has a story too."

Billy put his elbows on the table, leaned toward Rip and asked, "So what *is* his story?"

"Well, you wouldn't know it to look at him now, but Issy was once one of the best pool shooters in the world," Rip said. "Learned in Baltimore in the 20s and played against some of the best. Beat most of 'em, too. There was one guy he could never beat, though. Guy's name was Greenleaf. Issy played him for the world's championship a couple of times, but couldn't beat him. Funny thing. If not for that one guy, Issy probably would have just kept playin' pool for a livin'. They even had a nickname for him. They called him 'Hoppy' because of his limp."

"Well, what happened?" Billy asked. "How did he go from playing championship pool to selling tip sheets?"

"Apparently, there wasn't much money in tournament pool durin' that time. But Issy found out that he could make a comfortable livin' hustlin' unsuspectin' amateurs, so that's what he turned to. He took chumps for their money all over the east coast and as far out as St. Louis and Chicago. Worked with a set up guy, then he'd mop up."

"So, how did he wind up in this line of work?" Billy pressed.

"Well, I'm gettin' to it. Anyway, Issy took suckers in New York, Boston, Philly, Cleveland, you name it. Then one day in Detroit, he was leavin' a pool hall after fleecin' a couple o' marks, and who does he pass in the street but one of the all-time great hustlers, New York Fats. Issy always likes to tell how he could beat Fats anytime he wanted. Anyway, Fats recognizes him and asks 'Hey, what are *you* doin' here?' To which Issy says, 'Whaddya think? Same thing YOU'RE doin' here!' Well, New York Fats was no real fan of Issy's, seein' that Issy was a better pool shooter than him. So what do you think that fat bastard does? He goes into the pool hall that Issy just left and shouts, 'Hey, who played against the little man with the limp? 'cause you just got your ass hustled by Hoppy from Baltimore!' The suckers flew out of the pool hall and chased Issy, limp and all, down the street. Him and his set up man barely got away and decided things were gettin' too hot to keep up the hustle. After all, they were runnin' out of places where people didn't know 'em. Issy laid low for a while, then went to work for the *Lawton* sheet at the old Jamaica track in New York. He moved to the Jersey-Florida circuit when Monmouth opened in '46 and he's been here ever since."

Billy was enthralled by Rip's story. It was becoming apparent to him that he would be working with a very colorful cast of characters, and he could now hardly wait to get back to the racetrack and immerse himself in the business of selling tip sheets.

The two men had a leisurely dinner, dining on some of the finest seafood to be had anywhere on the Jersey shore, while chatting about the racetrack, tip sheets and the hustlers. All the while, Rip continued to drink double martinis, and had consumed four by the time dinner was completed.

Rip asked for the check and once again, produced a ball of cash. He called Kerra over to the table, paid the tab, and handed her a $20 tip.

"Have a nice evening, beautiful," Rip whispered to Kerra.

She smiled at Rip, then Billy, and replied, "Have a good night, gentlemen, and thank you. Drive carefully and I hope to see you again soon."

The two left the restaurant and, momentarily, the red Corvette was delivered to the valet area. Rip tossed the valet $5 and jumped into the driver's seat. Billy took the passenger's seat, and the car roared out of the parking lot and down Ocean Avenue.

Billy had not had a drink since leaving the track, and his buzz was wearing off. Rip, however, had never ceased his alcohol intake, and Billy began to worry if Rip was capable of driving. He was noticeably impaired and Billy could see the Corvette was beginning to weave.

Finally, the car pulled up in front of a big Victorian house a couple of blocks from the ocean as the final rays of sunshine were disappearing below the horizon.

"Well, here we are!" Rip shouted at Billy. "Time for a party!"

Rip and Billy strolled up the walkway, ascended the front porch, and threw open the door. A blast of loud music hit them, and the place was filled with people who were dancing, drinking, and singing.

The two hadn't been inside the door for more than a few seconds before a man greeted them and handed each of them an ice cold bottle of beer. Rip took a long swig of the brew, then began a ritual of exchanging hellos with everyone in the room, or so it seemed. Billy stood aside, taking it all in as Rip moved through the room, shaking hands, pointing, slapping backs and hugging women. Except Issy and Wingy, all of the Monmouth Park touts were there, as well as a great many others. It was apparent that Rip was well liked by all, and everyone seemed genuinely glad to see him.

Finally, Rip's eyes fell upon Reenie. She was standing alone in the doorway, smiling adoringly at him and waiting patiently for him to take notice of her. She wore a flaming red party dress and matching high heels, her flowing blonde hair nestled behind one ear and adorned with a red rose. If all that were not enough, Reenie's enticing lips were highlighted by a smooth and shimmering layer of luscious cherry lipstick.

In a gathering which featured many sexy and attractive women, she was easily the most gorgeous.

Rip smiled at Reenie, set his beer on a nearby end table, then made his way through the crowded room and took her outstretched hands in his. He whispered in her ear, "You've never looked finer, dear." He then kissed her on the cheek as Reenie asked, "Do you like my outfit?"

Rip, still holding Reenie's hands, backed off and took another look at the stunning creature, slowly moving his head up and down, finally settling with his eyes looking into hers.

"Oh lord, yes!" Rip said, "But then again, you're always beautiful, no matter what you wear!"

The music stopped abruptly, which brought a roar of protest from the room of partygoers. The man who had greeted Rip and Billy at the door, a thin fellow wearing an Adams Porkpie and dress shirt with a loosened striped tie, shouted, "Pipe down, pipe down, everybody! Make room in the middle of the floor! Big Mike has a special request!"

Billy, still standing inside the entrance with his back to the wall, wondered what could be coming up next. The freezing bottle of beer he had been holding was beginning to numb his hand, and he shifted it to the other to gain some relief. He stood silently, absorbing everything, as the crowd formed a tightly packed circle around the center of the floor.

The man in the Porkpie hat dropped a 45 r.p.m. onto the record player as Big Mike and his dance partner—a sexy brunette wearing snug jeans and black and white saddle shoes—took their places.

The opening strains of the popular Jerry Lee Lewis rock 'n' roll song, "Whole Lotta Shakin' Goin' On" blared out, and the couple immediately sprang into action as the furious piano lead-in boomed throughout the room. At once, the crowd of spectators began to whoop, holler and clap in unison.

Billy was amazed at how Big Mike took command and led his partner through a long series of intricate dance moves—spinning her, lifting her over his head, and tossing her side to side in jitterbug fashion. Billy was thoroughly impressed that Big Mike could execute the maneuvers with such a high degree of style and grace—especially given his hulking form—and thought that the couple could indeed be mistaken for professional dancers.

As the song ended, the room erupted in cheers for the excellent performance. Almost immediately, another loud, spirited, rock 'n' roll tune blared from the record player, and the group quickly filled the center of the room and resumed dancing.

Billy surveyed the area, looking for Rip and Reenie, but during Big Mike's dance the couple had apparently slipped away. He was a bit intimidated, being perhaps the youngest person at the party, and nervously swigged at the bottle of beer until it was gone. Not being accustomed to alcohol, Billy found his earlier buzz quickly rejuvenated. This had a calming effect on him, and he gradually felt more at ease despite not knowing a single person in the room.

The man in the Porkpie loaded a stack of 45's on the record player, then worked his way across the room near the spot where Billy stood. There was a shiny metal garbage can against the wall, loaded with ice chips and half-submerged bottles of beer, and the man reached inside and got himself a cold brew. He turned to Billy and said, "Look here.

I give you the first one when you come in. After that, you're on your own. Help yourself!"

Billy reached down and grabbed a beer. He pried off the cap with an opener nailed to the wall near the can, and took a drink from the bottle. The beer was so cold that it burned going down, but Billy didn't care. He was beginning to like it.

After another hour or so, and two more bottles of beer, Billy decided it was time to go. He hadn't made contact with his parents since leaving for the track that morning, and figured he was already in enough trouble. He made his way through the house, looking for Rip in order to get a ride home. He passed through every room on the first floor, having to push his way through wall-to-wall partygoers throughout, and finally saw Rip, holding Reenie in his arms, standing on the steps outside the back door.

Billy walked out onto the porch and tapped Rip on the shoulder.

"Rip, I really ought to get going. Could you give me a lift?"

Rip, retaining his hold on Reenie, looked over his shoulder at Billy and said, "Christ, Billy, it's still early. This thing is gonna go until the wee hours. Why the hell would you want to leave now?"

Billy felt juvenile giving the real reason—his concern about his parents—and came up with a more palatable story on the spot. "Um, I'm expecting an important phone call. Something to do with college. I have to be home to take it or things are gonna get messed up. Yeah, I hate having to leave. This is a great party."

Rip gave Reenie a peck on her lips. "I'll be back right away, sweetie. Stay beautiful." Reenie smiled at Rip, then turned to Billy and said, "See ya tomorrow, Billy."

Rip and Billy worked their way through the crowded house back to the front door. Rip grabbed two bottles of beer from the garbage can and opened them. "These are mine," he said. "One for the way there, one for the way back. If you want one for yourself, take it."

Billy had had enough beer for one day, and simply brushed past the can and followed Rip out the front door. The two jumped into the new Corvette and, after a quick set of directions from Billy, the car roared down the street. Rip turned the radio on and at once found a rock 'n' roll station. He turned up the volume and sang along, slurring the lyrics, while regularly taking swigs from one of the bottles. Billy got increasingly concerned by Rip's driving, as he occasionally swerved while driving at high speeds. Finally, the Corvette pulled up in front of the house, and a relieved Billy got out.

"Hey Rip, drive careful. I'm afraid you might get into an accident."

"Don't worry about a thing," Rip replied. "I know what I'm doin'. I'll see ya at the track tomorrow!"

Rip peeled out and headed back to the party. He continued to sing along with the music on the radio, and continued to drink the beer. His driving was getting progressively worse, and as he tilted the bottle toward the night sky to get the last few drops out, he lost sight of the road as a bend appeared. The beautiful new Corvette drove off the road and plowed—full speed—deep into a corn field, finally coming to rest in the middle of a sea of moonlit maize.

CHAPTER 2 – A Day to Remember

The sky was crystal clear and the sun shone brightly the morning after the big party.

"Caw, Caw!"

"Caw, Caw!"

Rip, who had been stretched out across the seats of the Corvette, sound asleep since driving into the cornfield the night before, opened one eye and saw a big, black crow peering down at him from its perch upon the top of the windshield.

"Caw, Caw!"

"Oh, shit," Rip murmured to himself. "Fucked up again."

Still with only one eye open, he tried to focus on his wristwatch, finally discerning that it was nearly 10:30—well past the time he should have been to work at Oceanport Avenue. He groggily uprighted himself, sat slumped behind the wheel of the car for a moment, and tried to shake the cobwebs from his aching head. His mind attempted to recount exactly how he had wound up in such a predicament—off the road and surrounded by cornstalks—and he finally accepted that his drunkenness had once again been the major contributing factor.

Rip shooed the crow away, started the car and made a "K" turn in the middle of the cornfield, eventually driving out the same way he had come in. He re-entered the roadway and drove off in the direction of the racetrack.

Billy's day had gotten off to a different start. He had awakened at the respectable time of 8 a.m. and had been able to get ready and catch the bus which brought him to Issy's truck with time to spare.

The side door of the big panel truck was wide open, and Billy stuck his head inside to find Issy hard at work on his tip sheets. The old man sat at a table, which was covered with racks containing small metal letters. The area was lighted by a lamp, and Issy carefully selected each letter, pushing it onto a metallic tube using some sort of a pointed instrument. Billy stood silently until he was noticed by Issy.

"Hi, Billy!" Issy called out.

"Good morning, Issy," Billy replied. "I didn't want to bother you while you're working."

"No bother, my boy. Why don't you come inside and you can see how we put these things together?"

Billy stepped inside the truck and took a position across from Issy where he could witness the production without interfering.

"It's really a simple procedure," Issy said. "First, I pick the horses I want to put on the sheet. I use a *Racing Form* to check the records, then decide which horses I think will win. That's the hard part. Sometimes I spend as much as three hours going over the charts."

Issy leaned back in his chair so Billy could get a better view of the table.

"Then, we have to go through the printin' process," Issy continued. "We all—except for the red, white and blue sheet which is done on a mimeograph—use printin' presses called 'multigraphs.' These metal letters are called 'type'. We basically take a hand pick and push the letters of the horse's name onto this holder, called a 'stick,' then slide them onto the 'drum,' clip them in place and put the drum onto the multigraph. Then we load it with paper and turn the printer on. What comes out is a finished tip sheet. That's all there is to it!"

Billy watched intently as Issy spelled out each horse's name with type and secured it to the drum with clips. Although it seemed to be a simple process, Billy did notice that it was a bit time consuming.

The squealing sound of a car rounding a corner at high speed filled the air, and within seconds Rip's Corvette screeched to a halt at the curb beside the yard where Issy's truck was located. Billy turned abruptly and was appalled at what he saw. Rip's beautiful, new car had scratches on its side and a large piece of cornstalk was sticking out of the grill. The door flung open and Rip, still suffering the ill effects of the previous night's binge, fell out of the car and onto the sidewalk. He got to his feet, then staggered in the direction of Issy's truck.

Billy jumped out of the truck and walked towards Rip. "What happened?" he asked, genuinely concerned.

Rip, his clothes totally disheveled, sporting bloodshot eyes and hair that looked as if it had been ravaged by a hurricane, replied, "It's a long story. I'll fill ya in later." He then brushed past Billy and stuck his head inside Issy's truck. "Hey Issy, I'm in a jackpot. Mind if I borrow the kid for a while to help me get my sheet out?"

Issy, upon seeing the condition Rip was in, covered his mouth with his hand and tried to subdue his laughter. "No problem, Rip. Just have him on the line before the break. Oh, I almost forgot. Bussey called in his picks and I wrote them down for ya."

Issy handed Rip a piece of paper, which he promptly crumpled up and tossed on the ground without even looking at it. Then Rip grabbed Billy by the arm and pulled him toward an old Volkswagen bus which was located in the rear of the yard. "C'mon," Rip said. "We don't have much time!"

Rip slid open the side door of the bus, which was equipped much like Issy's. He reached inside his top pocket and produced a folded white sheet, which he handed to Billy. He then took a seat at a table covered with type, and started to give Billy instructions.

"Okay," Rip began, "that sheet I just gave you is called an 'overnight.' It has all the entries for today's races. What I want you to do is this: in each race find the horse with the shortest name and give it to me. Then give me the second shortest name. Start with the first race and give me the two shortest names, then go to the second race. Got it?"

Billy paused for a second, then, remembering how much thought and analysis had gone into Issy's picks, replied, "Yes, but aren't you going to check the records in the Racing Form—like Issy does—before you make the predictions?"

"Goddam it!" Rip snapped. "I don't have time for that bullshit now! I want to get the sheet on the stand before the break! Now give me the shortest name in the first race!"

Billy was momentarily startled by Rip's tone, but regained his composure and scanned the overnight for the horse with the shortest name in race number one.

"Rumor," Billy said.

Rip quickly pulled the type onto the stick, slid it onto the drum and clipped it in place.

"Okay, next," said Rip in a more subdued tone.

31

"Ormand."

"Got it," Rip said.

Rip kept up a fast pace until the last race was completed. He then secured the drum onto the printing press, loaded it with green paper, and began to run off the sheets.

Rip spoke over his shoulder to Billy as he continued to print his "picks." "You'd better get over to the track. You don't want to miss the break. Business is usually real good when the track first opens. I'll be along shortly myself. Oh. And thanks."

Billy nodded and left to make his way to the track. He had noticed that all the other touts had already left their trucks, walked down the street and entered the racetrack. Not wanting to fail Issy again, he strode at the double-time until he was through the gates and at his spot on the line.

Issy had left a pile of sheets at his spot on the tip sheet counter, and Billy had barely finished counting them when Rip came rushing through the employees' turnstile and up to the booth.

Before Rip could catch his breath, the gates opened. A siren sounded and hordes of people flowed in, many of them running directly for the tip sheet booth.

All at once, a dozen hustlers yelled out their pitches, trying to attract the lion's share of the business to their respective sheets.

"I got the day-leeeee double! *New York Handicap!*"

"A winning card, a winning day! *Longshot Riley* heah!"

"Right here for *Turfmaster*! What do you want? Winnahs, or po-ropaganda?!"

Rip also joined the chorus. "Another big day, the old, reliable *Jack!*" he shouted.

Billy, determined to not repeat the disaster of opening day, held up an orange sheet and yelled, "Winners today on the *Lawton* sheet. Get 'em while they're hot!"

A throng of people pushed towards the counter, most with either a dollar bill or a couple of quarters in their hands, ready to make a quick purchase and departure. The fans began snapping up the tip sheets, and Billy was getting a fair share of the business. It was immediately apparent that today was going to be a major improvement.

A customer approached Rip to buy a *Green Sheet* and paid with a dollar bill. After collecting the dollar and dispensing the sheet, Rip took the customer's two quarters in change and pushed them over to Billy. "Now, see what he's got," Rip advised the customer.

Billy handed the man a *Lawton* sheet and pulled the two quarters into his pile.

"Wait a minute," the customer protested.

"Just play his top double and best bet!" Rip demanded. "Now go in there and get the money!"

The man didn't appear totally convinced by Rip's yarn, but took the orange sheet and headed into the grandstand anyway.

"Jesus Christ," Rip said. "You're gonna have to learn how to close the sale. If I push somebody's change over to you, take your pencil and circle a couple o' horses in the daily double and a top horse in the middle of the card. Then shove the sheet into his hand and keep hustlin'."

"Sorry, Rip," Billy replied. "I'll be sure to do better next time."

Shortly thereafter, another customer bought a *Green Sheet* with a dollar bill, and Rip pushed the change in front of Billy.

"Now, see what he's got," Rip said.

Billy scraped the quarters into his growing pile, picked up his pencil and began to write.

"I have a couple of good horses in the double and a horse for later on that oughta win. Here ya go!"

Billy shoved the sheet toward the customer. The man took it and quickly walked away.

"'Atta boy!" Rip said, smiling at Billy. "This is an easy game once ya get the hang of it! Now make sure ya always circle the same horses. Otherwise, if two people with sheets compare notes, it won't look good if ya gave out different horses."

A minute later, a woman stepped up to Billy and bought a *Lawton*, paying for it with a dollar bill. Billy handed the lady a sheet, then pushed her fifty cents change over to Rip.

"See what he's got," Billy told her as Rip quickly snapped up the quarters and began to write.

"Play what I mark," Rip commanded. "I have a honey for ya in the daily double. Now, take the money you win on the double and make a good bet on this horse in the seventh."

"Well, thank you!" the woman said, happily. "And if these come in, I'll be back to give you a tip!"

"Okay, lady," Rip replied. "You do that! Now get in there and get some of that cash they're givin' away!"

The woman softly giggled and headed off in the direction of the grandstand.

"I don't care what you give these people," Rip said, "they NEVER come back!"

The feeding frenzy continued for about twenty minutes, then gradually tailed off to the point where the hustlers had to compete for the "undecideds" who regularly approached the tip sheet stand.

A man stood in front of the booth, obviously ready to buy a sheet, but unsure of which one to choose. As he looked up and down the line at the sheets, the hustlers zeroed in on him and tried to lure him in with their pitches.

"Over here, pal! I got somethin' good for ya!"

"What are ya lookin' for buddy? A winner? You came to the right place!"

"Step right up, mister. I got a couple that'll put ya on easy street!"

Billy decided to join the fray. "I've got a good daily double for ya," he said, waving an orange sheet at the man.

The prospective customer stepped toward Billy to buy his sheet, but before he could get to the stand, Curly intervened. "That card ain't worth a piss hole in the snow!" he said, reaching far over the counter and into Billy's space. "Take this and play what I have marked!"

The man hesitated, then started to reach for Curly's sheet. But Billy, still smarting from the bruising he had taken from Curly the day before, pushed past him and shoved the orange sheet into the customer's hand. "Sir, you want to win, don't you?" Billy asked. "Then you certainly don't want *that* piece of garbage."

The man took the sheet from Billy, placed two quarters in his hand and walked away. Billy felt a sort of exhilaration, having won the battle.

"That's bullshit!" Curly shouted in protest. "You pushed me out of the way to get to that guy! Don't ever touch me when I'm goin' to make a sale!"

Rip, who had been watching the incident unfold, leaned back and pointed at Curly.

"Fuck you, Curly!" Rip said in Billy's defense. "You came over in front of him. If you don't want him to touch you, stay the fuck outta his space!"

"What are you, anyway?" Curly snapped back. "The fuckin' kid's father, or somethin'?"

"Yeah, right, you asshole," Rip shouted, still pointing. You don't like it when the shoe is on the other foot. Everything is fine as long as you're the one comin' out ahead. When the table gets turned, you can't handle it."

Jigger Higgins broke from selling his blue sheets farther down the line and quickly moved to defuse the situation. He reached under the counter, grabbed a frigid can of beer in each hand and walked down the line, handing one to Rip and the other to Curly.

"Okay, guys," Higgins said. "Have a beer and cool off. We don't need to bring any extra scrutiny on ourselves. Next thing ya know, somebody complains to management and they're out here hasslin' us."

Both Rip and Curly accepted the brew, and they quickly opened the cans and began to drink. Then they ignored each other and went back to hustling the slow, steady stream of fans who were entering the track.

Billy wanted to thank Rip for his support, but thought it would be better left for later, considering Curly still stood only a foot away from him on the stand. He looked over at Rip, who took a sip of beer, then silently nodded and winked.

It was almost time for the first race, so Rip picked up his remaining sheets and began to count them. Billy saw this, and mimicked the action. Once completed, Billy was inwardly excited about the results, but tried to keep calm on the outside.

"184 sheets today," Billy said, matter-of-factly.

"See, you're getting the hang of it," Rip said. "Won't be no time before you catch up to the rest of us."

Billy was surprised to learn that his total for the day was not on a par with the other hustlers on the line. Now curious as to the success of the others, Billy tried to formulate a question which would give him the answer, without being obvious.

Finally, Billy asked, "Well, what would be the average?"

Without looking up, Rip replied, "Oh, about three hundred, maybe four hundred, on a day like this. Saturdays would be more, naturally. I did almost four hundred today."

It was now 2:30 p.m.—time for the first race, and time for the hustlers to check out with the tip sheet owners.

As the others dropped big wads of bills and heaps of coins into the managers' sacks, Issy approached the stand, and Billy handed over the receipts, minus his commission.

"Oh, lord," Issy said with a smile. "I see you really turned things around. This is just the beginnin'!"

Billy then scooped up his remaining sheets and started to hand them to Issy.

"No, no, Billy," Issy said. "Those are yours now. Didn't any of the guys here explain it to you? Those are for your 'lates'."

"Lates?" Billy asked. "What are lates?"

"I'll explain it to him, Issy," Rip said. "Go ahead and finish checkin' out."

Issy departed the stand and headed toward the clubhouse.

"What's Issy talking about?" Billy asked.

"Lates? Man, that's one of the best parts of bein' a hustler," Rip said. "Everything ya sell late—that's after checkout—you keep. All of it. It's a beautiful thing!"

A man approached Billy to buy a tip sheet.

"Lawton," the man called out, tossing a pair of quarters on the stand in front of Billy, who quickly dispensed the sheet before any of the other hustlers could try to sway him.

"Now that's yours to keep," Rip said. "It's another way of makin' money around here!"

The tip sheet booth, which was located near the entrance to the grandstand, had no view of the track itself, but it did face a tote board which displayed the numbers of the leaders while a race was in progress. In addition, a loud speaker on the grandstand wall provided the call of each race, so the hustlers were able to monitor a race as it was being run.

The bell rang, the horses broke from the gate and the first race of the day began. The hustlers, most of whom had placed wagers on both the first race and the daily double, momentarily stopped their pitches and intently watched the tote board while listening to the announcer.

"And around the final turn and into the homestretch, the leader continues to be Rumor!" the announcer shouted.

"With a sixteenth of a mile to go, it's all Rumor! Rumor wins it by three and half lengths! Salute the Admiral was second, and Man of the Hour was third."

Billy looked up at the tote board and, remembering that Rip had placed Rumor on his sheet by virtue of having the shortest name, noticed that the horse had closed as a rank, 30-1 outsider.

Rip, who had shown no interest in the outcome of the race, stared blankly into space, oblivious to what had happened.

"Didn't you pick that horse on your sheet?" Billy asked.

Rip snapped out of his trance in order to respond to Billy's question. "Uh, damned if I know," he replied. "Let's take a gander and see."

Rip opened a copy of the *Green Sheet* and discovered that he indeed had placed Rumor in the win position on it.

"Now that's what I call handicappin'!" Rip chortled.

Onion Joe, who had been ripping up his losing tickets and muttering curses under his breath, overheard the exchange between Billy and Rip. "A $63 winner! Tell me. How in hell did you pull that horse out of your ass?" he demanded.

Rip looked over his shoulder at Joe and said, "Now, you don't expect me to be givin' out all my handicappin' secrets, do ya?"

He winked at Billy, then laughed to himself as he checked the *Green Sheet* for the second race "pick." A quick glance revealed that "Hasta" was the top choice in the second race - a horse which happened to be a 15-1 outsider in the program.

The men on the line continued to hustle their wares to the late fans. Those entering the track had dwindled down to a trickle by now, but still a surprisingly high percentage of them bought tip sheets. Before long, Billy had sold an additional thirty lates, which translated into an extra $15 on top of his earlier commissions of $37.

Rip turned toward Billy and said, "Okay. Now we have to try to squeeze the last few bucks out of this. Give me the rest of your sheets."

Billy had no idea what Rip had in mind, but by now he trusted him and asked no questions as he handed over the sheets.

Rip began to combine his green sheets with Billy's orange, folding one inside of the other to make pairs. Then, as the fans neared the stand, Rip called out to them, "*Jack* and *Lawton* here! Two for the price of one!"

The prospect of a bargain was too much for many of the fans to resist, and a steady stream of customers stepped up to Rip and took advantage of his offer. However, the increased business being generated by Rip resulted in fewer sales for the others, and this did not go unnoticed by the men on the line.

"There he fuckin' goes again!" Bullet Bob called out in Rip's direction.

"Hey, Rip! Why don't you cut that shit out!" Onion Joe roared.

"Why don't you just give the fuckin' things away for free?" Cockeye Sol chimed, his left eye staring straight at Rip, and his right eye pointing in the direction of the grandstand.

Curly didn't want to risk another confrontation with Rip and merely grumbled to himself in disapproval.

The Alligator, his hands on his hips, glared menacingly at Rip with his cigar tightly clenched in his teeth and hanging out of the side of his mouth.

Bernardo, Big Mike, Wingy and Jigger remained neutral.

Crazy Tommy seemed oblivious to the whole matter, and in a subdued voice held a conversation with himself, which was typical behavior for him.

"Ah, fuck off!" Rip said as he looked down the line. "If you jerkoffs had any brains, you'd do the same thing! Pair up and split the money! You'll make more together than yas will alone!"

Onion Joe and the Alligator saw the logic of Rip's argument and paired up to sell their sheets. The others either didn't care, or couldn't find anyone they could pair up with.

"Yeah, that's easy for you to say," Cockeye Sol complained. "You have somebody to team with!"

Rip, getting progressively annoyed with the situation, blared, "Well if you weren't such a shitheel maybe somebody would marry up with ya, Cockeye! Now leave me the fuck alone!"

Rip took the last drink from his beer as the field for the second race came out of the paddock and into the walking ring. He scanned the horses until he found Hasta, a small, skinny chestnut filly.

"Damn," Rip said to himself, slowly shaking his head. "She looks like a piss ant compared to the others. Some chance she's got in here."

He glanced up at the odds board and saw that the filly had drifted up to 20-1. Rip concluded that if she were somehow able to win, the daily double payoff would probably be in the neighborhood of $1,000 for a $2 ticket. A typical daily double paid in the $50 - $100 range, so Rip knew that such a big payoff would be a big boost for his business.

The jockeys mounted the horses and, after the bugler played "the call to post," they left the walking ring and strode toward the racetrack.

Within a few minutes, the second race field was in the gate and ready to go. The horses were dispatched, and one minute and forty one seconds later, Hasta charged down the middle of the track, stuck her nose in front at the wire, and won the race. Shortly thereafter, the result was declared official, and the payoffs were posted. Hasta paid $43.40 to win, and the daily double payoff was a whopping $1,107.

Rip stood spellbound for a moment, then alternately looked at the selections on the *Green Sheet* and the payoffs on the tote board, as if somehow there had been a mistake.

Suddenly, a man, furiously waving a *Green Sheet* in the air over his head and hopping up and down as he ran across the pavement near the walking ring, shouted, "GOD BLESS JACK! GOD BLESS *JACK'S GREEN CARD!*"

The man repeated his blessing again and again as he hopped around for a full minute. The hustlers, upon seeing this display, gathered around Rip and demanded to see the picks on the *Green Sheet*. Grumbles and comments of disbelief filled the air.

"No fuckin' way you had that!"

"Let me see that sheet. I don't believe it!"

"Who you tryin' to bullshit?"

Rip handed out green cards like a proud papa would hand out cigars. "Read 'em and weep, boys," he chuckled.

Onion Joe took the opportunity to throw one more barb at Rip. "Somethin's up here!" he said. "How the hell could YOU come up with horses like that?"

Rip took delight in his reply. "If you chumps knew how to handicap, maybe you could have had 'em, too. Whaddya want me to do? Apologize for bein' able to pick winners?"

Rip figured that this would be the perfect time to make his exit, quitting while he was ahead.

"Well, time to take off," Rip said to Billy. He counted the money they had collected from their "partnership," and handed Billy $11. All told, Billy had made $63 on the day—more than he would have earned from a week of selling tickets.

As the two were preparing to leave for the clubhouse, the Alligator tried to entice a fan entering the racetrack.

"Over here, pal. Give ya something good for today."

The man, who was apparently a blue-collar type, stopped in his tracks and pointed at the hustler.

"Why don't you get a REAL job," the man said. "Some job you got. Sittin' in a booth and aggravatin' people when they come into the track. You oughta be ashamed of yourself!"

"Don't quit your day job," the Alligator cackled.

This was the first time Billy had witnessed such animosity from a fan. "What was that all about?" he quizzed Rip.

"Well," Rip sighed, "You have to remember somethin'. Guys like that work in a hot, noisy factory eight hours a day and make a hundred bucks a week. We work in the fresh air for couple of hours and make $100 *a day*, then go drink and gamble. Half of the people who come into this place hate us, and the other half would if they knew how much money we were makin'. Jealousy is a terrible thing."

Like the day before, Rip led Billy into the clubhouse and into the bar where Reenie stood pouring cups of draft beer. He tossed a $5 bill on the counter as she put a couple of frosty brews in front of him.

"Hiya Rip," Reenie said. "What happened to you last night? I waited for more than an hour, then took a ride home from one of the girls. Is everything okay? You look terrible!"

Rip handed a beer to Billy, then turned back to answer Reenie.

"Yeah. Well, not exactly. I had a little "incident" on the way back to the party. Let's just say it's gonna cost me a few bucks to get my car fixed."

"Oh, no," Reenie said. "You didn't have an accident did you?"

"Nah, nothing like that, honey. Well, I drove off the road and my car got a little scratched up. No big deal. Nothin' serious. Nobody got hurt or anything."

"Well at least you're safe and sound," Reenie said. "That's the most important thing."

"You're gonna have to find your own way home today," Rip said to Billy. "I'm gonna have to drop my car off today to get it fixed up. Luckily, I know a good body shop up the street. I'll grease the manager with a sawbuck and he'll take it right in. Should be good as new by tonight."

Billy placed the beer on the bar next to Rip. "No problem," he said. "The bus goes right near my house and runs all the time. I'll catch one when I'm ready to leave."

Rip looked at the beer that Billy had placed on the bar and asked, "What's the matter? Had a little too much last night?"

"Um, well, yeah, um, no," Billy stammered. "I don't feel like drinking today, that's all."

Billy didn't want to disclose the real reason for his refusal to imbibe—his parents. He had gotten home late enough last night that he avoided the inevitable confrontation with them, and figured it would not do his cause any good to come home today with his breath reeking of beer.

"Gotcha," Rip said. "Drinkin' every day is an acquired activity. It's probably gonna take you a while before ya can run with the big dogs." Rip took a gulp of beer, then finished the thought. "Take your time, kid. Take your time."

Billy said nothing, but thought to himself that becoming an everyday drinker was not exactly a goal he should aspire to.

Rip leaned on the bar, chatting with Reenie and Billy until his beer was finished. He then glanced at his watch and said, "Okay. Time to check out. I'll be right back."

He left the clubhouse bar and headed back toward the grandstand. After a momentary silence, Reenie spoke to Billy.

"So, how do you like the job so far?"

"Oh, I really like it," Billy replied. "I think I'm getting the feeling for it. Rip's been showing me the ropes, and the money's fantastic. I still have a lot to learn, but I think I'll be okay."

"That's great that Rip has taken you under his wing," Reenie said as she drew a beer for a customer. "He's really a good guy. I think of him as an M & M candy; hard and colorful on the outside, soft and sweet on the inside. He's really one of a kind."

Billy, not sure of what kind of reaction he was going to get, asked a question that had been on his mind most of the day.

"Um, does Rip drink every day?" he asked.

Reenie sighed. "Yeah, pretty much. Most of the touts are either compulsive drinkers or compulsive gamblers, and some are both. It kind of goes with the territory, I guess. The guys all have cash in their pockets, time on their hands, and a constant opportunity to overindulge. I suppose the temptation is too much to overcome."

"Does Rip gamble every day, too?"

"Oh, no," Reenie said. "Rip can go days and days without making a bet. He's very smart about his gambling. He only bets when he thinks he has some kind of advantage. Some of the guys run up to the windows and make a bet every race. Not Rip. When he puts his money down, there's a good reason for it."

Rip re-entered the barroom and made a path straight for Reenie's station. He was carrying a bulging sack, like those that the tip sheet owners had been toting at checkout time.

"Throw this under the counter, will ya, hon?" Rip said, handing the bag to Reenie.

"Sure," she said, taking the sack with both hands and carefully placing it under the bar and out of sight. Billy was a bit confused by the transfer, and his curiosity got the best of him.

"What's in that bag?" Billy asked.

Rip glared at Billy and shouted, "WHAT ARE YOU, A COP?"

Billy was taken aback by the response. "Uh, no, I, um…"

Rip turned to Reenie and blurted, "DID YOU KNOW THIS GUY WAS A COP?"

Reenie, smiling softly, said, "Well, you know, he does ask a lot of questions."

Billy was momentarily flustered, but quickly realized he was the brunt of yet another of Rip's phony tirades. Before he could formulate a witty response, both Rip and Reenie erupted in laughter.

"Man, you are *too* easy," Rip said, slapping Billy on the shoulder.

Billy, feeling much more at ease at this point, gently laughed along with the others. He was finally getting used to Rip's sense of humor.

"Don't worry about the bag," Rip said. "You'll find out soon enough what's inside."

Rip picked up the beer he had originally bought for Billy and began to drink. The third race went by, then the fourth, and Rip was keeping pace—downing a beer per race. The trio chatted between races and the time went by quickly.

Then it was time for the fifth race.

The fifth went off, and a horse named Bongo led from start to finish at odds of 60-1. Shortly after the race, a man entered the barroom and plunked down a $50 bill on the bar in front of Reenie.

"Top shelf scotch—on the rocks," he directed. "and keep 'em coming!"

As Reenie poured the man a drink, he excitedly told her, "Made a bundle on the last race! You know, that *Green Card* had that big daily double AND had that longshot! Whoever handicaps that sheet is a genius!"

Rip was standing only a couple feet away and heard the man's comments. He pulled the *Green Sheet* out of his top pocket and opened it to confirm the good news. Sure enough, top choice in race five: Bongo.

Rip chugged down the rest of his beer, then turned to Billy. "Let's go. We have some work to do."

Reenie reached under the counter and handed Rip the bag which had been in her custody. Then, Rip and Billy said their goodbyes and headed out of the grandstand entrance, where Rip's car was parked. As he crossed in front of the tarnished Corvette, Rip stopped momentarily to remove the piece of cornstalk which was still hanging out of the grill, then opened the trunk and threw the "mystery bag" in.

Within a few seconds the car stopped aside the yard where Rip's Volkswagen bus was located. Rip walked briskly up to the vehicle and threw the side door open. He called out to Billy to join him as he stepped inside.

"We have to print pass-outs!" Rip barked.

"What are they?" Billy asked.

Rip seemed somewhat annoyed at the question, but sighed and said, "I keep forgettin' that you don't know shit. Pass-outs are just more copies of the sheet we printed this mornin'. When you have a big day pickin', ya come back and make a couple of stacks. Then, ya go back to the track and hand 'em out to people as they leave the track. It's for promotional purposes. If people see how good ya did today, then maybe they'll buy your sheet the next time they come."

The printing press already had the drum in place and was ready to make more copies. Rip loaded it with green paper and flicked the switch that made the press come to life. In no time, the press had spit out a huge stack of sheets. Rip divided them into two smaller stacks, hastily threw a rubber band around each, then handed one of the stacks to Billy.

"Time to go," Rip said. "It's gettin' late and people are leavin' now. I want to get rid of all these pass-outs!"

The duo jogged to the car and drove the short distance back to the racetrack. The car pulled up in front of the main grandstand entrance, where a steady stream of people were leaving.

"Stand in the middle of the exit," Rip instructed. "Call out, 'Jack gave ya that big double and longshots all day!' and hand out the sheets. I'm goin' over to the clubhouse side and pass them out over there."

Billy jumped out of the car and into the growing sea of departing fans as Rip pulled away and sped in the direction of the clubhouse. He took the rubber band off the stack of sheets and delivered his "pitch."

"Jack gave ya that big daily double and longshots all day!" he bellowed. People descended on him like flies on honey, grabbing up the pass-outs as quickly as he could dispense them. Within fifteen minutes, he had handed out hundreds of copies of that day's *Green Sheet*. Before he knew it, they were all gone.

Billy decided to would walk over the clubhouse side of the track to meet up with Rip, but before he could make a move, Rip pulled up beside him.

"Good timin'," Rip said. "Get in. We still have a little unfinished business."

Within a minute, they were back at the Volkswagen bus where Rip printed the *Green Sheet*. Rip opened the trunk and removed the bulging sack.

"C'mon in. I have to close the door behind ya. C'mon! make it quick!"

Billy stepped inside the bus and Rip slid the door closed. He flicked on the overhead light, which illuminated the table where he had set the type earlier that morning.

"Okay, now get on the other side of the table, across from me," Rip commanded. He then loosened the fastener on the bag, turned it upside down and shook it, dumping the contents onto the table.

Billy's eyes widened as money began to pile up before him. All sorts of cash—$5, $10, $20 bills—as well as tightly packed wads of singles filled the table. Change fell out, too; hundreds of quarters as well as numerous nickels and dimes. Many of the coins careened off the table and onto the floor as Rip emptied the bag. Even some bills spilled over onto the floor as the mound grew higher.

Billy had NEVER seen so much money! Heaps of cash, taking up every available inch of the table and piled high in the middle. "Where did all this money come from?" he asked, excitedly.

"Two day's receipts," Rip said. "Yesterday and today. Why are ya so surprised? You didn't think that the line in the grandstand was the only place we sell sheets, did ya?"

Billy, uncertain of how to respond, shrugged.

"We have five spots, all around the place," Rip said. "Everywhere there's an entrance, there's a tip sheet booth."

Billy stared at the mountain of money as Rip explained, "The place where Issy hobbles off to everyday—that's the train gate. Railroad tracks back right up to the end of the grandstand and two trains, loaded with suckers, pull up everyday. There's ten or twelve guys hustlin' back there."

Rip threw the empty bag onto the floor of the bus and continued to fill Billy in.

"Then there's the clubhouse. They only let three guys in there at a time, because they don't want all that noise and hustlin' to disrupt the character of the place. Everybody has to take turns. Even so, more sheets are sold there than anywhere else in the joint. The clientele there basically has the money and buy everything in sight."

Rip began to sift through the bills with his hands. "The ramp has two rows of booths, too. The guys there probably do about half of what we do on the main grandstand turnstiles. The last spot is the convention gate, right outside the clubhouse. They have a special entrance for groups there. The buses pull up and they herd 'em in through a side gate—right past a one-man booth. If you get that spot on the right day, you can sell hundreds of sheets. They get off the bus and line up, like sheep!"

Billy continued to stare wide-eyed at the bounty.

"Okay, now start separatin' the money," Rip instructed. "Ignore the coins for now and concentrate on the bills. Twentys over here, tens go here, and fives there. Leave the singles for last."

The two began to segregate the money and after a while had turned the huge mound of cash into several smaller, more manageable piles. Rip put the larger denominations into stacks, then counted them. He divided the singles into several stacks and counted them as well. Lastly, when the tedious exercise of accounting for the coins had been completed, Rip did a final inventory of the loot.

"Best as I can tell I have $622 for today. Not bad. Did a lot more yesterday, but that was opening day. All together, there's more than fifteen hundred bucks here, after commissions."

Rip took a pair of $20 bills from one of the stacks and flipped them to Billy. "That's for helpin' me out today. I wouldn't have been able to pull it off without ya. Thanks."

"Don't mention it, Rip," Billy said, stuffing the bills into his top pocket. On his first full day of hustling tip sheets, Billy had earned more than $100.

It was beginning to seem like a dream.

Rip banded up all of the money, threw it into the sack, then tossed the sack on the floor underneath the printing press.

"You're not going to leave all that money on the floor of this bus, are you?" Billy asked.

"Why not?" Rip said. "Same thing I've been doing for years. I drive down to Cherry Hill and meet the owner of the sheet once a week to give him his share. Not worth messin' around with a bank, so I keep it here. Nobody bothers it. That reminds me. Did I ever tell you the story about Bussey and *Jack's Green Card*?"

"No."

"Okay, well I'm not gonna stand around here chewin' the fat. Let's go up the street and I'll wise ya up."

Billy was torn. He knew that he ought to be going home, but at the same time, he wanted to hear more about the tip sheet owners. He hesitated only for a moment.

"Let's go," he said.

The two hustlers got into the Corvette and drove up Oceanport Avenue to the Route 36 traffic light. A quick left, a quicker right, and within two minutes they were in the parking lot of Running Brook Inn.

"We call this joint the R.B.I.," Rip said. "Nothin' fancy; it's a neighborhood bar that gets real crowded durin' racin' season. The last race hasn't let out yet, so we may be able to get a stool at the bar. Don't let on that you're not of legal drinkin' age. I'll order the first round of drinks, and everything'll be okay."

Rip and Billy entered the R.B.I. and had to look hard before they found two empty seats next to each other at the bar. They sat down and Rip waved at the bartender to get his attention, then threw a $10 bill on the bar.

"Hiya. A bottle of Bud for me, and whatever my friend here wants," Rip said.

The bartender carefully studied Billy as he waited for his order.

"Uh, I'll have the same," Billy said, trying to sound sure of himself.

The bartender paused, suspiciously. "Hold on, son. How old are you?"

"Um, 21," Billy replied, trying to conceal his nervousness.

"Let's see some proof," the bartender said.

Before Billy could make a move, Rip interrupted. "What the fuck! You know me! Ya think I'd come in here and sit down with some minor? He's with the show!"

Billy's wits instantly took over. "Fuck it, Rip," he blurted. "I left my wallet back at the print shop. Let's go back and get it!"

"Yeah, but if we do that, we're gonna lose our fuckin' seats!" Rip shot back, picking up on Billy's game and playing along.

The bartender was apparently swayed by the act. He reached into the cooler beneath the bar, opened two bottles of Budweiser, and placed them on cardboard coasters advertising Monmouth Park in front of the hustlers. "Forget it," he said. "Anything else? Need a menu?"

Rip shook his head as the bartender picked up the $10 bill and left for the cash register.

"Good thinkin'," Rip whispered out of the side of his mouth, as Billy nodded and took a sip of the beer.

Billy was a bit surprised at himself. He almost never used that kind of language, and certainly was not given to lying. But after that brief moment of introspection, his attention turned elsewhere.

"Okay. Tell me about the tip sheet owners," Billy said.

"Right. Well let me see. First and foremost, there's Bussey. He's the owner of the sheet I run—*Jack's*. He calls in his picks every day and I print and sell 'em for him, only not today for obvious reasons. Ray has been in the business his whole life. Ya see, his father, Charles, started the business in the 1890s. Story is that old Charles was a bookmaker at the Fair Grounds in New Orleans around that time, and had a fallin' out with his partners. In those days, there was no such thing as mutuel machines—like we have today—and all bets had to be placed with the bookmakers who set up shop in booths along the track and in the infield. Well, anyway, there weren't any papers back then—no *Racing Form* or *Morning Telegraph*—that had the records of the horses. The average sucker who came into the track only had a little info to go on—the trainer's name, owner's name, jockey—stuff like that. They could watch the odds quotes by the bookmakers to try to get clues, but the ordinary stiff didn't know much about doin' that. Well, one day, Charles was in a Turkish bath in the French Quarter talkin' to a couple of friends and they came up with the idea of puttin' out a sheet that would give the best horses to bet on. So Charles quit the bookmakers and started printin' his picks. It was an instant success, and he made a ton of money. He knew a lot about horse bettin', considerin' his background with the bookmakers, and put the suckers onto plenty of winners. Most people who knew Charles said he was the greatest handicapper ever. Take Issy, for instance. Issy knew the old man in his prime and said he was the best he ever saw. That's pretty big comin' from Issy, seein' that he's been one of the best in the business for years."

Rip broke from his monologue, took a couple of long gulps of his beer, then continued, "Anyway, Charles realized right away that if he could make money at the Fair Grounds, why not everywhere else? He started hirin' people, settin' 'em up with multigraphs, and puttin' 'em in almost every race track in the country. Before long, he had money pourin' in from everywhere. But that's not all. Because he had experience with printin', there were some tracks that hired him to print their programs. He built an empire—all based on racin' and racetracks—mostly owin' to the success of the *Green Card*."

Billy took a short sip of his beer and listened with great interest as Rip continued to spout information.

"Charles continued to expand the business as far as he could," Rip said. "He was in nearly every track as far north as Toronto, as far west as St. Louis and all up and down the east coast. He made '*Jack's Little Green Card*' a household word, at least with racin' fans. So, Raymond is born around 1905, his brother, Bobby, is born a year later, and the two boys grow up around tip sheets. The family raked in the dough all through the 20s, the 30s, and the 40s. Then, it happened."

"What?" Billy asked anxiously, "What happened?"

"Well," Rip replied, "the old man got a little long in the tooth. Gradually the boys took over the business, and pushed him farther and farther outta the picture. So in the mid 50s, the boys stuck old Charles in a room in Baltimore. They told him to stay there and not to come to the racetrack. So this old man—their father, the man who built the empire—was shoved aside by his own boys. He lasted a couple of years before he couldn't take it anymore. Brokenhearted, he walked down to Baltimore Harbor late last year, and jumped in. When they finally pulled his body out of the drink a few days before Christmas, he had blueclaw crabs hangin' off of him. There was an article in the *New York Times* about it. The article reported that the Bussey boys said their father had been 'nervous.' Nervous my ass. He was *despondent*. The poor old bastard."

Rip looked straight ahead, lowered his head, and whispered, "What a sad end for such a good old man."

The two sat in silence for a moment before Rip resumed. "Anyway, the boys split up the business; Bobby runs the Maryland tracks, Delaware Park, Charles Town and the tracks to the west. Raymond is in charge of Florida, New Jersey, New York, and points north. They hire managers, like me, for the most part. That's why I meet him every week and give him his cut."

Rip chucked softly, then added, "The assholes did do one smart thing. The *Green Sheet* has always had a picture of the old man on it. Every *Jack's* card has the slogan, 'None genuine without Charles Bussey's photo—beware of bogus imitators' printed on it. At least they realized who made the sheet what it was, and who the people identified with."

"Wow," Billy said. "What about the other sheets?"

"Alright, take the sheet you're sellin'—*Clocker Lawton*. That was the promotion of a guy named Tex Stenersen. The story is a little complicated, but see if ya can follow. At one time, one of the biggest sellin' sheets in New York was a sheet called *Lawton*. Stenersen gets this bright idea one day to change his legal name to "Lawton." Not his last name—his first name. So he legally becomes "Lawton Stenersen." Then, he puts out a sheet called *Lawton*. Well, the guy from the original *Lawton*, a lawyer by the name of Lawton Garside, goes berserk. He sues Stenersen for some kind of trademark shit, you know, infringement or somethin', but the judge who hears the case sides with Tex. So now, there are TWO *Lawton* sheets for sale in New York, and naturally, people get confused. Garside goes to the management at Belmont Park and complains. So they compromise. Management refuses to go against the court, but they demand that each sheet make changes to reduce confusion. So Garside starts to call his sheet *'New York Lawton'* and prints it in red, white and blue. Stenersen puts out an orange sheet and calls it *'Clocker Lawton'*. He throws a picture of his mug on the sheet, takin' a page out of Bussey's book. But Stenersen is a much better promoter and hustler than Garside and, before too long, he has everybody believin' the orange sheet is the original *Lawton*. His sales took off, and he's been head and head with *Jack's* ever since."

"So a guy named Tex owns the sheet that I sell?" Billy asked.

"Well, no. Let me finish. I told ya this was complicated. So, Tex, who is a big gambler—mostly cards, not horses—and a heavy drinker, gets into debt from some bad bets he made, so now he needs cash in a hurry so he doesn't wind up with a bullet in his head. There's a guy from New York who has been tryin' to buy an established tip sheet, a guy named Schroeder. Anyway, Tex goes to this guy and tells him he'll take him in as a partner for a quick cash settlement. Schroeder comes up with the cash, Tex gets out of his jam, and everything is honky-dory. Except Tex keeps drinkin' and gamblin' and borrowin' from Schroeder. Before too long, Schroeder basically owns the whole sheet by himself. Eventually, Tex drinks himself to death and what little bit of the sheet he still owned fell into Schroeder's hands. So that's the guy who owns the sheet now—Schroeder. But make no mistake about it. The guy who made the sheet was Tex. He was a master promoter."

Rip finished his beer and motioned to the bartender for a refill. He took a long drink and continued, "Tex was a helluva nice guy. I met him once years ago. He told me when he was a kid in Baltimore, he got sent to St. Mary's school for incorrigible boys. Tex was good friends with another guy you might have heard of."

"Yeah? Who's that?" Billy asked.

"Babe Ruth," Rip said. "Only he didn't get the nickname 'Babe' until he got into baseball. Tex told me that Ruth's nickname at St. Mary's was 'niggerlips'!"

Billy sat engrossed in Rip's tale.

"One thing about all of this," Rip said. "You keep all of this to yourself. About the sheets, the money, everything. One thing none of us want is for info on our business to

50

get out. At some point, you're gonna get asked about it. There are a lot of nosy people around, tryin' to get the skinny on what we do and how we do it. We have a nice little racket goin' here and we don't want anything to mess it up. No matter what question you're asked, tell 'em, 'I don't know. Call Lawton.' There ain't no way for them to do that, so that'll stonewall 'em but good. And for Christ's sake, never tell them where we print the sheets. The last thing we need is for somebody to come snoopin' around there in the mornin'."

The last race at Monmouth Park was apparently over, as evidenced by the large number of fans who were steadily crowding into the barroom. Among the customers filtering through the front door were several of the touts—first Jigger Higgins and Bernardo, then the Alligator and Crazy Tommy, and finally Big Mike. By the time the touts got to the R.B.I, there were no seats left at the bar, and they had to stand to get a drink. Each of the hustlers searched the bar for somebody they knew and, upon seeing Rip and Billy, worked their way through the crowd to where the two were sitting. Before long, Higgins, Bernardo, the Alligator, Crazy Tommy, and Mike stood in a tightly packed semi-circle directly behind them.

Rip dispensed drinks to the touts as Chuck Berry's "*Rock and Roll Music*" blared from the Wurlitzer jukebox in the corner of the barroom.

The hustlers huddled around, guzzling beer and discussing the usual subjects—business, the races, betting and the like—as the bar gradually filled to capacity. The close quarters made for many uncomfortable moments as customers banged and nudged each other while trying to navigate the room. Inevitably, drinks were spilled, often on unsuspecting people, and occasionally tempers flared.

The sounds of a scuffle emanated from a corner of the barroom, loud enough to be heard above the pounding rock n' roll music. Big Mike scanned the room above the heads of the crowd and spotted three men surrounding another. The men were shouting obscenities at the encircled patron, who was distressed and cringing from his predicament.

On closer inspection, Mike recognized the embattled man. It was Bobby Landon, the nephew of a top official at Monmouth Park.

51

Big Mike turned and shouted, "Rip! Bernardo! Come with me!" The trio, with Big Mike leading the way like a snow plow and a curious Billy trailing, forged their way through the crowd to the corner where the fracas was taking place.

"Okay, what's the beef here?" Big Mike growled.

One of the men turned and, waving a thumb in the direction of Landon, shouted, "this jerkoff just spilled a whole beer on me! Fuckin' idiot! Why? Is he a friend of yours, or somethin'?"

"I'm askin' the questions here!" Mike roared.

Big Mike, flanked by Rip and Bernardo with Billy standing closely behind, took turns staring menacingly at each of the perpetrators. As his eyes caught those of the men, one by one, they became intimidated and glanced toward the floor. Although the men were all of good size, within an inch or so of six feet, none of them was a match for the hulking figure of Big Mike.

"Well, here's how it's gonna go down," Mike commanded. "You guys have a choice. Either Bobby here can buy you a round of drinks and you forget the whole thing, or, the three of you and the three of us can go out in the parking lot and settle it that way. What's it gonna be?"

The decision was instantaneous. None of the three men wanted any part of Big Mike.

The man who had suffered the spillage spoke up. "Hey, we don't want any trouble with you guys. A round of drinks sounds fine. Whaddya think, fellas?"

The man's comrades immediately replied in unison.

"No problem here," said the first.

"Fine with me," the other said.

Big Mike turned to Bobby. "Alright. Get these guys a round of drinks, then scram," he instructed.

"Okay," Bobby said. He then whispered so only Big Mike could hear, "And thanks, Mike. If you ever need anything done at the track, let me know."

"Yeah, yeah," Mike replied, repeatedly waving the back of his hand at Landon. "Now take care of this business and get the hell outta here. I don't want to be disturbed any more today with this kind o' bullshit."

The touts returned to their places at the bar. Mike kept a close eye on the proceedings, until such time that Bobby delivered the drinks and left the bar for the day.

Billy was impressed. Although only a couple of years his senior, Big Mike commanded the respect of all of the older touts. It was apparent that Mike would be a good person to be acquainted with, especially if some "muscle" were needed.

The time passed quickly and, little by little, the number of patrons waned. Billy glanced up at the barroom clock and saw it was fast-approaching 9 p.m.

"Say, Rip," Billy said. "I'm gonna get going. I'll catch up to ya tomorrow."

"Where you goin' so soon? Things are just gettin' started!" Rip replied.

Billy hadn't had a real conversation with his parents since beginning his plunge into the tip sheet world, and did not want to aggravate the circumstances by coming home late with the smell of alcohol on his breath. He surmised that disappointment and disapproval were in the offing once his parents knew what he had become involved in, and he also knew that he could not delay the moment of reckoning forever.

He said a round of quick goodbyes to the other touts, exited the bar, then walked down the street to the bus stop. The bus arrived momentarily, and quickly whisked Billy to within a block of home.

Billy proceeded down the street, paused for a few seconds in front of his house, then took a deep breath, hoping to muster the courage to enter.

The evening was rather warm for mid-June, and the screen door was the only thing between Billy and his parents who sat watching television in the living room. Billy ascended the few steps that led to the front porch, slowly opened the door and stepped inside.

Billy's father, lying back comfortably in his recliner, and his mother, who sat in the corner of the sofa, glared at Billy as he stood inside the doorway, looking like the proverbial "cat who swallowed the canary." There was an awkward silence for a moment as Billy stood mute and his parents continued to simply look into his eyes. Finally, Billy's father broke the stalemate.

"Well?" he said.

"Well, what?" Billy responded timidly.

"Well, what the hell is going on here?" his father blurted. "What the hell have you been doing for the past couple of days?"

"Umm, I've been working. Why, what did you think I've been doing?"

Billy's father disengaged his recliner, sat for an instant then stood, pointing his finger at Billy. "Well you sure weren't selling tickets at Monmouth Park, were you? I called Chip James at the track today and he said that he couldn't use you on opening day because you got there late and that he hasn't seen you since. So, I'm asking you again. What the hell is going on here?"

Billy gulped. "I found another job, Dad. I was lucky enough to get on with a tip sheet at the track. I sell the sheets and get commissions. In the past couple of days I've made about..."

Billy couldn't even finish the sentence before his father shouted, "What! Have you lost your damned mind, boy? I know a lot more about that kind of stuff than you think I do. Those guys–they're called tipsters–are a bunch of bums who gamble all day and drink all night! That's no kind of job for a boy like you!"

"Actually, Dad, they're called 'touts.'"

"I don't give a good goddam if they're called Santa Claus, they certainly aren't the kind of people that members of *this* family should be associated with! Now you forget about that tip sheet nonsense. I'll talk to Mr. James and try to get you back on with the mutuels."

Billy stood silent for a moment, his head bowed. He loved and respected his father, but he had made up his mind on the subject.

"I'm not quitting, dad."

Billy's father stood quietly for a few seconds—a few seconds that seemed like an eternity to Billy—then responded in a slow, deliberate, calculating manner. "Billy, I'm trying to remain calm and talk some reason into you. You are a college boy with a bright future in front of you. The guys you are involved with now are nothing of the sort. They have no talent, no ambitions, no standing in society. Associating with them can only diminish what you have. Certainly you can see that, can't you?"

Billy glanced at his mother, who had been silently witnessing the exchange, all the while displaying a look of utmost concern on her face, then looked at his father and replied, "Dad, I know you care about me and want the best for me. But I'm not a little boy anymore. I have to make some decisions on my own. I know you have doubts about the guys who sell the sheets, but they aren't nearly as bad as you think they are. Actually,

54

they seem to be a fairly intelligent, resourceful group. And the money, Dad. The money is terrific. I made more money in the past couple of days than I could have made in weeks of selling tickets."

Billy's father was taken aback by Billy's remarks. He was used to dictating all family matters, and did not like this challenge to his authority.

"Well, Billy, I thought I could talk some sense into you, but apparently not. I suppose you think this is the end of it, don't you? Well, I can assure you, it is not. What about the little matter of your college tuition? What about the fact that you live under this roof by my good graces? Before you go making any "decisions" you might want to take those factors into consideration. I surely wouldn't like to have to crack down on you to get you to do the right thing."

Billy was appalled that his father would threaten such dire consequences should he fail to comply with his wishes. He turned and started up the stairway, with his father shouting at his back, "Think about it, son! It would be a shame if you had to look for another place to live and somewhere else to get the money for college!"

Billy's mother, who had remained mute throughout the entire exchange, finally broke her silence once she was sure that Billy was closed inside his room and out of earshot.

"Do you have to be so harsh with him, Kerwin?" she said.

Billy's father was livid that his wife would question his actions.

"What? Are you taking *his* side in this, Colleen? Are you actually saying that you *approve* of what he has been up to? I'm sorry, but this is totally unacceptable. And you had better get onboard with my decisions. The last thing we need now is for him to think that there is some legitimacy in what he is doing!"

Billy's mother was not accustomed to engaging her husband in debate, normally deferring to his wishes. This instance would be no different. She silently resumed reading her magazine, which Billy's father recognized as her tacit acceptance.

"Good," Billy's father said. "I will handle this. How difficult things will be for Billy is totally up to him. Hopefully he will see the folly he is involved in and take the right path from here on."

CHAPTER 3 – Choices and Consequences

Billy awoke after an evening in which he had gotten only sporadic periods of sleep. He had tossed and turned for much of the night, mulling over what could lie ahead for him if his father carried out his threats. Would his father really withhold tuition if he didn't get his way? Would his father actually cast him out of his home? Billy wasn't completely certain, but his father wasn't usually given to idle threats. When Kerwin Mulray said something, he meant it.

Billy was torn over what to do next. The prospect of disappointing his father was unpalatable, but Billy also understood that he was capable of making his own decisions, and the decision he faced now would be the biggest of his life so far.

It was nearly time to leave for work, so Billy hastily showered and got dressed. He descended the stairs and went out the front door without a word to his mother or father, both of whom were having morning coffee in the kitchen.

As Billy walked to the bus stop, he could not shake the feeling that in some way he would be betraying his parents if he continued to work as a tout. He entered the crowded bus, remaining silent and solemn despite being surrounded by boisterous riders on the way to the track. At one point, he considered turning around and returning home, but quickly dismissed the notion. He also contemplated going back to the track and asking Mr. James for another chance at the mutuels—something that would certainly satisfy his father and cure his dilemma. Billy had a big decision to make, and by the end of the trip, he had made up his mind.

The bus pulled up in front of the track, the door flew open and the riders poured out and headed toward the entrance where they were willing to stand for nearly an hour before the gates opened. Billy stepped off and began the short walk to where the touts were printing the day's selections.

The decision had been made.

Billy's routine was beginning to take shape. He got his tip sheets from Izzy, hustled them at the track, earned more than $50, added another $26 in lates, then joined Rip at the bar for a drink. It was beginning to seem easy to Billy, and he was getting to like the situation quite a bit.

Another part of the routine was Rip's excessive drinking. As Billy took intermittent sips of his beer, Rip guzzled his as if it were coming from the last keg on earth. Before long, Rip had gulped down three beers by the time Billy had finished one.

"C'mon, kid!" Rip chided. "You have to pick up the pace a little. It's lonely drinkin' by myself!"

Billy tried to manage a smile, but the attempt simply telegraphed his malaise.

"What's the matter?" Rip asked in a genuinely concerned tone. "Ya had a good day today, didn't ya? Ya should've. First Saturday of the meet and there was a slew of people. What's wrong?"

Billy looked away as he spoke.

"Well, it looks like my father is going to retaliate for me choosing to sell sheets. He's threatened to cut off my tuition payments and even to throw me out of the house if I don't give it up. I never thought he would do something like that to me."

"Oh, I get the picture," Rip said, taking a big swig of beer between sentences. "Your old man doesn't want ya associatin' with the likes of us touts."

"Oh, well, no, umm, I don't think it's exactly like that," Billy stammered, trying not to insult Rip.

"Hell, can't say that I blame him!" Rip said. "A young guy like you with college and a future, well, this really isn't any place for you. Tell him that you'll quit at the end of the meet in plenty of time to get to school in the fall. That oughta make 'im happy."

Billy shook his head. "No, I don't think that would make any difference," he replied, still looking down. "He seemed to be insistent on me quitting right now, or else."

"Okay, then ya gotta make a decision. Remember, though, once ya make your bed, you're gonna have to sleep in it."

"I know, Rip. I know. And I really have no idea what I'm going to do if I go home and get thrown out. I have no place to go, and my dad knows that. That's part of what he's banking on to get his way."

"Not so fast, pal," Rip said. "You have a place to go. See where we all live—the place where we had the party—on the other side of town?"

Billy had an idea which direction this conversation was heading.

"Yes, what about it?"

"There's always room at the inn, so to speak. You can stay with us if ya get tossed out. We split up the rent, so you would have to pay your share. Not bad, though. A lot cheaper than tryin' to get a place on your own."

"Uh, I don't know," Billy said. "I don't know if I'm ready for that."

"Well, ya may not have too much choice in the matter," Rip replied. "I'm just sayin', in the event that you get stuck, ya have an option. Don't forget, this is resort territory in the summer. Prices for rents are high and at this stage of the game, ya probably won't be able to get a place within 10 miles of this joint. At any rate, if ya need a place, I'm sure ya'd be welcomed to flop with us."

Reenie, looking as lovely as ever, placed another beer—his fourth—in front of Rip.

"Well, thanks," Billy said as he finished his beer. "It's good to know I at least have a way to cope if worst comes to worst. Hopefully, my father will not take it to that point."

With that, Billy said goodbye to Rip and Reenie and walked to the bus stop to make his way home. He rode silently, constantly mulling over the choice he had to make. By the time the bus reached the stop near Billy's home, he had made up his mind. He made the short walk to the house and stopped on the sidewalk. He stared at the front door for a moment, unsure of what would transpire once he went in.

Billy knew he was standing at the crossroads of his life. Although he had settled on which direction he would take, a nagging doubt still made him uncomfortable with his decision. He gulped, took a deep breath, and slowly moved up the walkway, up the steps and through the screen door.

Billy's parents were in their customary spots—his father in his recliner and his mother in the corner of the sofa—watching television when he entered.

There was an awkward silence as Billy and his parents exchanged stares. Finally, Billy's father spoke up.

"So, what's the story here?" Mr. Mulray demanded.

Although his mind harbored many doubts about his decision, Billy tried his best to impart an air of confidence when he replied, "I'm going to continue to sell the sheets, and I'll go back to school in the fall."

His father's face became flushed as he tried to contain his inner rage. The elder Mulray thought for a moment, stalling while he regained his composure, then rose from his seat and walked to within a couple feet of Billy. He folded his arms and looked directly into his son's eyes.

"So, I suppose you think that's all there is to it, right?" Billy's father said, his piercing eyes plainly demonstrating his displeasure.

Billy stood steadfast, his silence providing the answer to the question his father had asked.

"Well," his father continued, "it hurts me to have to do this. But you apparently are bent on ruining your life, and we will not idly stand by and allow you to do so. Therefore, I must insist that you remove yourself from this house until such time that you come to your senses. When, and if, you return will be entirely up to you."

Billy's mother covered her mouth as she gasped at her husband's address. Billy's father turned and sternly glared at his wife as she vainly tried to suppress her tears. But within seconds, Mrs. Mulray was openly weeping, her hands covering her face in a attempt to contain the suffering which had overcome her.

Billy momentarily ignored his father and sat next to his mother on the couch. He put his arms around her in an effort to ease her sorrow. Billy loved his mother very much, and it caused him pain to see her in such distress. He fought back his own tears as he did his best to comfort her.

"It's alright, mom," Billy said. "I'll be okay. You don't have to worry. I can take care of myself."

Billy kissed his mother on the cheek, rose, brushed past his father, and ascended the stairs to collect his belongings. He quickly packed and made his way back downstairs to where his mother and father were silently waiting in the living room. He gave his mother a hug and kiss goodbye, grabbed a suitcase in each hand, and made his way to the front door. As he pushed the screen door open, his father spoke up.

"You'll regret this someday, boy," he said.

Billy glanced over his shoulder and continued out the door.

As he made his way down the walkway, Billy's father moved to the screen door to witness his exit. In his heart, he was sure that Billy would soon see the error of his ways and come back with his "tail between his legs." In his mind, this was the only logical outcome to the situation.

All the while, Mrs. Mulray ruefully stared at her husband through a stream of tears. Of all the demanding, domineering episodes she had endured at the hands of her husband over the years, this was clearly the worst. Her heart sank as she could see Billy walking away through the living room window. In *her* heart, she was worried that she would never see her son—her only child and the light of her life—ever again. In *her* mind there had to have been a better resolution to the dilemma than this.

In a moment, Billy disappeared down the street as he headed for the bus stop.

CHAPTER 4 – Somethin' Like a Lunatic Asylum

Billy took the bus to the racetrack stop, then caught a connecting bus that brought him to within a block of the touts' house. In a couple of minutes he found himself at the big, oak front door, and he grasped the dingy brass door knocker and gave it a couple of raps.

Nothing.

He gave it a couple more raps.

Nothing.

Finally, he gave the knocker a quick, repetitive hammering, but before he could finish his volley the door opened abruptly and Curly stood in the doorway, glaring at him.

There was an awkward silence as Billy expected some sort of greeting and Curly expected some sort of explanation. Finally, Curly broke the stalemate.

"Well?" he snapped.

"Is Rip here?" Billy asked.

"What do you think I am," Curly smirked, "the personnel director around here? How the hell should I know? Come in and look for him yourself!"

With that, Curly turned and left, the front door remaining wide open for Billy to let himself in. Ordinarily Billy would have thought Curly's actions crude and ignorant, but he was beginning to realize that such demeanor was standard procedure for many of the touts and quickly dismissed it as he entered the house. He placed his suitcases against the wall and looked around the room as he began his search.

It was early evening now. Crazy Tommy and Bullet Bob sat across from each other in the living room, drinking beer and discussing Gallant Man's victory in the Belmont Stakes which had been run in New York that afternoon.

Billy interrupted the chat. "Either of you guys see Rip?"

Crazy Tommy, obviously drunk, looked up from his seat on the couch and raised the beer in his hand. "Hey, it's the college kid!" he slurred. "What the hell are you doin' here, college kid?"

"Well, right now I'm looking for Rip," Billy responded.

"Rip, right, Rip," said Tommy, scratching his head. "I think he's takin' a nap upstairs… second room to the left once you get to the hallway. Walk in and give him a shake. Rip hates it when ya knock. Puts him in a bad mood to get woke up that a-way. Don't worry, college kid. He likes to get up around this time anyway."

Billy thanked Tommy and trudged up the long stairway to the landing on the second floor. He paused momentarily at the second door on the left, then opened the door and stuck his head inside.

Billy couldn't believe his widening eyes. Lying on a bed was a bare naked Big Mike and mounted on him vertically—also totally nude—was the girl he had done the jitterbug with a couple of nights earlier at the party. Her round breasts bounced wildly as Big Mike gyrated her rapidly by the hips.

Billy stood with his mouth open, paralyzed by the sight before him.

Big Mike paused long enough to look at Billy staring through the door and yelled in his deepest, most intimidating voice, "Get the fuck outta here, ya fuckin' asshole!"

Realizing his horrible mistake, Billy slammed the door shut and beat a hasty retreat back down the stairs to where Crazy Tommy and Bullet Bob sat howling with laughter.

"Oh, you think that's funny?" Billy screamed at Tommy.

"What?" Tommy replied, still snickering. "What happened? Didn't you find Rip?"

"I think you know exactly what happened," Billy shouted. "Rip asleep in the second room, my ass!"

Tommy looked momentarily at Bob, who was now in tears from laughter, then looked squarely at Billy and said, "Oh, did I say the second room? Damn. My mistake. I meant the *third* room. Big Mike has the second room. Oh, and I remember now. Rip isn't here yet, and Mike doesn't want to be disturbed."

Tommy took a sip from his beer and nearly choked on it as he giggled at the success of his little prank.

Billy was somewhat less amused. He thought of thoroughly engaging Tommy but remembered what Issy had told him: *"He's been in and out of the nut house and even gets a check from the government every month for being a lunatic."* Billy realized that to have any further exchange with the maniac would be fruitless and unnecessarily incendiary. He turned and left the room, serenaded by the guffaws of Bob and Tommy.

Billy had nothing to do now but hang around until Rip showed up. He walked through the empty dining room and toward the kitchen where he heard the sounds of several men talking and laughing. He stopped at the doorway and saw that several of the touts were sitting around a table playing poker.

Onion Joe, the Alligator, Jigger, and Bernardo turned in unison and looked at Billy quietly standing in the portal.

"Hey, Billy,"Bernardo chimed in. "Lookin' for a card game? We could use a fifth man!"

"Wait one minute!" the Alligator shouted around the cigar clenched in his teeth. "How about ya take a vote before you let somebody into the game? You don't run this table, Bernardo!"

Onion Joe mumbled something to himself then slammed his cards down on the table in front of him. "Yeah! He's right! Who died and left you king of this card game, anyhow?"

"What the fuck is wrong with you two?" Jigger protested. "The kid is one of us now. If he wants in, I say *let* him in!"

"Exactly!" Bernardo said. "The more, the merrier, I always say! What about it? Wanna get in?"

Billy shook his head. "No, I'm just waiting for Rip to get in."

"Alright, that settles it!," shouted the Alligator. "Now can we get back to the game? You guys don't mind if we get a couple of hands in here, do yas?"

The game resumed with Billy observing, indifferently. After a few hands, Bernardo called out to Billy. "Hey, would ya mind gettin' us a round of beer? They're right in the fridge. Opener is on the counter. Get yourself one, too."

Billy followed Bernardo's instructions—except for getting himself one—and got the men their beer. Besides Issy and Rip, Bernardo seemed the most affable of the touts, and Billy didn't mind doing him the favor. It was apparent that if he was to work with this group he'd need some allies, and Bernardo was potentially one.

As Billy finished placing the last of the beers on the table, he saw someone in the doorway out of the corner of his eye. He turned and saw Big Mike standing there, tucking his shirt into his pants and glaring menacingly at him. Billy gulped and stood silently.

Big Mike pointed at Billy, motioning for him to come into the dining room. Billy was fearful of what would come next but complied and followed Mike.

Mike drew close and towered over Billy. "What are you, a fuckin' wiseguy?" Mike said.

"Um, no," Billy stammered. "It was a joke. I mean, it was a joke that Tommy came up with, that is, he told me that Rip was in your room, um, what I mean is…"

Mike poked Billy in the middle of his chest with his finger, and it felt like a roll of silver dollars being shoved through his breastbone. "Shut the fuck up!," Mike commanded. "I don't like jokes, ya understand? So, there better not be a 'next time.' Ya dig?"

The last thing Billy wanted was to have Mike's big right hand unceremoniously remove a number of his teeth. "Of course not, Mike. I'm sorry. It was a big mistake. It'll never happen again, I promise!" he replied.

Big Mike backed away from Billy, but shoved his shoulder before turning and heading toward the living room. Billy let out a sigh of relief. All things considered, he felt lucky. The outcome could have been far worse, in his estimation.

Billy could hear Big Mike confronting Crazy Tommy in the living room. As could be predicted, the weasel denied having anything to do with the caper, instead saying that Billy had misunderstood his instructions.

"I told him to check the *third* door, Mike, I ain't lyin'! *He* fucked up! I had nothin' to do with it! Your beef is with him!"

Mike gave Tommy similar admonishments to those he had given Billy, then returned upstairs.

The episode now officially over, Billy went back to the kitchen to watch the card game and wait for Rip. He helped himself to the ice cold beer that Bernardo had offered him earlier, reasoning a drink or two might help to get his nerves back to normal.

Bernardo's curiosity got the best of him. "Say, what was that all about? You do somethin' to rub Big Mike the wrong way or somethin'?"

"Yeah," Billy said, taking a sip of the frosty brew. "But it's all settled now. No big deal."

Bernardo could sense that Billy didn't want to elaborate on the incident, and simply shook his head slowly as he watched the next hand's cards being dealt.

Most of the money on the table appeared to be in a pile in front of Jigger and, after several more hands, Jigger had almost all of his adversaries crushed as his luck was apparently running strong this particular evening. Finally, with a large pot at stake, Onion Joe matched each raise until he called Jigger, and Higgins turned over a pair of aces. A dejected Joe flung his cards onto the table, revealing a pair of kings.

"Looks like it's my lucky day!" Jigger chuckled.

"Fuck you, Higgins!" Joe shouted.

"I've had enough of this bullshit!" the Alligator said.

"I'm out," Bernardo muttered beneath his breath.

Higgins raked in the pile and chortled, a wide smile on his face.

"Nice doin' business with you *suckers!*" he said.

The three losers got up from the table and headed for the refrigerator to get a round of beers. One by one they left the room, with Jigger still lowly cackling as he tallied up his bounty.

"Sit down, my boy!" Higgins said as he nodded in the direction of the empty chair next to him. "Let's have a little chat!"

Billy took the seat next to Jigger.

"So, Rip was tellin' us that you're a college boy from Rutgers, is that right?"

"Yes," Billy said. "I'm in my third year—or I will be—when I go back in September."

"Your name's Mulroy, isn't it? Pretty common Irish name, especially in the old country."

"Well actually, it's Mulray. And yes, I'm Irish."

Jigger put his hand on Billy's shoulder. "Don't worry, kid. You're in good company. Plenty of Irishmen around here. We'll show ya the ropes and help ya out any way we can."

Billy felt that Higgins was sincere, and began to think that maybe he was making inroads with some of the touts. Of course, some of the others seemed downright hostile to him.

"Um, can I ask you a question, Jigger?" Billy asked. "What's the story on some of these guys—Crazy Tommy, Bullet Bob, Alligator, Onion Joe, Curly? Why are they so mean and nasty most of the time?"

Jigger sat back in his chair and sighed. "Well," he said, "you're dealin' with some pretty extreme personalities here. First off, some of these guys have serious mental and emotional problems. That's why this place seems somethin' like a lunatic asylum most of the time. Then, most of these guys consider you an outsider. This is a game where everybody plays it close to the vest—no card pun intended—because the only thing that could upset the apple cart is people findin' out about our racket. It might take a long while before some of these guys accept ya. Maybe they never will."

Billy took a sip of his beer and waited for Higgins to continue.

"Ya know," Jigger said, "most of these guys, despite their personality flaws, are pretty good eggs once ya get to know 'em. You asked about Bob and Tommy. Well, don't let them bother you a bit. A couple of knuckleheads for sure, but harmless. Just don't loan 'em any money. Good chance it'll be the last you see of it. Now that I think of it, don't lend money to *any* of the touts, except me, of course."

Billy and Jigger both chuckled at the quip. Billy was beginning to feel at ease with Jigger and wanted to hear more of what he had to say.

Higgins took a long drink of his beer, then continued. "Where was I? Oh yeah. The others. Okay, Curly can be a stone cold asshole most of the time. He's basically a surly bastard. Fuckin' know it all, to boot. Don't get into any arguments with him, boy. It's not worth it. Once that prick gets something in his head, there's no changin' it. On top of that, he's the worst poacher of 'em all. If somebody goes to buy your sheet, he'll try to steal 'em, *every* time!"

"Yeah, I know," Billy said. "he killed me the first day on the line."

"I saw it," said Higgins. "It wasn't pretty. But hustlin' sheets is kinda like learnin' to walk. You fall at first until ya can stand on your own two feet. Ya did a pretty good job puttin' that turd in his place the past couple of days."

Jigger raised his beer as a salute to Billy, then took a sip.

"Uh, let's see," Higgins said. "I guess you have a pretty good handle on Big Mike. He's the tough guy around here. Nobody wants to get on the bad side of him, and he usually gets his way on things. Havin' Mike here is kinda like livin' with a monster in the house. Ya just have to try to avoid him if ya can. One thing I can tell ya: if there's trouble, it's good to have Mike on your side. He's bailed out almost every one of us at one time or another."

66

Billy could hear the front door open and within seconds, Rip staggered into the kitchen. He stood for a moment, then got himself a beer and sat at the table across from Higgins and Billy.

Rip looked at Billy and said, "Well, look what the cat dragged in. What the hell are you doin' here? Didn't you get enough of us touts today?"

"Well," Billy replied, "remember what we talked about today? That's what I'm here about."

"Uh oh," Rip said, "I guess the shit hit the fan already, huh? Well don't worry. We got ya covered!"

Rip turned to Jigger and said, "Billy here needs a place to flop. His folks cast him out on account of him workin' with us touts."

"Ha!" Jigger shouted. "Where the fuck are we gonna put him, on the roof? In the back yard? I know… under the porch!"

"Whaddya mean," Rip protested. "You tellin' me we don't have an extra room around here?"

"That's what I'm tellin' ya," Jigger said. "The last room we had went to that stooper from Hot Springs. The guy that Cockeye Sol knows."

"Oh, fuck that guy!" Rip shouted. "Billy is one of us. Throw that asshole out and give Billy his room. If anybody is gonna sleep on the roof or in the backyard, it should be that stooper, not the kid here!"

"You know we can't do that to the guy," Higgins said. "Tell ya what, though. We do have room in the attic. It's a little hot and dusty, but it's a flop. We can set him up with a foldin' cot and a big fan. Not exactly the Taj Mahal but it beats a sleepin' bag in the alley!"

Rip turned to Billy and said, "I'm sorry. I forgot about the stooper. Looks like the attic is the best we can do for ya. If somethin' opens up, you'll be the first to get the room. Whaddya say?"

Billy didn't exactly have a lot of choice in the matter. He nodded his head in agreement.

"Okay, it's settled," Rip said. "Now get your stuff and let's get ya set up."

Rip opened a closet door off the kitchen and removed a flashlight. He held it up for Billy to see and said, "I almost forgot. We're gonna need this. The light in the attic is blown out, and if I know the assholes around here, nobody's replaced it."

Billy and Rip walked through the dining room and living room where Billy grabbed his two suitcases. Rip led the way as they climbed the stairs, then walked down the hallway to a door at the end.

"This is the door to the attic," Rip said as he opened it. "Now normally, this switch here would turn on the light, but as ya can see, it's busted right now. All ya need is a bulb. I'll see if I can find ya one later."

Rip flicked the flashlight on and climbed the steps to the attic. Although it was not abnormally hot outside, with each step the heat increased until it was exceptionally hot once the two stood on the dusty attic floor.

Rip used the flashlight to find the cot, which was situated a couple of feet across from a window. The fan lay, still plugged in, nearby.

"There ya go!" Rip said over his shoulder to Billy. "Open that window, throw the fan in, and you'll be set. Oh, and I'd brush the dust off that cot before gettin' in it, if I were you."

Billy laid his suitcases aside and went to the window to open it and get the fan in place. The window was shut tight, and he had to rap it repeatedly to loosen it. Finally he was able to pry it open high enough to fit the fan inside. Rip shone the light on the control dials, and Billy turned it to the "high" position. The old fan whirred into action and immediately began to blow cooler air from the outside into the hot, musty attic.

The fan also caused the dust in the attic to take flight. The two began to cough as they inhaled the particles.

"It's been a couple o' years or so since anybody's been up here," Rip said between heaves. "Leave the fan blowin' and we'll come back later. Let's get the hell outta here!"

Rip and Billy moved quickly down the stairs to the second floor where fresh air greeted their ravaged airways.

"Sorry, kid," Rip apologized. "This is the best we can do on short notice. I'll get you a decent spot as soon as I can. We have to work on gettin' that goddam stooper outta here so you can get a real room."

"Hey, I understand," Billy replied as he wiped the residual dust from his face. "I'll make do. And I appreciate you helping me out. Hey, Rip? What's a stooper, anyway?"

"Oh, they're the bottom feeders of the racetrack," Rip said. "They spend the whole day walkin' around the track pickin' up tickets that people throw away. They hope to find either a winnin' ticket that somebody tossed or a ticket with a scratched horse on it that would get 'em a refund. They're parasites, if ya ask me."

"Why would anybody throw away a winning ticket?" Billy questioned.

"Geez, boy," Rip replied. "They don't throw 'em away on purpose. A lot of drinkin' goes on at the track, and by the end of the day people are doin' all sorts of stuff without thinkin'. And sometimes, when there's a late scratch, people don't hear the announcement, and when they don't see their horse's number on the board, they chuck out the ticket."

The two then retraced their earlier steps which took them down the stairs and into the living room.

Tommy and Bob, who had been joined by Bernardo, sat drinking beer and were now watching a Brooklyn Dodgers game on television. Rip stalled and looked at the TV, which featured a very small screen within a large wooden cabinet.

"Hey," Rip said to Billy, "get us a couple of beers and let's watch the game for a while."

Billy got a round of beers and returned to the living room. He handed one to Rip, who had taken up a seat in a chair at the end of the sofa, and sat on the opposite end of the couch from Crazy Tommy.

"What inning, Bob?" Rip asked.

"Just started," Bullet Bob said. "Yas haven't missed a thing."

"Who's pitchin'?" Rip asked.

"Roger Craig is startin' for the Bums," Bob replied. "I think it's Sam Jones for the Cardinals."

"Oh, Craig." Rip said. "He was okay a coupla years ago when he was a rookie, but he sure hasn't been much since then. He walks too damn many guys."

As the game went on, some of the other touts filtered into the room. Curly came downstairs and sat on the sofa next to Tommy, leaving as much room between himself and Billy as he could. The front door opened and the Alligator, followed closely by

69

Onion Joe, entered and pulled up chairs within view of the TV. It appeared that most of the touts were baseball fans, something that sat very well with Billy. He had cut his teeth wearing a Dodger's cap, and was a lifelong Brooklyn fan.

The Dodgers had fallen behind early by a score of 4-0, damaged by home runs from Stan Musial and Del Ennis. When Ennis nicked Roger Craig for a double in the bottom of the third inning, Craig was removed from the game and replaced by Carl Erskine. Erskine got Ken Boyer to hit an easy fly ball to left fielder Elmer Valo and the Dodgers were out of the inning.

"Ha!" Rip crowed. "I told yas that Craig wasn't no good. Couldn't even make it out of the third inning!"

Once again, the front door opened and an agitated Cockeye Sol charged into the living room, stopping directly in front of the Alligator.

"Okay, buddy, what kinda bullshit do ya have up your sleeve for Monday?" demanded Sol, pointing at the Alligator.

"What the fuck are you talkin' about?" the Alligator scowled.

"You know damn well what I'm talking about! BULLDOGGIN'!" shouted Sol.

"Bulldoggin'? What are you, outta your fuckin' mind? Where in hell did ya get an idea like that?"

"Never mind," Sol growled, shaking his finger at the Alligator. "I hear things, and what I heard is that you and your guys are plannin' to bulldog on Monday!"

The other men ignored the game as all eyes in the room zeroed in on Sol and the Alligator. Billy had no idea what the term "bulldogging" meant, but it seemed to be a serious subject among the touts.

"Is this the truth?" Rip asked the Alligator.

"Of course not!" the Alligator responded. "I'd never do anything like that! Only a real scumbag would try to pull somethin' like that!"

His statement was met with universal silence.

Rip turned to Sol and said, "Ya know, this is a serious accusation. What proof do ya have of any of this, anyway?"

"I ran into one of my sources down at the news stand. He told me that he overheard the Alligator and his flunky planning a bulldoggin' session for Monday. He said that they said that Monday would be the best because it would set up for a whole week of big sales. The guy never bullshits me, so I take it as gospel when he tells me somethin'.''

"Well, bulldoggin' hasn't been attempted around here since the early days of this track," Rip said in a general address to the gathering. "It's somethin' we don't put up with. I doubt anybody would be stupid enough to even think of trying it nowadays. So let's put this thing to rest. It's over. Now let's watch the rest of the game."

"What? Is that it? Is that all there is to it?" Sol protested.

"Now you look here, Cockeye," Rip shouted, "the Alligator didn't do anything. You haven't proved that he *was* gonna do anything. 'He said that they said that you said that I said' is *not* proof. For all we know your "*source*" could have a beef with the Alligator and wants him in a jackpot. Now drop it."

"Yeah, sure," Sol said. "If you heard it from one of your guys, you'd be singin' a different tune!"

"Alright, Cockeye." Rip pointed at Sol and said in an elevated voice, "I'm gonna say this, and I'm only gonna say it once. You're gonna drop this shit right now, and if ya don't like it, get the fuck out!"

Sol glared at Rip for a moment then left for the kitchen.

"Oh," Rip shouted through the doorway at Sol, "and if you're thinkin' about drinkin' some beer, you better put some in first, ya cheap bastard! We're tired of buyin' beer so you can guzzle it all down!"

Rip returned to his chair next to Billy.

"Hey, Rip," Billy asked, "what was all that stuff about bulldogging? I guess that's bad, huh?"

Rip took a long gulp of his beer then said, "Shit yeah, it's bad. Bulldoggin' is about the worst thing a tout can do to another tout. Here's how it works: A guy sets the type from the fifth race on—he leaves the first four races blank—and doesn't print his sheets for the day. He goes to the track and stays for the first four races. He writes down all the winnin' horses and goes back to his print shop, puts those winners on the drum, then prints up a big stack of sheets. Then he goes to the track and passes 'em out. The suckers see that the sheet had the first four winners and think the guy is a genius. The next time they come to the track, naturally they want that sheet. It could mean big sales for quite a while. It used to be done once in a while in the old days, but not anymore. We have strict rules against it for obvious reasons."

The game went on, and Brooklyn tried to rally from the early 4-0 deficit. The Dodgers scored a run in the bottom of the third, fourth and fifth innings—mostly owing to the bat of Duke Snider, who hit a sacrifice fly and a home run during that span—and narrowed the Cardinal lead to 4-3. But a Wally Moon two-run blast off Erskine in the top of the sixth extended the St. Louis lead to 6-3. Once again, Brooklyn faced an uphill battle, and time was running out.

"Well," said Higgins, "looks like the Bums are finished. They finally close the gap, then the Redbirds tack on a couple more."

"Not so fast, pal," Rip responded. "There's plenty of baseball left to play here. The Dodgers have one of the best lineups in the game and they can score a lotta runs quick, especially at Ebbets."

Within minutes, Jones walked the first two batters leading off the bottom of the seventh.

"See!" Rip shouted. "I told yas! Here comes dem Bums!"

Cardinals manager Fred Hutchinson strolled slowly to the mound after the second walk. He motioned to the bullpen with his right arm, and the voice of Dodgers announcer Vin Scully boomed across the room. "So, after two walks to lead off the inning, the Cardinals will be making a pitching change. Righthander Lloyd Merritt comes in from the bullpen to replace Jones."

"Who the hell is Lou Merritt?" Rip asked. "Never heard of 'im!"

"It's Lloyd. He's a rookie," Billy explained. "He was buried in the Yankee farm system and the Cards picked him up. He hasn't pitched too much, but he's been pretty good, so far."

"Holy shit!" chortled Curly. "What do we have here? A fuckin' walkin', talkin' encyclopedia?"

Billy, beginning to tire of Curly's incessant barbs, glared at him and said, "No. I just happen to know a little bit about baseball. Tell me Curly. What do you know about—other than how to insult and aggravate people?"

The gathering let out a collective "Whoa!" and all eyes focused on Curly to see what his response would be.

Curly jumped to his feet and shouted at Billy, "Well, I do know one thing! I know I'm gonna put my foot up your ass if you keep mouthin' off!"

Billy quickly rose to his feet, also. He momentarily lost his balance and had to steady himself on the arm of the sofa. "Talk is cheap!" Billy shouted back. "Let's see ya do it!"

Before the two could get at each other, Jigger placed himself in front of Curly and Rip grabbed Billy by his arms to restrain him.

"Hey, would all you assholes sit down?" the Alligator called out. "You're blockin' the TV and some of us want to watch the game!"

"Alright, alright," Rip said, trying to inject a degree of reason into the situation. "Calm the fuck down, you two. We aren't gonna have any of this kind o' bullshit around here. Now everybody sit down and watch the game."

Billy and Curly exchanged glares, and the dislike they harbored for each other was obvious and growing by the day.

With the incident over, the touts resumed viewing the game. Merritt was able to get three straight batters, but not before a couple of ground balls had scored Junior Gilliam to make the score 6-4 in favor of St. Louis.

Wingy, who had been nursing a beer since the beginning of the game, chirped, "Hey, what's everybody gonna do next year after the Dodgers and Giants skip for California? What are we gonna watch then?"

"Never gonna happen!" Bullet Bob smirked. "Maybe the Giants'll go, but both of 'em? No fuckin' way! The Dodgers want a new ballpark in Brooklyn, and my money says they get it. That cocksucker Moses wants to stick 'em up by the old fair grounds in Queens, can you believe that? I can't. I think it's some kinda ploy to get what they want. The Brooklyn Dodgers playin' in Queens. Now if that don't take the fuckin' cake!"

"Moses...who's Moses?," Wingy asked.

"Some councilman or somethin'," Bob replied. "He's the guy who decides that sort o' shit, that's all I know."

"Well," Wingy said, "I read in the Herald Tribune a couple o' weeks ago that the National League okayed them to *both* move to California. I got a C note that says they both go. Now if ya lay me 10-1, I'll make the bet!"

"You got it!" snapped Bob. "Gonna be the easiest hundred I ever made!"

The Dodgers were able to scratch out a run in the bottom of the eighth and going into their half of the last inning trailed the Cardinals by a score of 6-5.

"Okay boys, you better hold onto your seats!" Rip said. "The Bums'll put up a pinch hitter to start the inning, then it's the top of the order! I told yas they weren't finished!"

But, despite all of Rip's best wishes, Merritt only needed 11 pitches to finish off the Dodgers, three up, three down. The final score: St. Louis 6, Brooklyn 5.

By the time the game was over, everyone in the room was totally, and undeniably, drunk. Even Billy, who had lagged far behind the others in the amount of alcohol consumed, was well on his way to a serious degree of inebriation.

Rip turned off the TV then walked over to the radio—an old hardwood console set from the 1930s—and turned the knob. "You're listening to WINS. This is Alan Freed bringing you the latest and greatest in rock n' roll. Here's a song that's been causing quite a buzz since we debuted it a couple of weeks ago. *Yes*, it's by Buddy Holly and the Crickets, and *yes*, it's called 'That'll Be The Day'."

"I love this song!" Billy blurted out, as the voice of the crooner from Texas filled the air.

Everyone in the room laughed in unison.

"Yeah, I suppose you college kids do love this shit," Rip said. "We keep it on here mainly because the chicks—most of which are younger than us touts—like it too. Now take me for instance. I'd prefer Dinah Shore to this crap any day."

"Yeah," Onion Joe said while waving his hand at the radio, "This guy is a bustout hillbilly singer. He couldn't carry Hank Williams' guitar case. That's why he got into this stuff. No talent."

"Sinatra is tops in my book," Bernardo offered.

"Well, it figures a wop like you would say that," Rip chuckled.

Bernardo scowled and shook his head.

Billy ignored the opinions of the older touts and lowly murmured the lyrics of the song. He was feeling the effects of the many beers he had consumed, and closed his eyes as he muttered the words to himself.

There was a knock on the door, and Rip walked over and had barely opened it when Reenie jumped inside and threw her arms around his neck. "Surprise!" shouted Reenie, her dazzling smile now inches from Rip's face.

"Hey, cutie!" Rip chuckled.

"Well, I don't know if you realize it," Reenie said, "but tonight *is* Saturday night! I sure wasn't gonna stay home on a Saturday night!"

Standing behind Reenie were a couple of young women that Billy recognized from the opening night party. The three females entered the room to the welcoming salutations of the touts.

Rip, holding out a bottle of beer that seemed to be omnipresent in his right hand, shouted, "Okay, everybody! I have now officially declared this a par-*tee!*"

One of the girls, wearing a colorful circle skirt and a tight blouse that put her womanly form prominently on display, walked over to the radio and turned the volume up. She began to sing along while snapping her fingers and tapping her foot to the rhythm. She seemed a little younger than the others, and Billy couldn't help but take notice of her.

"Billy, why don't you get the ladies a round of drinks?" Rip asked.

"Sure thing. What can I get you?"

The women universally responded "beer," and Billy went into the kitchen to get a round.

Rip picked up the telephone receiver and quickly dialed a number which was apparently well established in his memory bank. "Hiya. This is Rip. Can you guys bring us over a cold keg of Bud on the double? You know the address. Thanks."

Billy returned from the kitchen with a round of frosty brews and distributed them to the ladies. The last beer went to the girl with the circle skirt. She took the beer from Billy and wasted no time introducing herself.

"By the way, I'm Lorraine. Thanks for the beer," she said. Then she leaned nearer and whispered into his ear. "I saw you at the party the other night and I think you're cute, Billy. Why don't you be my date for tonight?"

Billy was a little taken aback by Lorraine's forwardness. It was apparent that the women associated with the touts were not exactly the kind he was used to.

"Umm, well, uh," Billy stammered.

Lorraine giggled at Billy's state of fluster. "Relax, relax," she said. Then, leaning against him with her large, firm breasts pressing against his chest, she whispered, "I don't mean to come on so strong...I just figured we might be able to have a little fun together."

Lorraine turned and left Billy, flushed and standing alone, and joined the others who were mingling in the living room.

Billy felt overwhelmed. In the space of a few days, he had gone from a schoolboy living at home and looking for a summer job to a racetrack tout being accosted by women at booze parties.

It seemed a bit surreal to him.

More and more people joined the party, the cold keg of beer arrived, and before long, it was nearly as crowded as the soiree the touts threw on opening day. Rock n' roll music blared from the old radio, and Billy continued to imbibe in the cold beer until he couldn't stand straight without leaning against the wall.

Billy had been sneaking glimpses of Lorraine during the evening, and as his inhibitions decreased, his opinion of her elevated. It was inevitable that Lorraine was going to catch Billy in one of his stares, and when she did, she quickly seized the opportunity to cross the room and talk to him. She once again pressed her ample breasts against Billy's chest and whispered into his ear.

"So, are you havin' a good time so far?"

Billy whispered back to Lorraine, unsuccessfully trying not to slur his speech, "Why yes. How 'bout you? Enjoyin' yourself?"

"Oh sure," Lorraine replied. "But we could be havin' an even better time."

"Oh really? How so?" Billy responded coyly.

"Well," Lorraine whispered, running her lips across Billy's earlobe, "we could go up to your room. I'm pretty sure we could come up with some fun things to do."

Billy closed his eyes as Lorraine continued to nibble on his ear and, within seconds, the room began to spin and Billy felt a swirling in the pit of his stomach.

Billy opened his eyes abruptly and stammered, "Um, err, not tonight. Maybe some other time."

Billy put his beer on a nearby end table, turned, and headed up the stairs to his room.

Lorraine was livid. "Well, don't hold your breath on that one, Buster!" she shouted at him as he made his retreat. "If you think I'm gonna be at your beck and call, you're outta your friggin' mind!"

Billy ignored Lorraine's remarks and stumbled up the stairs and into the stifling attic. He flopped onto the cot and tried to find the best way to lie in order to take advantage of the fan's cooling breeze. After closing his eyes for a few seconds, Billy could once again feel the sensation of spinning and his stomach, filled to the maximum with beer, resumed swirling.

Billy knew he was about to hurl.

He reached over, quickly dislodged the fan from the window and lunged halfway out in an attempt to get the vomit away from the house and down into the alley.

Billy violently heaved and it seemed like a gallon of hot, nasty, puke shot out of him and down into the narrow corridor below.

Immediately, a voice echoed from below. "MOTHERFUCKER!"

Unbeknownst to Billy, the window was directly above where the garbage cans were stored, and apparently at the exact moment of Billy's expulsion, Curly was depositing some trash into the cans. When Curly heard the heaving above him he instinctively looked up, and his face and head became the unfortunate recipients of the bulk of Billy's eruption.

Billy looked down in drunken silence for an instant, wiped his mouth with the back of his hand, and mumbled, "Excuse me."

Curly took his hand and forearm and wiped as much of the disgusting slime from his face as he could, then bolted out of the alley and toward the front door, fuming and intent on retribution. Big Mike, who had been leaning on one of the pillars at the top of the front steps and smoking a cigarette, had heard all the commotion from his vantage point and surmised the whole incident. As Curly rushed up the stairs and toward the entrance, Mike stuck his big arm out to halt Curly's advance. Curly stopped and shouted, "I'll kill that son of a bitch! Did you see what he did? I'll kill him!"

Big Mike calmly exhaled a billowy cloud of smoke, then, looking past Curly and towards the road in front of the house, said, "Yeah, I know. But this is gonna have to wait 'til tomorrow. The kid's in no condition right now. Cool off and take it up with him tomorrow."

"But Mike," Curly protested, "the bastard just..."

Curly stopped mid-sentence when Big Mike slowly turned his stare from the road and fixed it menacingly on Curly's eyes. Curly, thoroughly intimidated, looked away and said sheepishly, "Okay, okay. But tomorrow that kid's going to get his."

Sunday's big altercation turned out to be a bust. The anticipated confrontation wound up being little more than a series of loud and caustic threats by Curly followed by a tacit apology by Billy. Before long, things were back to normal—or at least what passed for normal at the touts' place.

CHAPTER 5 – Bug Out Time

The summer at Monmouth Park passed quickly. Each day, Billy became more and more confident in his abilities and his sales—and income—showed it. He was very comfortable with the routine and was quite happy with the decision he had made.

It was mid-August and an even more difficult decision loomed. The meet at Monmouth Park was rapidly coming to an end. He now had to decide whether he would move on to Atlantic City Racecourse and continue to sell tip sheets, or return to Rutgers in September. If he did opt for college, that would mean asking his forgiveness from his father. Although Billy had made very good money all summer and had actually managed to save some, he would need Kerwin Mulray's financial support to return to school.

Crawling back to his father and begging was most definitely unpalatable to Billy. After much thought, he came up with something he believed would be a good compromise. He would continue to work the tip sheet circuit and return to college at a later date.

The last day of the Monmouth meeting fell on a Saturday, as always. There was superb racing, a large and enthusiastic crowd, and a big day of sales for the hustlers. The touts always looked forward to the windfall of "getaway day" and termed the cash earned that day "shipping money."

As with opening day, closing day meant a big bash at the touts' residence. All of the usual party-goers were there: Reenie, Lorraine and their friends, guys and girls from the mutuels and, of course, all of the touts. Also as customary, the party was loud and raucous with plenty of drinking, dancing and merriment. The touts' house was packed to the rafters, and after a couple of beers Billy walked out of the front door and leaned on one of the big, ornate pillars in an effort to get some air and put some space between himself and the throng inside. Dusk was fast approaching, and the last rays of sunlight struggled to illuminate the rooftops nearby.

Although Billy had experienced a monetarily successful first season at the track, on the social side of the ledger he had not connected with any of the women who hung out with the touts. The youngest of the group, Lorraine, had washed her hands of Billy after their earlier episode. None of the older females had shown interest in Billy, and he was not attracted to any. All that summer Billy had observed Rip and Reenie's relationship, and at times he had secretly and silently yearned for the same.

A warm summer breeze softly wafted off the ocean and gently flowed through Billy's hair as he stood staring blankly into space, silently contemplating all that had taken place over the past couple of months. He was about to go inside and get another beer when a shiny Chevy Bel Air convertible pulled up to the curb in front of the house. As Billy approached the vehicle he recognized the driver, a brunette wearing a kerchief and a big pair of sunglasses, as Kerra, the server. Billy and Rip had visited her restaurant several times over the summer, and Rip had always professed an extreme fondness for her. Billy stopped next to the door of the Bel Air and said, "Hi, Kerra. I'll go inside and get Rip."

As Billy turned toward the house, Kerra spoke up. "Billy, wait." she said. "I'm not here for Mr. McKenna. I'm here for you."

Billy felt a jolt throughout his body as if he had been subjected to an electrical shock. He stood confused and speechless for a moment, then looked over his shoulder at the house.

"Don't over-think this, Billy," Kerra said. "If you don't want to come with me, that's fine." Then, lowering her sunglasses and looking directly at Billy with her shimmering, seductive, emerald eyes, she said, "But if you do want to come with me... that would be much better."

Billy thought for a second, then took a deep breath and gulped. Whatever reservations he may have had were overcome by the allure of Kerra's tantalizing smile. He walked around the front of the Bel Air and slid into the passenger's seat.

He was now undeniably entering uncharted waters.

Kerra proceeded to drive the short distance to Ocean Avenue. Billy couldn't help noticing that Kerra was wearing a tight white blouse that accentuated her voluptuous breasts and black shorts which showed off her firm and shapely legs. He repeatedly stole glances at Kerra until finally she caught him, causing her to chuckle over his boyish escapade. Billy was mildly embarrassed at first, but got over it quickly when he realized that not only had Kerra accepted his conduct; she also seemed to welcome it.

The two silently drove along the coastline for a while, then Kerra parked next to a high stone seawall. She removed her kerchief and, as she gently shook her head side to side to free her flowing jet black locks, Billy detected the flowery scent of her hair. He inhaled slowly, covertly yet unashamedly partaking in the pleasure he derived from it.

Kerra exited the car and opened the trunk where she had stored a blanket, a bottle of champagne, and two glasses. The couple climbed the stairway and quickly found themselves standing on a secluded beach in the waning light. Billy helped Kerra spread out the blanket, and two laid down on it. Through the blanket, the warmth of the sand produced a soothing and comforting feeling.

Kerra guided Billy through the process of opening the champagne bottle. He poured a glass for her and one for himself. After months of drinking primarily beer, the champagne tasted bitter to Billy, but he continued to sip it nonetheless. The couple engaged in small talk, mostly about what had happened during the summer, and they lamented how quickly it had passed. The sun finally slipped below the horizon, and the two found themselves bathed in moonlight as the last drops of champagne dripped from the bottle.

Billy was lying on his side, propped up on one elbow next to Kerra, who lay on her back, viewing the night sky. She looked up at Billy and as their eyes met, she reached up and ran her hand through his hair. She gently pulled Billy toward her and he willingly complied. Their lips met, and as Billy felt the warm succulence of Kerra's tongue around his, he instinctively began to reciprocate, slowly swirling his tongue around hers.

Billy had kissed and fondled girls before, but he knew that what would transpire this night was something he had not yet experienced.

The two continued to kiss, and Billy's anticipation—as well as his erection—increased quickly and dramatically. He ran his hand under Kerra's blouse and cupped her breast.

"Billy, wait," she said, gently pushing him off her and into a sitting position, "there's a better way."

Kerra sat up, pulled the blouse over her head and removed it. She then turned her back to Billy and whispered, "unhook my bra."

Without a word, Billy unhooked the bra, which she removed and tossed aside. Billy quickly pulled off his shirt and threw it clear, also. Kerra then resumed her position on the blanket and once again pulled Billy near. As they kissed, Billy began to fondle

Kerra's incredible breasts. He ran his fingers around her aureoles until her nipples were erect and virtually begging for his attention.

Billy put both of his hands on one of Kerra's breasts and began to suck her nipple. He did so with great enthusiasm, so much so that it prompted Kerra to whisper, "Not so hard, Billy. Use your tongue a little. Lick it, and then suck it gently."

Instead of being insulted, as many young men would, Billy welcomed Kerra's instruction. He swirled his tongue around her aureole and nipple, then gently sucked as he continued to softly move his tongue back and forth.

Kerra closed her eyes and sighed. "That's good, Billy," she whispered. "That's very, *very* good!"

Billy continued for a couple of moments, then proceeded to her other breast. Kerra softly moaned and sighed appreciatively as she held Billy's head in her hands.

Although Billy and Kerra had enjoyed themselves to this point, they were both ready to escalate the experience to the next level. Kerra lifted Billy's head and whispered to him through the gloaming, "Help me with my shorts and panties."

Billy's heart began to pound in earnest now. Kerra unbuttoned her shorts and lifted her buttocks off the blanket. Billy reached over and slid the shorts down her legs until they were free.

Now, only her panties remained.

Billy hesitated for an instant, straining to see her lying there in the moonlight. It was as if he were trying to preserve the moment, to burn it indelibly in his memory forever. He placed his fingers inside the waistband of the panties and again balked. Kerra, sensing a bit of insecurity on Billy's part, said softly, "It's okay, Billy. Go ahead." With that, Kerra once again arched her back and Billy slowly pulled her panties down and placed them on the growing pile of garments.

Kerra lay on the blanket in front of Billy totally nude now, and even with the scant illumination Billy could appreciate the beauty of her breathtaking form. She was, in Billy's estimation, a goddess, and he harbored serious doubts that he could ever be worthy of such a gorgeous creature.

Kerra realized it was time for her to take control, and she instructed Billy to lie down beside her. She unbuckled his belt, and in one swift and decisive motion she pulled both his pants and underwear down his quivering legs and removed them.

The two lovers were now naked to the night, and Kerra leaned over and kissed Billy with the deepest, most passionate kiss he had ever experienced. Billy's erection felt nearly ready to burst now, and at that precise moment Kerra mounted Billy and guided his throbbing penis toward her.

As she slowly lowered herself onto him, Billy felt a white hot ripple of pleasure begin to engulf his entire body. He unconsciously gasped as Kerra expertly maneuvered herself into position, taking full possession of him. Sensation rushed not only to Billy's brain and body, but indeed it seemed as though he could feel tingling in the farthest reaches of his very soul.

This was a far greater, more euphoric experience than he dreamed it would - or even could - be.

Kerra began to rock back and forth on Billy, settling into a slow, smooth, rhythmic motion. Billy reached out and placed his hands on Kerra's hips in an effort to help perpetuate her movement.

It only took a few minutes of this bliss before Billy's climax was near. He began to moan increasingly louder now, and Kerra recognized his cue and began to move her hips faster and faster.

Billy was on auto-pilot now. He clutched Kerra's buttocks and furiously rocked her back and forth as he growled in the grips of ecstasy. This propelled Kerra to the apex of her excitement and she, too, rapidly spiraled to orgasm. The lovers continued to rock, groan, growl, and squeal until Billy erupted with a massive explosion inside Kerra, filling her and causing her to shriek with pleasure.

Kerra fell off of Billy and onto her back, now satisfied and looking up at the starlit sky. Billy continued to hyperventilate, bathing in the rush of endorphins which coursed through every atom of his body. The two lie silent for some time, until Kerra leaned over Billy and ravished him with a long, slow, deliberate kiss.

Kerra then ran her finger down Billy's bare chest and said, "It's time we got going. I have to be somewhere early tomorrow, and you should get back to the party before someone misses you."

Billy wasn't sure what Kerra meant by someone "missing him", but he complied with her directions and began to get dressed without question. In short order, Billy and Kerra were clothed and cruising back down Ocean Avenue towards the touts' place.

Billy couldn't help but feel awkward at this juncture. He was as unsure how to act after engaging in sex as he had been before it. He remained mute all the way to the house, as did Kerra, and when the Bel Air came to a stop in front of the touts' place, he felt compelled to say something, although he had no idea what that should be.

He looked directly at her and said, "Um, Kerra." But Kerra turned and smiled at Billy, then interrupted his uncomfortable declaration. "Billy, don't say anything. You go around the circuit and I'll see you when you get back here next summer." She then pulled Billy near and kissed him goodbye.

Relieved, Billy slowly got out of the car. He turned around to say goodbye to Kerra, when she said, "Oh, and I had an excellent time tonight, Billy."

Billy looked down and smiled. "Me, too, Kerra. Goodbye. And thanks."

With that, Kerra drove away and Billy watched her disappear into the darkness. He stood for a minute, then returned to the party inside the house.

Billy didn't much feel like drinking anymore and retired to his room. Despite intense noise and loud music he was able to drift off to sleep as the party below continued into the morning hours.

The following morning Billy woke to an empty house, except for the myriad of beer bottles, pizza boxes, and overflowing ash trays which seemed to be everywhere. There were also a couple of empty beer kegs lying on their sides in the living room. Somehow, he was able to maneuver around the trash and make his way into the kitchen. There he witnessed a sight that epitomized the evening before: Bullet Bob and Crazy Tommy sat on the floor, slumped against the refrigerator, both out cold to the world. Tommy's head was resting on Bob's shoulder, and Bob's head was all the way forward on his chest. Bob still clutched a half-drunk bottle of Jim Beam, which he had apparently been sharing with Crazy Tommy when the drunken duo lost consciousness.

Realizing the likely debacle which lay before him, Billy forgot about the glass of orange juice he had imagined and instead opted to go sit on the porch in the fresh air. He sat contemplating the events of the previous evening when the door behind him opened and Rip staggered out and sat across from Billy on the top step.

"Where the hell were you all night?" Rip asked. "That dizzy chick Lorraine was lookin' for ya. She said she walked out front here and saw you get into a convertible with some brunette. Last anyone saw of ya all night."

"No," Billy said, "I came back and went right up to my room. I didn't feel much like partying last night."

"So you *did* go with some broad last night, huh? Say, that convertible wasn't a Bel Air by chance, was it?"

Billy was very uncomfortable with Rip's grilling. First, he didn't want to divulge any details of something he felt was quite personal. Secondly, he didn't know how Rip would respond if he were able to deduce that it had been Kerra he was with last night.

Billy began to stammer, and Rip jumped to his feet and shouted, "It was Kerra you were with last night, wasn't it! You son of a bitch! You son of a bitch!"

Billy didn't know what was coming next, and turned away from Rip.

Rip began quickly walking in tight circles on the porch. "I don't believe it! I don't fuckin' believe it!" he yelled. Then he approached Billy and shook his shoulder from behind. "You fucked Kerra? Are you actually tellin' me you fucked Kerra?"

Billy said nothing. He was sure that Rip was about to unleash a barrage of some kind on him, but instead, Rip began laughing. "You lucky bastard! You are the luckiest bastard who ever walked the earth! Tell me! Was it good? What were her tits like? Did she give you a blowjob, too? Holy shit! This is one for the books!"

Billy was thoroughly embarrassed now and couldn't face Rip or even muster a verbal response. He looked away and slowly shook his head.

Rip was relentless. "Man, that is one wicked babe! Un-fuckin-real that you nailed her!" Then Rip leaned over Billy's shoulder and whispered, "Hey, that wasn't your first time, was it?"

Billy remained silent, his back still turned towards Rip.

"Oh my god!" Rip roared. "First time out of the fuckin' box and you score a morselette like her? Oh, you lucky, lucky bastard!"

Billy had had enough of this nonsense and ran into the house and up the stairs. Although he had become quite fond of Rip, there were times—like now—when his crassness was unbearable. As Billy ascended the stairs he could hear Rip continue to laugh and chuckle while professing his incredulity of the situation.

One by one, the touts stumbled out of bed and shook the cobwebs out of their heads. Aspirin was the breakfast of choice for half of them, while alcohol was the choice of the other half. Regardless of the course of medication, all were functional when it came time to pack up and move on to Atlantic City.

The men packed their luggage and placed it on the front porch. Then they made their way to Oceanport Avenue to prepare the trucks for the move. There wasn't much to do with the trucks except secure all of the equipment, so by late morning everything was set. In succession, the trucks pulled out of the lot and the caravan crept up the avenue and through Long Branch until it reached the touts' house. There was a flurry of activity as the touts loaded the luggage into the trucks, and within minutes the hoard was ready to go.

Billy was sitting in the passenger side of Issy's truck awaiting the departure when Rip walked up to the window. "You wanna ride down with me?" Rip asked. Billy looked over at Issy for his approval. "Sure, go ahead Billy." Issy said. "I don't mind drivin' down there by myself. I've done it many times before. I have the radio for company. Don't worry. Go ahead."

Billy thanked Issy and got into the passenger side of Rip's Corvette.

"Time to bug out!" Rip hollered as he pulled away from curb and began to drive off. The duo quickly left the others behind, speeding toward the Garden State Parkway with the top down and the mid-day sun beaming on them.

"This road is a god-send," Rip said. "They've been workin' on it for the past few years and recently finished it up. Before this came along we had to drive down Route 9, which was a fuckin' nightmare. Lights every couple o' feet, traffic bumper to bumper. It took hours and hours. The only alternative was to drive down to south Jersey and take the White Horse Pike in. That was no picnic, either. Now with this new road, we go right down to Atlantic City without any problem."

Billy wondered how Rip's truck was going to get to Atlantic City and asked him about it.

"Well, I throw one of guys a double sawbuck and have them drive it down for me," Rip said. "Wingy didn't have such a great day yesterday, so he volunteered. He can use the shippin' money and I can use the help."

"I didn't see much of Wingy at the track," Billy said. "What was up with that? He worked every day, didn't he?"

"Sure," Rip said. "But Wingy is kinda like an in-between sorta guy. He only rarely worked the front stand with us. He's more of a second string hustler. He works for the blue *Dan Carter* sheet. Not a bad seller, only not close to the top cards. And Wingy usually works the train gate or the ramp. He's not as big a drinker as the rest of us, so you don't see him hangin' at the bars. When he finishes up, he normally joins Issy in a corner of the second floor. He's more like Issy than he is like the rest of us. A little older and more interested in privacy. One thing, though. He's not afraid to flap the wing at ya. Whenever he needs a little sympathy, out comes the wing, flappin' under your nose. He's sold a lotta sheets over the years by flappin' the ol' wing."

The new road was meticulously paved and on this early Sunday afternoon the traffic was light. Rip could not resist putting the powerful Corvette through its paces, and as the fine automobile roared down the parkway Billy noticed that the speedometer steadily rose into the eighties.

Rip and Billy chatted sporadically as they drove toward their final destination. The two had to shout to converse above the combined roar of the engine and rushing air caused by their high velocity. All told, though, the journey was an enjoyable one. Besides, there would always be plenty of time for talk later.

As the exit for Mays Landing approached, Billy assumed they would get off and find their way through the pines to the racetrack. However, Rip ignored the exit and motored right past, continuing his southbound trek.

"Um, Rip," Billy shouted. "Wasn't that the exit we should take for the track?"

"Well it would have been," Rip replied, "if we were goin' straight to the track. We aren't."

"Where *are* we going," Billy asked.

"It's a place I usually stop on the way down here." Rip said. "No big deal. Why? You in a hurry or somethin'?"

"Well, no," Billy said. "I just thought..."

Rip interrupted him in mid sentence. "Let me do the thinkin', will ya? Jesus Christ. Would I give ya some kinda bum steer?"

Billy looked straight ahead. He wasn't sure what adventure Rip had in mind, but he was in no position to protest now.

The red Corvette continued south until Rip slowed down to take the Wildwood exit. He paid the toll and drove directly to the parking lot of Zaberer's Restaurant.

"This is our fine dinin' joint for the Atlantic City meet," Rip said. "This place is not only famous for seafood, but steaks, too. Oh, and they have the biggest drinks to be found anywhere. They call them "Zaberized" cocktails. It's only been open for a couple of years, but it's already known from Philly to New York."

"Say, Rip, it's only a little past three o'clock. Are we going to eat this early?"

"Well," Rip said, "This place will be impossible to get into in another hour or two, besides I have to get to the truck and make sure everything is workin' because I have to put the sheet out tomorrow."

The restaurant was a huge building with two cigar-store Indians standing guard at the doorway while a gigantic wooden bald eagle appeared ready to swoop down from above. Rip and Billy entered and found themselves immersed in the colorful interior; the walls were covered with photos of famous people—entertainers such as Bobby Vinton, Liberace, Bob Hope, and Frank Sinatra, politicians Richard Nixon and Dwight Eisenhower, and athletes Robin Roberts and Richie Ashburn. In addition there were many photos of winning horses from Atlantic City Racecourse. The champion three-year-old and Kentucky Derby winner of 1956, Needles, got his first stakes win at Atlantic City the year before and his picture was prominently displayed. So was the photo of Career Boy, who was named Champion Grass Horse of 1956 in large part to his victory the previous summer in the United Nations Handicap at Atlantic City. Billy was impressed by the photos and memorabilia that filled the restaurant, and continued to take in as much as possible as the two strolled toward the Maître d's podium.

The restaurant was very crowded, but the maître d' recognized Rip and led the two directly to a table with a window view. The man smiled and said "enjoy your evening, gentlemen," as Rip pressed a bill into his hand.

The two took their seats and Rip said to Billy, "Flippin' the maître d' a sawbuck seems to work wonders. Ya know the Jews have an old sayin'. Translated from Yiddish it goes something like this: 'If you grease the rail, you slide.' I learned that one from Issy."

The waitress appeared at the table and before she could accept any orders, Rip chimed in, "I'll take a Beefeater martini, and Zaberize it." Rip then turned to Billy and said, "Why don't you try one of these special drinks? I know, give him one of those sweet Piña Coladas, and make sure you put a little paper umbrella in it."

Billy waved his hand. "Never mind that," he said. "Give me one of those martinis, and no umbrella, if you don't mind."

Rip chuckled. "Are you sure about that? You're really movin' into the big leagues with a drink like that."

"Yeah, I'm sure," Billy replied. "And I'm ready to order. Prime rib—medium well, baked potato, *au jus* on the side."

"This is a man who knows what he wants!" Rip howled. "Okay then. Fried seafood sampler, crinkle cuts, tartar and cocktail sauces on the side. Oh, and we'll take those drinks a.s.a.p."

Within a couple of minutes, Rip and Billy had been served Zaberized martinis, minus the paper umbrellas. Rip began to guzzle his while Billy took a more measured approach, sipping his martini until he had an idea of what he was doing.

The drink was very strong to Billy, and he could feel the alcohol burn his throat on the way down. Before long, Rip was finished, but Billy wasn't even halfway through his drink. Apparently, Billy thought to himself, a martini is a drink that one must "develop a taste for."

By the end of the meal, Rip had polished off three of the huge martinis. Billy, on the other hand, had not even finished his drink when it was time to go. Not wanting to look like a weakling in front of Rip, Billy downed the remainder of his martini, threw a five dollar bill on the table and grabbed the check.

"My buy," he said as he got up and walked to the cashier.

"Hey, no argument from me, guy," Rip said.

They left the restaurant and as they walked across the parking lot towards the Corvette, Rip reached in his pocket for the keys. He yelled, "Think fast!" as he tossed them to an unsuspecting Billy. "It's time you did some drivin'," Rip said. "Things are more spread out down here than they were up north. Means more drivin' so you're gonna have to pull your weight."

Billy got into the driver's seat and started the car as Rip settled down on the passenger's side. No sooner had Rip entered the car than he reached into the glove compartment and produced a half-pint bottle of Seagram's VO whiskey. He opened it and took a long gulp as Billy drove out of the parking lot and headed back towards the Parkway.

Billy had learned to drive on his father's 1954 Crestline Town Sedan Ford, a model equipped with a three-speed manual transmission which was shifted from the column. Billy had to make some adjustments to handle the four-speed floor shift, and drove quite slowly at first until he got used to the different mechanism.

A couple of things had become evident to Billy by the time the two had reached the Parkway: he was getting used to shifting the Corvette, and the effects of his "Zaberized" martini were now in full swing. The Corvette roared up the entrance ramp and onto the Parkway, where Billy quickly accelerated the car and banged through all four gears within seconds. The Corvette was flying along in excess of 80 miles per hour now, but Rip could not be more disinterested in the speed of the car. He simply gazed at the pine trees which lined the road, occasionally taking a swig from the bottle of liquor.

The traffic was light and apparently the new road was not heavily patrolled, either, which proved to be a stroke of luck for Billy. He approached 90 miles per hour at times and had the police pulled him over, the evidence for drunk driving would likely have been enough to arrest him on the spot.

The two continued up the Parkway, silent and trance-like, with Billy focused on the road ahead and Rip staring blankly into the surrounding pines. Suddenly, as the car approached an exit, Rip shouted, "Get off here!"

There was a screech of wheels as Billy swerved the car onto the exit ramp. He threw the transmission into neutral and applied the brakes while desperately attempting to keep the vehicle from flying off the ramp and into the trees on either side.

After a couple of seconds, it was evident that Billy was successful. He put the car in gear and slowly drove up to the toll booth, his heart still pounding from the ordeal.

"What the fuck!" Rip shouted while glaring at Billy.

"I'm sorry," Billy said. "I didn't know that was our exit. I thought you'd let me know in advance."

"Well, I hope you know what this means!" Rip yelled.

Billy looked down. He was certain that Rip was going to make him relinquish the wheel and he would never let him drive the convertible again.

"This means," Rip continued, "that you owe me a drink! That little maneuver made me drop my bottle and the last few gulps spilled onto the floor!"

Rip held his half-pint bottle upside down, thereby proving to Billy that it was indeed empty.

"Now, be more careful next time," Rip admonished. "Good liquor doesn't grow on trees, ya know!"

Billy, relieved that he hadn't been banned from driving the Corvette, paid the toll and drove to the main road. A large sign—Atlantic City Racecourse—pointed to the left, and he followed the directions. After driving a few miles through roads surrounded by thick pine forests, Rip and Billy came to the intersection of a major highway.

"Make a right at the light," Rip instructed. "That's the Blackhorse Pike. Right around the corner is the track. Things are a little different here. We put our trucks on the grounds of the racetrack out of view of the public. This is a short meet, so it works out good that way."

Rip directed Billy and within a couple of minutes, they were driving across the huge parking lot of Atlantic City Racecourse. Rip pointed to a gateway in a long chain link fence and Billy drove straight for it. As he drove the Corvette through, he slammed on the brakes. A bit inside the gate Wingy was bent over, frantically trying with his one good arm to pick up type that was scattered all over the ground.

"What the fuck happened here?" Rip shouted.

"Everything was goin' fine 'til I got here," Wingy explained, while swinging the stub of his left arm back and forth. "I drove through the gate and tried to shift and there was a goddam cinder block in the way. I tried to swerve around it, but a front wheel caught it and damn near tipped the whole shootin' match over. The door flew open and out the type went."

"Cinder block? I don't see any cinder block around here," Rip said.

"Well, um, it was there a minute ago. How the hell else would this have happened?"

Rip, realizing the futility of trying to get a satisfactory explanation, simply threw his hands in the air. "C'mon, let's help this sorry old fuck gather this stuff up."

The sandy soil made it difficult to pick all of the type out off the ground, but the three men were able to get the vast majority of it into a bag and back into the Volkswagen

91

bus. Rip gave Wingy $20, then drove the bus to its parking spot as Billy followed in the Corvette.

"Geez, that was weird," Billy said. "I mean, he hit a cinder block and then somebody took the cinder block away. Maybe somebody saw what happened and didn't want anyone else to hit it."

"Yeah, maybe," Rip said. "And maybe we'll get a foot of snow tonight. There wasn't no cinder block. What happened is that the poor old bastard lost control of the bus and almost tipped it over. He only has one arm, don't forget, and I'm guessin' that when he took his hand off the wheel to shift, the bus hit a rut or somethin'. He doesn't want anybody to think that havin' only one wing means he can't do what everyone else can. Don't ever say anything about this to anyone. I wouldn't want to embarrass the old prick. I guess things could've been a lot worse. He could have lost control on the Parkway and hit another car and maybe killed somebody."

Rip quickly organized and tested his equipment, and satisfied himself that all would be ready for tomorrow's printing.

Rip motioned for Billy to take the driver's seat of the Corvette. From the passenger's side, he directed Billy back to the Black Horse Pike and to the nearby town of May's Landing.

"Another thing that's a little different here is that we don't have one big house to flop in," Rip said. "There's a row of roomin' houses and we all get a room for the meet. Costs a C note for the month. And we ain't close to the ocean here, either. It's a few miles to the east. There are a couple of pluses, though. The Irishmen get rooms in the same joint and the Jews congregate at another. After a couple of months up north, it's a pleasure not to have to look at Cockeye Sol and Curly's sour pusses for a while."

"What about Issy? Or Bernardo? Or Wingy?," Billy asked.

"Bernardo is a pape and he flops with us," Rip said. "Issy and Wingy are older and don't want to be bothered with the hijinks from the rest of us. They stay in a roomin' house that caters to an older crowd."

Billy followed Rip's instructions until they arrived on a tree-lined street containing a long row of massive houses. Many of them had signs in front: *Rooms by the week or month. Vacancy. Inquire within.*

"That's our flop right here," Rip said, pointing to a huge two story house with brown shingle siding and a long, covered porch.

Rip led Billy up the stairs and to the front door. He rang the bell and an elderly, heavy set woman with white hair answered the door.

"Mrs. Moriarty!" Rip said. "If you aren't a sight for sore eyes!"

"Yeah, yeah," the old lady responded. "After what ya pulled here last year, I'm not sure if I should even give ya a room."

"Aw, c'mon Mrs. Moriarty. You know I didn't do anything wrong with that girl I brought here last year. I was only showin' her my photo collection. Besides, ya know I apologized. It won't happen again. I swear."

"You smell like a gin mill," the old lady said. "You aren't tipsy already, are ya? 'Cause I don't need any drunkards stumblin' in here in the middle of the night."

"Oh, my, no," Rip said. "I had one small drink with dinner, that's all. I'm fine."

"Well, alright," the old lady said. "But you know the rules. NO females in the house—I'm not running a brothel here. NO loud music or noise and NO coming in all hours of the mornin'—I don't want my boarders disturbed. NO cookin' in the rooms—if I find out you are, out ya go immediately. NO boozin' in the room—this ain't no cocktail lounge. Finally, you keep your room CLEAN. I run a roomin' house here, not a maid service. And that goes for the rest of your friends. I'm sure I'll be seein' them pretty soon."

"God bless ya, Mrs. Moriarty!" Rip said. "You won't be sorry. I promise." Rip then turned to Billy and winked.

Mrs. Moriarty looked at Billy and asked, "Who's this young fella? Does he need a room, too?"

"He's Billy Mulray," Rip said. "Yes, he's workin' with us, so he'll be needin' a room here."

"Alright. You fellas take the first two rooms at the top of the stairs. That would be rooms three and four."

Rip and Billy returned to the car, got their bags out of the trunk, and carried them up the stairs.

"Hey, Rip," Billy said. "Do you mind if I take room four?"

"No, why?" Rip said. "You think it's gonna bring ya some luck or somethin'?"

"Well, kinda," Billy said. "My favorite baseball player is Duke Snider. He wears number four for the Dodgers. I figured if it doesn't make any difference to you..."

"Nope," Rip interrupted. "besides number three is closer to the stairs. Ya never know, maybe bein' a few feet closer will come in handy when I stagger home some night. Hey, lock up and let's get outta here."

Billy locked up his room and the two returned to the Corvette. Rip, still feeling the effects of being "Zaberized," gave the keys to Billy, and within a couple of minutes they were in the parking lot of a square, one story bar on the Blackhorse Pike.

They entered, and the first thing Billy noticed was that the air was so filled with smoke he could barely see his way. The jukebox was blaring rock n' roll music and the sound of pool balls crashing into each other echoed throughout. In the corner, two men argued over a game of shuffleboard. The two touts worked their way to the bar and were lucky to find a couple of seats near the center. The bar had a very odd look, Billy thought. Unlike most taverns, there were no rows of bottles against the wall, only a single bottle on a narrow shelf. There were about a half dozen wooden barrels lined up and each one had a spigot which released a black liquid that slowly filled pint glasses beneath. The bartender, a huge man with a receding red hairline and a sour expression on his face, met them at the bar.

"Ya wanna drink?" the bartender asked in an unmistakeable Irish brogue.

"Yeah," Billy said. "I'll have a Beefeater martini and..."

Before Billy could finish his sentence, the bartender put shot glasses in front of Rip and Billy, picked up the lone bottle and poured them each a shot. He then took two pints of the black liquid and placed one in front of Billy and the other in front of Rip.

Rip picked up the shot glass and raised it towards the bartender. "Here's to ya, Eoin!" he said, then downed the whiskey and took a long gulp of the brew.

Billy stood speechless for a second, then turned to Rip and said, "Rip, don't you usually get a martini?"

Rip cackled, then looked at Eoin and said, "Say, you want to fill this rookie in?"

"Ya, I s'pose," Eoin said. "We have whiskey and stout in this place. The whiskey is Jameson's and the stout is Guinness. If ya don't like it, ya can get the hell out." Then the bartender added with a wry smile, "We don't cater to piteogs around here."

Billy had heard the term "piteog" bandied about by some of the Irish touts over the summer and knew that the word roughly translated to "sissy." He glared directly into the bartender's eyes, picked up his glass and, as Rip had done, raised it to Eoin. He drank the liquor straight down, then took a drink of the stout. The whiskey burned going down, and the cool stout was soothing as it helped alleviate the fire in Billy's chest. He turned away from the bar, and a tear slowly trickled down his cheek. Billy covertly wiped it away and hoped that Eoin hadn't witnessed it.

Billy looked around the barroom and noticed that some of the other touts were there. Higgins and Big Mike, with his omnipresent cigarette, were shooting pool on the other side of the room. Bernardo and Onion Joe sat talking on one end of the bar while Crazy Tommy sat alone at the other.

"Say," Billy asked, "where are the other guys? Curly, Sol, and Bob? Their trucks were parked back at the track. Don't they come in this place?"

"Hell no," Rip said. "This is kinda like the roomin' house as far as that goes. This is an Irish bar for the most part. Maybe a couple of wops and pollocks here and there, but most of the guys who come here are Irishmen. And these guys are blue collar papes, so let's just say they don't have any love affair with Jews. It works out better for everybody concerned if they go somewhere else for a drink."

Rip downed another shot of Jameson's and chased it with stout. Then he turned to Billy and said, "Don't beg, don't kiss ass, and don't hang around where you're not wanted. If you follow that advice, you'll always be able to sleep at night and you'll always feel good about yourself."

Billy and Rip hung around the bar for a couple more hours, drinking and chatting. It was now dark, and Rip had finally had enough to drink. The two touts left the bar and began to walk to the car, when Billy realized he was being bitten by what seemed like a torrent of mosquitoes.

"Holy shit!" Billy shouted. "The mosquitoes are eating me alive!"

"Me, too," Rip said. "Let's get the hell outta here on the double!"

As the Corvette roared out of the parking lot, Rip spoke up. "Yeah, I forgot about those little bastards! This joint is the world capital of mosquitoes this time of year! After dark they come out in droves and pounce on any livin' thing they come into contact with.

They make a spray that keeps them at bay, but ya have to remember to put it on. God help ya if ya don't!"

"Goddam!," Billy said. "I have welts all over and they itch like hell!"

"You don't have to tell me anything about it," Rip said. "There's swampland all around this place and the mosquitoes have the perfect place to multiply. The people who live at the track like to say that the mosquitoes are so big they use the home stretch for a landin' strip!"

Within a couple of minutes, Billy and Rip were in front of the rooming house.

"They're here, too," Rip warned. "Hurry up and get in the house before they zero in on us!"

They hustled up the stairs and into their rooms, where they spent a good portion of the night applying witch hazel to the multitude of bites they had suffered.

CHAPTER 6 – Atlantic City

The touts assembled by the trucks on Monday morning and began to get the sheets ready for opening day. Billy walked up to the truck where Issy was busy printing his *Lawton* sheet, and the old man greeted him with a smile.

"Oh, you made it," Issy said. "I have some good news for ya."

"Really? What is it?" Billy asked.

"Well, we drew the clubhouse today. You get to work it. Should be terrific sales on openin' day. They only let two guys work the clubhouse at a time. You and Rip will be workin' together."

"I'm a little confused, Issy." Billy said. "Are we going to be the only sheets on sale there today?"

"Well, no," Issy said. "I forgot. You never worked the clubhouse at Monmouth. Okay. Here's the setup. You get some of the sheets from the other guys and you have yours. If somebody comes in and asks for somebody else's sheet, well, you give it to 'em. But all the undecideds you try to sell for yourself. That's a powerful thing, Billy. You get to push your sheet in the best spot of 'em all."

"Okay," Billy said. "I'll be working with Rip, so I'm sure he'll wise me up."

Issy gave Billy a big stack of sheets and said, "Alright. Now take these up to the clubhouse and show 'em how it's done!"

Billy took the sheets and began the long walk from the parking area to the racetrack. He had only taken a few steps when he heard Rip's voice coming from behind, "Hey! Wait up!" Rip quickly caught up to Billy and the two continued to advance toward the track.

"So," Billy said, "Issy seems to think today ought to be a good day in the clubhouse."

"Oh, for sure," Rip replied. "Could be one of the biggest days of the meet. Everybody seems to like to be at the track on openin' day. And we got the best spot to be had, my boy! We're gonna have a picnic today, you watch and see!"

After a few minutes, the two reached the track and already there was a crowd gathered outside the gate waiting to gain admission. The touts pushed through the employees' gate and into the clubhouse where a pair of large stands with signs that read "Selections" above them faced the doors. Rip motioned for Billy to get behind one and he settled in behind the other. One by one, the other touts came in and dropped off their sheets—one stack for Rip and one stack for Billy. Rip instructed Billy to count each stack and to record it on a piece of paper.

"Now here's how it goes," Rip said. "When it's your day for the clubhouse, you get all you can get. When the other guys are in here, they get all they can get. Don't worry about hurtin' somebody's feelin's or anything; everyone knows the score in here. Have two sheets—one of yours and one of mine—in your hand at all times. No matter what the customer asks for, push our sheets at 'em, and don't take no for an answer. If you can't sell both, then sell your own. Listen to how I operate, then you do the same thing. And for Christ's sake, don't be afraid to use your pencil in here. These are the easiest people in the world, but you have to tell 'em what they need. The power of suggestion goes a long way in here!"

The bell rang and the gates opened, unleashing a throng of fans who steadily poured into the clubhouse.

"Right this way for winners!" Rip bellowed. "All cards here! Give ya that Daily Double! Step right up for winnahs!"

Billy followed Rip's lead, and within seconds people were lining up at the stands anxious to get their sheets before taking their seats in the clubhouse.

"Have a dollar ready!" Rip shouted to the crowd forming in front of the stands. "Let's try to move this along so's you all can get in there and start makin' money!"

As each person stepped up in front of Rip, he pushed two sheets into their hands—one of his and one of Billy's. The people seemed like sheep, simply stepping up, handing over a dollar bill, and walking off with the sheets Rip gave them. The same was happening at Billy's stand, and every once in a while he would shout out, "Please! Have a dollar ready so we can get you on your way without a delay! Step right up!"

Then, a man stepped up in front of Rip and said, "Give me a *Turfmaster* sheet."

Rip sprang into action. "You don't want that sheet here, bud. He was stone cold at Monmouth and he's usually worse down here. *Jack's* and *Lawton* always get off to a good start here at Aycee. Give 'em a shot!" The man threw Rip a dollar and took the sheets.

This scenario was repeated many times over. Only when someone continued to insist did they sell any sheets other than their own.

After the initial rush was over, a steady flow of fans continued to enter the clubhouse. Rip and Billy had more time to use their pencils and were able to steadily pile up the sales of their sheets, to the detriment of the others.

With twenty minutes to first post, Rip called out to Billy. "Okay. Time to tally up all the sales. Take a copy of each sheet and write down how much you sold of each one. Then put the cash in a sheet, fold it up, and put a rubber band around it. Somebody will be by soon to pick 'em up. Then figure out how many of your sheets you sold, take your commission, and put the rest aside for Issy. Once that is finished, the rest is ours for lates, so hurry up!"

Billy followed Rip's instructions, and when it came time to make the payouts, Billy opened the cash drawer in front of him and was amazed. The drawer was overflowing with money—mostly one dollar bills, but many fives, tens, and even twenties. All of the sheets did some business but, as expected, Rip's and Billy's sheets—*Jack's* and *Lawton*—out sold the others combined by nearly ten to one. The final count for *Lawton* was 242, and *Jack's* sold 234. Billy's commission came to $48, and lates were yet to come.

Billy handed over $117 to Rip for the sales he had made. As he handed the money to Rip, Rip in turn handed over $135 to Billy for the sheets he had sold.

"Now," Rip said. "You get commissions for those sales, too. Just because I was the one who sold them for ya, doesn't mean you're not entitled to be paid for it. I take my commission for the ones you sold, too. As far as lates go, we keep everything we take in and split it." Then Rip smiled and added, "Welcome to the gravy train, lad."

Billy could hardly believe it. He hadn't even realized that the sheets sold by Rip would be credited to him, too. In addition to the $48 he got from his own sales, he would receive $54 for the sales Rip had made.

As post time for the first race drew near, a couple of tourist buses pulled up in front of the clubhouse and people began to pour out. Rip looked up from his racing program and yelled over to Billy, "Get ready! Here they come!"

The doors flew open and wave after wave of people came through. Rip and Billy were energized by the throng and started to yell their pitches. "Have a dollar ready! Only a few minutes to the first race, so step right up! Get those winnahs right here! Still got time for that daily double!"

The customers did as they were told, and lined up with money in hand. Rip and Billy dispensed the sheets as fast as they could and shortly there were people standing all around with tip cards in their hands.

Then, from behind the crowd, a tall man stepped to the center of the vestibule and in a deep voice blared, "DON'T BUY ANY SHEETS! I GET EVERYTHING AROUND HERE FOR FREE! NOW, FOLLOW ME!"

As quickly as the sheets had been sold, they were returned for a refund. Those who had been in line with a dollar ready to buy stepped away, put their money back in their pockets, and followed the tall man up the escalator.

The tall man's maneuver had cost the touts nearly $100 in late sales.

Billy looked quizzically at Rip, who appeared disgusted and inflamed at the man's actions. Once the last of the refunds had been made, Billy turned to Rip and asked, "What was that all about? Who was that guy?"

"That guy," Rip said, "is a guy named Ed McMahon. Let me tell ya a little somethin' about him. He's another Irish shitheel from New England, somewhere around Boston. A few years ago, he winds up sellin' some kinda vegetable slicers or some shit down on the Atlantic City boardwalk. A bust out, two bit hustler if there ever was one. Well, he always wanted to be an announcer—TV, not horse racin'—and one mornin' he was gettin' ready for an audition. He was walkin' around outside his apartment building in Philadelphia, holdin' some kinda script and mumblin' to himself, you know, sorta practicin'. So, while he's doin' that, a guy goes to take his garbage out and sees him and asks 'are you in the television business?' To which this guy—McMahon—says 'well, I'm off to an audition today.' Long story short, the guy takin' out his garbage is Dick Clark—you probably heard of him. Anyway Clark uses his connections in Philly to get McMahon a try out as an announcer on WCAU. McMahon gets the job and he's been creepin' around ever since. The fuckin' mooch. You'd think he'd leave us guys tryin' to make a buck alone, but no, he's gotta play the bigshot. Like I said, just another shitheel from New England."

Billy thought for a minute and said, "Dick Clark, yeah, I've heard of him. He has a show called 'American Bandstand.' I think I saw it on TV once or twice this summer."

100

"Yeah, that's the guy," Rip said. "He's been on TV in Philly for years doin' that sorta stuff. Finally they put the show on the network, so that's why you saw it up north."

The late sales were fairly good, but the two buses that they lost to the McMahon maneuver made a great day out of what could have been a record breaking day. The two were about to close up and were counting up the late sales when the elevator door opened and a man stepped out. He walked directly to the stand where Billy and Rip stood counting.

The man stood patiently waiting for the touts to acknowledge him. Finally Billy looked up from his sheets and was stunned at what he saw.

Frank Sinatra was standing in front of the stand with a pair of crisp, $100 bills in his hand.

"Sorry, fellas," Sinatra said. "I heard what that guy McMahon did with the sheets and I wanted you to know I felt bad about it." Then Sinatra held out the bills for Billy to take. "I hope this makes up for it some way."

Billy was so taken aback that he could not speak. Rip finally looked up when he heard the voice, and he, too, was shocked. The two stood silently for a moment, then Rip reached out and took the bills.

"Great," Sinatra said, "have a good day and wish me luck!"

Billy and Rip said, "Good luck!" in unison and watched as Sinatra returned to the elevator and disappeared.

"Oh, man," Billy said. "I can't believe it. I just saw Frank Sinatra live and in person!"

"Yeah, he's quite a guy," Rip said. "He's known to be a big tipper and generally a nice man."

"I guess he likes the races, huh?" Billy asked.

"Likes the races? He *owns* part of this place. Him and a lot of other celebrities. One guy who brought them all together is a guy named Jack Kelly from Philadelphia. Ever hear of him?"

"Um, I don't think so." Billy said.

"Well, he's a little before your time. He started out as a bricklayer in Philly in the early part of the century. While he was a young man, he learned to row on the Schuylkill River. Anyhow, he became so great at rowin', he won gold medals in three different

Olympic games. Well, he becomes a multi-millionaire in the brick business, and in the mid-forties he helps put together a bunch of other rich people and they build this place. If you never heard of him, I'm sure you heard of his daughter."

"Who's that?" Billy asked.

"Grace Kelly. First she was a movie star, then she married the Prince of Monaco last year. One of the most beautiful women ever! And I have a little story about her, too. Years ago, a boy who lived in my neighborhood in Philly—Kensington—got to visitin' Grace up where she lived in East Falls. I'd say they were both about fourteen or fifteen at the time. I can't remember his name, O'Donnell or O'Connell, somethin' like that. A real good lookin' Irish lad, tall and thin with wavy hair. Anyway, she lived in a big brick house near the Schuylkill that her father built. Well, old man Kelly was always very protective of his 'golden girl' Grace. He desperately wanted to break into high society and he figured she was his ticket in. So when this kid—a blue collar boy from a workin' class Irish neighborhood—comes a callin' on her, Kelly finds out and he doesn't like it one little bit. So this kid—O'Donnell or O'Connell—gets a knock on his door one day. When he opens it up, he sees two big thugs standin' there. One of 'em says 'We know you've been up in East Falls.' Then the other guy grabs him by his shirt, gets right into his face and says 'You won't go back up there if you know what's good for ya.' Well this kid isn't just handsome, he's pretty smart, too. Smart enough to know not to go lookin' for Grace anymore. So, she goes to private schools, gets into actin' and winds up a big star in Hollywood—her dad has all those connections. Then she meets up with the Prince of Monaco and in no time she's a princess."

"Wow, that's some story," Billy said.

"Yeah, and that's not the end of it," Rip said. "Old man Kelly wanted her to marry that guy more than anything in the world, 'cause that would have made her royalty. That's the pass into high society he always wanted. So what do you think the Prince does? He shakes the old bastard down for a couple o' million bucks in order for him to marry Grace. They call it a "dowry" to make it sound nice and proper, but in reality it's nothin' more than a payoff. Take it from me, Grace's father is not a great guy by any stretch of the imagination. He's a relentless social climber. I guess he got what he wanted in the end but, the truth is, he's just the son of an Irish workin' stiff, like me or that O'Donnell boy. And another thing I bet you—or the Prince of Monaco—didn't know. Old man Kelly's sweet little golden girl was known as the biggest fuckin' whore in Hollywood when she was there. I was talkin' to a guy who worked in the industry and he told me that Grace fucked just about every leadin' man she worked with... along with plenty of others. Nowadays she's the royal knob polisher of Monaco. But if you read the papers, you'd think she was some kind of wholesome virgin who lived next door. Amazin' what the truth is sometimes."

Rip pointed toward the ceiling and said, "By the way, the old man is upstairs in the VIP room right now. He's up there with Sinatra, Bob Hope, and other Hollywood people and celebrities. They always come on opening day. Lots of 'em are investors in this joint."

The two touts closed up the stand and headed into the clubhouse for the customary drink at the bar. As it had been at Monmouth, so it was at Atlantic City; Rip met up with barmaids, patrons, and horsemen that he hadn't seen since the previous year. He introduced Billy to everyone and in no time, Billy felt at ease with his new acquaintances.

The barroom door opened and a rotund, middle-aged man who was wearing a big office wall clock around his neck suspended by a chain, walked in. Rip, upon seeing the man immediately called out, "Hey! What time is it?" The man pointed directly at Rip and without a second's hesitation shouted, "Time for a drink!" The patrons laughed as the man strolled up to the bar to get his drink, compliments of Rip.

Rip and Billy continued to chat and drink until the last race of the day was on the track. The barroom door opened and Crazy Tommy and the Alligator entered and took up a spot at the bar. They whispered to each other for a moment, then Tommy left and went into the clubhouse.

"I don't know what those two assholes are up to right now, but ya can be sure it ain't no good," Rip said.

A minute or two later, Tommy returned accompanied by a well-dressed, younger man. Tommy led the young man to the Alligator and introduced him, then the Alligator began to whisper into his ear.

"I recognize the swindle now," Rip said. "They're runnin' the old 'former jockey inside info' scam. Here's how it goes: Tommy finds some sucker and convinces him he knows an ex-jockey who has information on a fixed race. Then he brings the guy to the ex-jock who promises to give him the info in exchange for a ticket on the horse, usually

103

$50 worth. If the sucker is desperate enough, he might just go for the hustle. They give him a horse they think will win and, if it does, everybody's happy. If it doesn't, well, at least one of the parties to the transaction—namely the sucker—won't be. I'll let ya know soon if they had the winner or not."

The young man left the barroom and returned a couple of minutes later with a ticket for the Alligator. The race went off and the young man ran into the clubhouse to root for the horse. Crazy Tommy and the Alligator stayed behind, drinking and laughing having pulled off the scam.

As the horses entered the stretch and headed for the finish, Tommy and the Alligator gulped down their drinks and, after the Alligator threw the ticket on the bar, made a hasty retreat to the door leading to the parking lot.

Rip watched it unfold and roared with laughter. "Nope. No winner for 'em this time!" He then walked over to where the Alligator had been standing and picked up the discarded ticket. "Fifty bucks to win, exactly as I thought."

The door from the clubhouse flew open and the young man charged in. His face was red and his teeth were clenched in anger. He held a fistful of tickets in his hand.

"Did you see where those guys went? The ones that were standing here?" the man asked Billy and Rip.

Billy began to raise his hand and point to the outside door when Rip quickly pushed it down.

"Yeah," Rip said. "They went back into the clubhouse on the double. They were mad as hell and I heard 'em sayin' somethin' about bettin' the wrong horse or askin' for the wrong number or somethin'. They're probably lookin' for you right now. Say, ya didn't do somethin' like buy the wrong ticket, did ya? 'cause if ya did, I'd beat it outta here before they catch up to ya."

The young man appeared confused for an instant, then threw his tickets on the floor and joined the throng of people who were heading for the exits. In an instant he was gone.

"Okay," Rip said. "I know you must already know this by now, but I'm gonna refresh your memory. We don't rat on anybody, but *especially* not on our own. Now, I'm no fan of those two jerkoffs but the truth is, maybe someday you'll need them to do somethin' for you. Besides don't forget what W.C. Fields always said."

"What's that," Billy asked.

"You can't cheat an honest man," Rip said. "The truth is, that young prick thought he was gettin' in on some kind of larceny and instead he got robbed himself. Serves him right for gettin' involved with those two shit heads."

Billy and Rip quickly fell into the same routine that had been established at Monmouth earlier in the summer. They would hustle the sheets, drink until the races were over, go for dinner, drink some more, sleep it off, then do it all over again the next day. The only day that was different was Sunday, because racing was outlawed on that day of the week.

The Atlantic City meet was short in duration—a few weeks—and it was over almost as soon as it began. The crowds at the track dropped off precipitously after Labor Day, and with it the sales dropped, too. Billy hadn't managed to save much of his earnings; adopting Rip's lifestyle had been costly.

During the meeting, only a few incidents of note took place. Jigger Higgins grabbed a woman's buttocks at a bar on the Atlantic City boardwalk and spent a night in jail before Bernardo could bail him out. Crazy Tommy and the Alligator tried to pull their infamous "ex-jockey info" scam and weren't as lucky the second time; they were caught in the parking lot and both got a well-deserved whipping. Big Mike tried his hand at hustling fake watches on the boardwalk and did quite well until he sold one to an undercover cop. He was fortunate to get away with a fine and a warning, along with the loss of his inventory, of course.

Billy had escaped any trouble—except for a couple of minor skirmishes with Curly—and put some of his time to good use during the Atlantic City meet. Issy recognized that Billy had a natural curiosity about racing and took him under his wing to teach him how to handicap the races. Issy was as generous with his time as he was with his money, and the master handicapper patiently instructed him on the basics of picking winners at the racetrack. Billy had learned how to read the *Daily Racing Form* by the end of the meeting and, following Issy's advice, had become a fairly proficient handicapper.

Now that the meeting was near an end, Billy had a decision to make. Every year, half of the touts went to Garden State Park after the Atlantic City meeting and the other half went to Florida to get ready for the winter season there. Issy always went to Garden State while Florida was Rip's perennial destination. Billy obviously had a job with Issy if he wanted one, but Rip convinced him that he could catch on with a sheet in Florida and team up with Issy when he made the trip south.

Billy really wanted to go to Florida—it seemed like a better place for adventure—but he had a fierce loyalty to Issy. There was no question that Billy would continue to Garden State if that is what Issy wanted.

On Saturday, the final day of the meet, Billy was waiting for Issy to provide him with the sheets for the day when the question came up.

"I suppose you have a decision to make, huh, Billy?" Issy said. "Word has it that Rip has offered to take ya with him to Florida. I'm goin' to Garden State. I always do. You can come over there with me if ya want. But that's for you to decide."

"Well, Issy," Billy said. "I would like to go to Florida, but if you want me to go with you, I will. You've been very good to me, Issy, and I wouldn't want you to think less of me or think I'm not thankful for all you've done."

"Don't mention it," Issy replied. "The Garden State meet is only a few weeks. They race a short meet in the spring and another in the fall. Once it's over, I'll be comin' down to Florida myself. If you want, you can take back up with me down there."

"Really?" Billy said. "That would be great! As long as you're sure you won't need me, I'll go down there and wait for you to get there. Thanks, Issy. Thanks a lot."

Issy gave Billy the sheets and he walked directly to the racetrack. As luck would have it, Billy and Rip had the clubhouse stands on the final day of the meet, as they had on opening day. Sales were brisk and the two touts earned a good amount of cash for "shipping money."

As they were ready to leave the stand for the day, a man with a big burlap bag walked by and went straight to an admission booth. He took the cash from the admissions for the day and deposited it in the bag. Then he briskly walked through the side door and into the parking lot.

"See that guy?" Rip asked.

"Yes. Who's he?"

"His name is Joe Toscano," Rip said. "He's the head admissions man here. Some little racket *he's* got goin' in this joint. That rat-faced bastard is in charge of all of the parkin', admissions, and program sales. He basically handles a lot of the cash around here. He probably doesn't think anybody knows it, but he's been skimmin' for years. That bag of cash he just absconded with is goin' home with him, not into the track's coffers. That turnstile right there is his, and his alone; no sharin' with the racetrack. God knows how much of the program and parkin' dough he gloms! Ya know, I figure he's gettin' away with it because of his connections. He's datin' the daughter of Eugene Mori—the president of Garden State Park—and word is they're gonna get married. Now, Mori is a great guy—he's been super with us touts—but the truth is, his daughter is not exactly the prettiest girl in the world. But, Toscano knows she's the ticket to easy street, so to speak, and is more than willin' to overlook that minor inconvenience. Besides, he's no matinee idol himself. Anyway, word is that once he marries her, he's probably gonna wind up the general manager at Garden State, and that's a prestigious and lucrative job."

"Geez, some people will do anything for money, won't they?" Billy said.

"You bet," Rip said. "That's not all this prick has pulled. He's done even worse than this shit."

"Really?" Billy said."What else did he do?"

"Not too long ago, a guy who works in the parkin' lot came up with this new kinda counter that registers cars as they go into the lot—I'm sure you've seen 'em. Anyway, before this thing came along, it was hard to keep track of the cars enterin', and the fear was that the guys workin' the lot were shortin' the number and keepin' some of the cash. So this parkin' lot guy comes up with a counter that the cars have to drive over. It has the counter inside a housing and it's locked, so nobody can tamper with it. Well, this is exactly what companies who have parkin' lots have been lookin' for; racetracks, ballparks, jai alai joints, you name it. So this guy—Toscano—realizes the market for the thing, so I heard he steals the idea from the guy who invented it. In no time, he's rentin' the fuckin' things to everyone, and pullin' in a ton of cash. The guy who came up with the idea in the first place? I don't know what—if anything—he ever got out of it, but from what I was told the general feelin' is that he got porked."

Billy and Rip spent the remainder of the last day at Atlantic City at the clubhouse bar, saying fond farewells to all the people they knew.

The next day those touts who were moving on to Garden State packed up and left, Issy included. Those who were going to Florida had much less urgency in leaving because the Tropical Park meet near Miami wouldn't begin for a few weeks. Instead of a flurry of activity, the southbound touts filtered out one by one according to the schedule they chose for themselves.

Rip was in no hurry to "bug out" this time. Unlike Monmouth Park, where he had basically dated Reenie exclusively, Rip had several love interests at Atlantic City. On any given night during the meet, Rip could be seen with one of a variety of women. Rip had crudely mentioned that his shiny new Corvette was a "pussy magnet," and the results seemed to confirm the hypothesis.

Billy, on the other hand, had not made any connections. Instead, he found himself thinking about Kerra a great deal of the time. There were several occasions he considered borrowing Rip's Corvette and driving back north to see her, but he was not sure how that would have been received. After all, she had instructed him to "see her when he gets back next year," and he thought that could have meant "don't come back looking for me once you leave." As much as he wanted to see her again, he resisted returning.

Billy also realized that as soon as he left for Florida, he would have no opportunity to see his parents for many months. He was certain that his father, in his absolute stubbornness, would not care, but it was his mother that concerned him. He felt terrible about not saying goodbye to her.

Rip needed a week to "say goodbye" to the women he had kept company with during the meet. Night after night he would stagger back to his room in the wee hours of the morning. Finally, he was finished and quite worn out from those efforts. When the two touts left for Florida, it was with Billy behind the wheel of the Corvette; Rip apparently needed a rest.

Rip instructed Billy on the route to Florida. He guided him to the New Jersey Turnpike where they headed south. Outside of the state the Turnpike turned into Interstate 95, and once Rip was satisfied that Billy was going in the right direction, he slumped in his seat and fell into a sound sleep.

Over the next several hours, Billy drove south through Baltimore, Washington, Richmond, and the mostly rural state of North Carolina. As the borderline of the the Carolinas approached, Rip sat up in his seat, almost like clockwork. "We'll be stoppin' right over the border," he said, rubbing his tired eyes.

A sign that read "Next Exit Dillon, SC," appeared alongside of the interstate. "That's it," Rip said. "Get off here."

Billy slowed down and took the exit, which quickly revealed a building with a sign that said "Cold Beer" in huge red letters. At once, Billy realized why it had been so vital to Rip to stop at this place.

"This joint has the only beer for miles and miles," Rip said. "It's surrounded by dry counties on all sides. The guy that runs this place started out with a small gas station and a little stand—like a fruit stand—that he sold beer from. I've been stoppin' here for years. Now he has a big buildin' he works from. He's added some other stuff, too... food, soda, stuff like that. This joint has become a gold mine."

Billy parked next to the building and the two men went inside. Behind the counter, a middle aged man stood ready to take orders.

Rip recognized the man and smiled. "Hiya, Alan," Rip said.

"Well, howdy do!" the man said in a heavy southern drawl. "Mus' be that time o' year, I 's'pose. Y'all headed down to Flor'da already?"

"Yup," Rip said. "Say, have any of the other guys stopped here yet?"

"Nope." the man said. "Y'all the first to come this a'way so far. What can I git y'all t'day?"

Rip got a couple of six packs of cold beer and a can opener. He and Billy hadn't eaten since leaving New Jersey and were now thoroughly famished. "What do ya have that's quick that we can take with us?" Rip asked.

"Well how 'bout a couple o' nice smoked ham po' boys and some chips? Ham is smoked local and it's mighty good if'n I do say so myself!"

"Yeah, that'll be fine," Rip said. Then he added, "Say, is the nearest motel still 10 miles down the road?"

"'Fraid so. Ya know, we's buildin' some rooms right here but they ain't gonna be ready 'til next spring. Next time y'all come this a'way y'all can stay wid us!"

"Will do, Alan," Rip said as he handed over the cash for the goods he had bought.

"I'm a gonna give this here place a name, too," Alan said. "I was thinkin' of callin' it 'Alan's State Line.'"

"Why don't you call it 'South of the Border', Alan," Rip said. "No matter whether you're goin' north or south, it's still just south of the NC border."

"Ya know, I kinda like that, and it do make sense. Maybe that's what we'll call it," Alan said.

Billy and Rip left the store and made the 10 mile drive to the motel where they were able to eat and get a good night's sleep. Rip, as could have been predicted, drank a six pack before bed while Billy only had one can with his sandwich. Billy expected to do most of the driving the next day, and didn't want to contend with a hangover.

If the first part of the trip had been difficult, the second part was even worse. In several places in South Carolina and Georgia the interstate was incomplete and the touts had to detour onto local highways before the road reconnected. This caused substantial delays in a trip that was already overly long. On a couple of occasions, the touts were forced to get gas in small, out-of-the-way towns where the attendants were downright hostile to northerners. Despite all of the adversities, the travelers arrived in Miami having spent nearly 30 hours on the road.

CHAPTER 7 – Florida

Rip and Billy checked into the house on the outskirts of Coral Gables that the touts rented for the winter season. They were the first to show up in Florida and were able to enjoy the large building all by themselves for the time being. After moving in and showering, the weary travelers walked down the street to the local bar for a couple of drinks and dinner.

The two touts sat at the bar and the bartender greeted Rip on sight. As with most taverns near a racetrack, Rip was on a first name basis with those who served alcohol.

"So, anything go on since the last time I was here, Davey?" Rip asked.

The bartender placed mugs of cold beer in front of Rip and Billy, then thought for a second. "Yeah," he said. "Remember that guy that one of the touts shot a few years back? The guy that worked in the admissions department?"

"Sure," Rip said. "What about him?"

"He died a couple of months ago. Not from being shot. From other causes. Heart attack or somethin'."

"No shit!" Rip said. "Good thing he didn't croak from the gun shots. Pokey would be up for murder if he did. It's bad enough he got serious time for shootin' him."

Rip took a long gulp of his beer and asked, "Say, is he buried nearby? I'd like to go pay my respects."

The bartender pointed down the street and said, "I think he's right over at Graceland Memorial. You know where that is, don't you?"

"Sure do," Rip said. "When we get finished here I'll go over and visit him."

Billy was curious about the story and asked Rip to explain it to him.

"I'll fill ya in later," Rip said. "There'll be plenty of time once we get outta here."

The touts had a simple but tasty meal at the bar, got a couple of six packs of cold beer, then walked back to the house to get Rip's Corvette. Rip took the wheel and in a few minutes the car pulled into the Graceland Cemetery. The touts parked and began to walk—six packs in hand.

"This joint ain't too big," Rip said. "Maybe 10 acres. Some graveyards in cities are five times that big. We shouldn't have much trouble findin' the guy."

As predicted, the touts easily found the grave of the man Rip was looking for. The grave still had disturbed soil on it and a headstone that appeared to have been recently placed.

Rip stood silently at the foot of the grave and continued to drink his beer. Billy, in an effort to show his respect—even though he knew nothing of the man in the grave—stood next to Rip with his hands folded in front of him and his head bowed. The two touts stood for a few minutes, silent except for the sound of Rip guzzling his beer. Dusk was now descending on the cemetery.

Then, Rip threw his empty beer can aside and walked up to the marker. He unzipped his pants and began to urinate all over the headstone, then the grave itself.

Billy couldn't believe his eyes. "What the hell are you doing!" he shouted.

"Payin' my respects to this old, dead, cocksucker!" Rip replied. "I promised this motherfucker I'd piss on his grave and, luckily, I got the chance!"

Billy wanted no part of this fiasco and started to walk back towards the car. "Wait!" Rip shouted. "I'll tell you the rest of that story now."

Billy stopped in his tracks and returned to where Rip stood zipping his pants.

"Okay," Billy said. "What could this guy have done to deserve that?"

"Well," Rip said, "that guy was one of the biggest pricks to the touts at any track anywhere. He always hated the tip sheet guys and hassled 'em every chance he could. He tried to get the sheets thrown outta the track a few years back but failed because the customers almost threw a riot. Anyway, he was always lookin' for ways to fuck with the guys on the line. The one guy he hated the most was a fella named Pokey. Well, Pokey ran the *Jack's Green Card* down here at the time, and this asshole buried here constantly harassed him. One day, the son of a bitch was walkin' near the paddock and Pokey strolled right up to him, pulled out a pistol, and pumped three or four shots right into him, point blank. The scumbag fell to the ground and somebody who was there told me that every time he took a breath, blood would shoot out of the holes in his chest."

"Oh my god," Billy said. "And he lived through that?"

"By some miracle, he did," Rip said. "So Pokey gets hauled in on some type of attempted murder charge and, of course, he gets convicted. When the judge goes to sentence him, he asks Pokey, 'Do you have anything to say before I impose sentence?' To which Pokey stands up and says, 'Yes, your honor. I shot the son of a bitch, I'm *not* sorry,

112

and I'd do it again if I had the chance. My only regret is that I didn't kill him. Thank you.' So, Pokey gets the maximum sentence. Pokey wasn't a bad guy, he just couldn't stand any more of the abuse. Truth is, if this bastard had died then, none of the touts would have shed a tear for him. I had my share of run-ins with the asshole, myself. During one of our tussles, I told him I'd piss on his grave. At least you can't say I don't keep my promises."

Rip took the can opener out of his pocket, opened another beer and began to guzzle it. Then, he wiped his mouth and said, "Remember one thing, kid. When a guy who's been a a motherfucker all his life dies, he doesn't suddenly become a good guy. He just becomes a dead motherfucker."

As Rip and Billy returned to the car, Rip added, "Oh, there's a little post script to this story. Crazy Tommy was at the track the day Pokey shot the guy and within a couple o' minutes he was on the phone. He called Bussey and said, 'Your manager just shot the admissions guy and the cops took him away. Can I have his job?' Only a dickhead like Tommy would do somethin' like that."

Over the next couple of weeks, the other touts began to trickle in; Crazy Tommy and the Alligator, Curly and Cockeye Sol, and Big Mike. The meeting was only about two weeks away now and activity began to pick up at Tropical Park. Horses were training over the track and workmen were busy setting up everything for the big opening.

On the Sunday morning before the Tropical meet, Billy was awakened by Rip shaking him in bed. "Get up," Rip said. "We have someplace to go."

Billy sat up in bed and rubbed his eyes. "What are you talking about," he asked. "Go where?"

"You'll see," Rip said. "It's a beautiful mornin' and this is gonna be a great day! Now get up and let's get goin'!"

Billy pulled himself out of bed and quickly got dressed. He met Rip outside of the house and the two touts got into the Corvette and roared down the street.

Billy said nothing while Rip did the driving. Within a half hour, the Corvette pulled into the Miami International Airport.

"Where are we going?" Billy asked. "We aren't going to fly somewhere, are we?"

"Yes, we are, and it's a surprise," Rip said.

Billy had experienced some of Rip's "surprises" and secretly hoped this one wouldn't end badly, as many had.

The men entered the airport and Rip led Billy straight to the Cubana Airlines counter. "Two round trip tickets to Havana," Rip said.

"Havana!" Billy shouted. "You mean Havana, Cuba?"

"On no," Rip said. "Havana, Mississippi. Of course Havana, Cuba, you nitwit! Have you ever heard of a Havana anywhere else?"

Billy wasn't sure he should even get on the plane. "I don't know, Rip," he said. "I don't have a passport or anything, and..."

Rip interrupted Billy in mid sentence. "You don't need any passport! Jesus Christ! How many times have I told ya, let me do the thinkin', will ya?" Then Rip added, "I have everything under control!"

"Yeah, that's what I'm afraid of," Billy mumbled.

Rip took the tickets and the men walked to the Cubana Airlines gate. Within 20 minutes, they were on board and ready for takeoff.

"Ever been on a plane before?" Rip asked.

"No," Billy said. "I'm a little bit nervous."

Rip waved to a stewardess and she approached the two touts.

"Can we get a couple of cocktails?" Rip asked.

"Surely. What would you gentlemen like? Seeing that it's still early, would you like to try a Mimosa?"

"No," Rip said. "Give us each a Jim Beam and Coke. And make each one with a two ounce airline bottle, will ya?"

Within minutes the drinks were served, the plane took off, and the Cuban excursion was underway. The two touts were able to have a couple of drinks during the short, 45 minute flight to Havana. By the time the plane arrived, Billy was very calm, and well on his way to a significant buzz.

At the airport, Rip looked for a certain driver among the many cabs that lined the curb. Finally, his eyes landed on the man he was looking for. "Juanito!" he shouted.

"*Señor* Rip!" the man called back, then got in his cab and drove to where the touts were standing. "How have you been, *señor* Rip?"

"Fine Juanito." Rip said. "You know the first place I always go when I come to Havana, don't you?"

"Why yes, *señor* Rip. Calle Empedrado. I will take you there right away!"

The cab weaved its way past the Spanish colonial buildings and through the narrow streets of old Havana until it came to a stop in front of a small Cuban bar. Rip paid the fare and instructed Juanito to return in two hours.

Rip led Billy into the crowded room and up to the bar. "*Dos mojitos*," Rip said.

"*Ahora mismo, señor* Rip." the bartender replied.

"Welcome to Cuba," Rip said, holding up his drink to Billy and waiting for him to do the same. They sipped the cold drinks and as Billy lowered his to the bar, his eye caught the sight of a man across the room talking to what appeared to be one of the natives. The man looked somewhat familiar, and as Billy studied his face, the identity of the man came to him.

"Rip, Rip," he said in an excited whisper. "Over there... across the bar...that man...that's Ernest Hemingway!"

Rip turned and looked in the direction of the man. "Sure is!" he said. Then he shouted in the man's direction, "PAPA!"

The man, Ernest Hemingway, stopped chatting with the native and smiled back at Rip. "Well, hello, Rip!" he said. "This can only mean one thing: the Florida racing season is upon us! How have you been?"

Billy and Rip picked up their mojitos and walked around the bar to where Hemingway was standing. "Fine, Papa," Rip said. "Meet my friend here, Billy Mulray."

Billy was awestruck. He had studied this man's works throughout high school and college, and considered him an icon. He shook Hemingway's hand and, in a semi-trance, managed to say, "glad to meet you."

Rip and Hemingway quickly got into a conversation, and Billy was content to stand by and quietly absorb it all.

"Do you still go fishin'? Do you still have your boat?" Rip asked.

"Hell, yes." Hemingway said. "I still have the Pilar, and the fishing has been quite good. Last month I landed a couple of blue marlins—big fuckers—over a grand apiece." He took a sip of his drink, then continued, "I still live at Finca Vigia, and I've been writing quite a bit lately."

Another topic of discussion was the state of affairs in Cuba, and which direction the island nation was headed. A civil war was underway between Cuba's dictator Fulgencio Batista and rebel forces under the control of an insurgent named Fidel Castro.

"I spend a lot of time with the common people and they tell me that things are getting worse and worse under Batista," Hemingway said. "His regime is corrupt, and he's in bed with those fuckin' American mobsters who control gambling, dope, and whores. This past spring, a group of brave students attacked the National Palace, trying to overthrow the bastard. Forty-four of them were slaughtered and, obviously, the attempt failed. Poor sonsa bitches never had a chance. But the rebel attacks against government targets are increasing now, led by Castro. He's been promising reforms and a return to the Cuban constitution which was suspended when Batista took power. I suppose only time will tell."

Hemingway ran his hand across his white beard and took another sip of his drink.

"Say, Papa," Rip said. "That's not a mojito you're drinkin'. What is that stuff?"

"This," Hemingway replied, "is absinthe. It's a tasty little drink, and it has a hell of a kick to it. I used to get the best absinthe in the world years ago in Paris. Then the bastards who control the wine industry over there got it outlawed because it was getting too popular and cutting into their sales. This comes from Spain. Not bad, but not as good as the Parisian kind. Spain is one of the only places in the world where it's still legal. One of the only good things under Franco, as far as I'm concerned."

Time passed quickly and before the two touts knew it, it was time to leave. Juanito pulled his cab up to the front door of the bar, beeped his horn and called from his window, "*Señor* Rip! Two hours! Just like you said!"

Billy and Rip finished their drinks, said their goodbyes to Hemingway, and hopped into the waiting cab. As Billy looked over his shoulder he could see the sign hanging in front of the bar which read "La Bodeguita del Medio." As the cab drove away from the curb, Billy couldn't help but talk about what had happened. "I can't believe it!" he said. "I just spent a couple of hours drinking with Ernest Hemingway!"

Rip laughed and said, "Well, there are probably more people who can say that than ya might think. Papa drinks nearly every day. He used to say 'done by noon, drunk by three.' He always did his writin' in the early mornin' and his drinkin' afterwards. You wouldn't know it to look at him now, but that man is only in his late fifties. He looks much older because he's been livin' life at 100 miles an hour since he was a teenager. After decades of doin' that, it shows. He's also been fucked up a few times—car accidents, plane crashes, bombs in the wars, you name it. He even shot himself by accident once.

Oh, and he's also been a great cocksman; you rarely see him without a hot babe nearby. He's been married somethin' like four times and god knows how many women he's had that he didn't marry."

Juanito expertly made his way through the Havana traffic which consisted not only of cars and cabs, but also donkeys, bicycles, and an inordinate amount of pedestrians. Finally he drove up to a building with a big sign that read "Oriental Park." Billy didn't even need to ask; he knew that they were about to enter a racetrack. Rip paid Juanito and instructed him to return after the races.

"They have horse racing here, too, huh?" Billy asked.

"Of course," Rip said. "This joint has been open since World War I. Pretty soon, some of the better jockeys will be coming down here. Joe Culmone, Willie Shoemaker, Bill Hartack. No track races on Sunday in the states, so this joint does big business on that day of the week. On Sundays a lot of the riders from Florida will be racin' here."

Men were entering the track in droves as time for the first race approached. Billy had never seen so many white panama hats and white suits; it almost seemed like a type of "uniform". Many of the men puffed on cigars, and a mix of Spanish and English chatter filled the air.

The two touts walked into the old wooden grandstand where they were able to buy *Racing Forms* and programs for the day's races. As they stood studying the charts, Billy could hear Rip begin to howl with laughter. Billy looked up from his program to see what could be causing Rip's hilarity, and saw a scene he would never forget. Staggering through the crowd, each of his arms wrapped around a gorgeous, young, raven-haired Cuban *señorita*, came Issy. He had a half-drunk bottle of Crown Royal whiskey in each hand, and the young ladies were obviously the only thing between him and falling flat on the floor.

"Hiya, Billy boy," Issy said in a drunken slur. "Fancy meetin' up with you here!"

"Man, I'll say," Billy said. "What are you doing down here?"

"Whaddya think? Same thing YOU'RE doing here, " Issy said.

Billy couldn't help but chuckle. He had never seen Issy drunk before and to encounter him under such circumstances seemed very odd—and comical.

"No," Billy said. "I mean I thought you were going to stay up at Garden State until they closed. I'm just surprised to see you already."

"Well," Issy said, "I was puttin' out the sheet at Garden and I get a call from the boss. He tells me he wants me to get to Florida right away for the Tropical meet. So they sent some guy from New York to handle the Garden and I came down here. No problem. I love Florida in the winter, and I *really love* Havana on a Sunday!"

Issy took a drink from one of the bottles of whiskey, then took a swig from the other. He was drinking with both hands, apparently trying to keep the amounts in each bottle equal.

"Hiya, Rip," Issy said, holding out the bottles. "You guys want a drink?"

"No," Rip said. "I'm gonna get myself an ice cold daiquiri in a minute. Thanks anyway."

Billy shook his head in the negative.

"Well, suit yourselves," Issy said. He took a sip from the bottle in his left hand followed by a sip from the bottle in his right. He then handed one bottle to each of his young admirers—both of whom were less than half his age—and they took a drink. Issy motioned for Billy to come closer and when he did, Issy whispered in his ear. "A lot of 'business' goes on at this track, and I have some good contacts down here. Word is they're gonna let a couple of apprentice jockeys win the daily double. Linda Cubana is supposed to win the first race and Jet-Ray is the horse in the second. Put a couple of bucks on it. My information in Havana is normally pretty good."

"Okay," Billy whispered back. "Thanks. I'll give it a try."

With that, Issy said goodbye and staggered off—a young woman under each arm—and disappeared into the crowd.

"What was that Issy told you?" Rip asked.

"Issy thinks he has info on a couple of fixed races," Billy said.

"Alright!" Rip shouted. "What did he say? Which races?"

"The daily double," Billy said. "He gave me the names of the horses."

"Holy shit!" Rip said. "We could make a major score today!"

Billy couldn't understand what all the excitement was about. He had been told about supposedly "fixed races" at every track and found that most of the time the information wasn't worth the time of day.

"Let me tell ya somethin'," Rip said. "This joint is run by the mob. An American Jew named Lansky controls the races here. The Jews in his organization take care of each other. One of 'em is a pal of Issy's, so if Issy says he has information, more than likely, it's golden. This is our chance to make a killin'!"

The first race field was on the track, so Billy and Rip got in line to buy daily double tickets. They each bought ten two-dollar tickets on the 4-4 combination, Linda Cubana and Jet-Ray.

The first race went off and the outcome was never in doubt. Linda Cubana took the lead as soon as the starting gate opened and she stayed in front the entire race, paying $4.00 as the even money favorite. Billy and Rip were "alive" in the daily double. Now, if Jet-Ray could win the second half, it would mean a big payday for the two touts.

Rip and Billy headed straight to the nearest bar and ordered a couple of daiquiris. They stood there and sipped their cold drinks until the horses were being loaded into the gate, then walked outside to watch the race. Billy marveled at the beauty of the old track; there were palm trees in the infield and large, colorful, tropical flowers everywhere. The midday sun shone down warmly on the thousands of fans assembled for the day's races, and Billy closed his eyes and basked in the comforting sunshine.

The bell rang and the field for the second race was released. The 8-5 favorite, Bull Leader, immediately took an easy lead while Jet-Ray, an 8-1 longshot, struggled to stay in contention. Around the final turn, Bull Leader held a four length advantage over Jet-Ray and time was running out.

Halfway down the stretch, the rider of Bull Leader began to look behind him, then he inexplicably dropped his whip. It was then that Jet-Ray finally kicked into high gear and began to close the gap with every stride.

"Cmon, girl! Run at 'em!" the touts shouted.

Nearing the wire, the jockey of Bull Leader seemed to pull in on the reins when Jet-Ray went by on her way to a narrow victory.

Billy and Rip congratulated each other and waited for the race to be declared official to see what their winnings would be. The old odds board finally lit up and the payoff for a two-dollar daily double ticket was $73.60 , which rewarded each of them with $736.00. Apparently Issy's information was indeed very good in Havana.

The two touts returned to the bar where they put down one daiquiri after another. Billy and Rip half-heartedly handicapped the races but didn't make a bet until Billy saw something that he thought would win in the last race.

"Hey Rip," Billy said. "I really like a horse in this race. I think I'm going to bet some win money on it."

"If you're gonna do that," Rip said, "be sure to check with the bookmakers out front. Sometimes ya can get a better payoff from them than you can from the mutuels."

"Bookmakers? What do you mean, bookmakers?" Billy asked.

"I forgot you don't know shit," Rip said. "Did you see the guys out front with the chalk boards? Those are the bookmakers. They offer odds on horses and ya get whatever price they're givin' when you buy your ticket. Sometimes—not always, but sometimes—they give a higher price than you wind up gettin' with the mutuels. So, if you're bettin' a win ticket, it's always best to compare and see which gives ya the best deal. At one time, those guys handled all the bets at the tracks in the U.S. Then along came the mutuel machines and the bookmakers were on their way out. They still have 'em here and in Mexico."

Billy saw the logic in Rip's explanation and decided it would be best to compare. "Will you go out there and show me what to look for?" he asked.

"Goddam it," Rip said. "I just want ya to know that if ya take a dump, I'm not gonna wipe your ass for ya. Let's go."

The two touts walked to the front of the grandstand where there were a line of chalk boards and men feverishly taking wagers and writing tickets. Every so often, they would erase the odds listed next to each horse and replace them with updated odds. Bettors stood around, checking each bookmaker's board to compare them with each other, then looked at the odds board in the infield to check the odds coming from the mutuel machines.

"Okay," Rip said, "now we stand here and check the various bookmakers' odds to see who's givin' the best price on your horse. Then, we see what the odds on the mutuels are. The thing ya have to remember is that the odds on the mutuels change all the time and you get the final odds, naturally. With the book, you get the odds at the time you place your bet. Ya have to be careful. Sometimes ya can make a mistake and make the wrong bet. Now which horse do ya wanna bet?"

"La Gitana," Billy said. "The number four horse."

"Alright," Rip said. "The guy on the left is offerin' 5-1. The guy in the middle has that horse listed at 5-1, too. Over on the right, you get 5.5-1."

Rip overheard a wager that the middle bookmaker accepted and said, "Wait a minute! The guy in the middle just took a big bet on the six horse. He's gonna change his odds right away. He's gonna raise the odds on all the other horses so he can balance the book and make a profit."

As predicted, the man in the middle booth quickly did some calculations on a notebook, then shouted, "New board! *Carta Nueva!*" He then erased the prices on the chalkboard and posted updated odds. The new odds on La Gitana were now 6-1 with the middle bookmaker.

Rip glanced out at the infield odds board to check the odds. "Only 9-2 with the mutuels," he said. "You hafta make up your mind now. The horses are movin' towards the starting gate."

"What do you think I should do?" Billy asked.

"Well, your best price is the man in the center booth. C'mon let's get closer so ya can make a bet. Do you want to place the bet, or do ya want me to do it for ya?"

"Maybe you ought to do it the first time," Billy said.

"Fine," Rip said. "I'll make this one, then you can see how it's done."

Rip and Billy closed in on the center booth where men were taking bets and writing tickets.

"How's the four?" Rip called out.

"6-1," a man with a pad and pen called out. "Last chance, amigo. No more than $100 to win. Want the bet?"

"Yup," Rip said. "Gimme $100 to win on the four."

Rip turned to Billy and said, "Gimme a C note. You're lucky we're gettin' this in under the wire."

Billy looked horrified. "But, um, I was only going to bet $5 on it. I didn't want that big of a bet."

"Jesus Christ!" Rip yelled. "Ya make hundreds on Issy's tip and ya don't even want to re-invest a lousy C note on somethin' you really like? Don't be a fuckin' cheapskate!"

"C'mon, c'mon," the man said, "here's your ticket, now hand over the cash! You're down now and the book is closed!"

Billy hated to be considered a "cheapskate" and reached in his pocket for a $100 bill. He handed it to the man who in turn gave him a hand-written ticket that read $100 win, #4, race 9, 6-1 odds.

Billy and Rip were barely in position to watch the race when the bell rang. The final race of the day was a long one—one mile and sixty yards. La Gitana was patiently ridden behind the pacesetter then took the lead turning for home and lasted at the wire by a diminishing length, giving Billy a $600 win. It was the first race that Billy ever handicapped *and* bet on.

After a round of back slapping and congratulations, the two touts walked back to the bookmaker's stand and collected the winnings. As they were leaving the track, Rip stopped at a cigar stand on the way out to buy some coveted Cuban cigars.

"Let me have a box of Rey d'Mundo's," Rip said. "Make it Choix Supremas. They're the best."

Billy stepped up to the counter and said "Let me get this for you, Rip. I wouldn't have made as much on that bet if you hadn't have helped me."

The cigars were $25 for a box of twenty five, and Billy paid the amount and gave the vendor a $2 tip. Then the touts—quite drunk by this time walked outside where Juanito had his cab waiting.

"We're gonna get some good Cuban food before our flight back," Rip said. Then he said to Juanito, "El Floridita, amigo."

Rip opened the box of cigars and handed two to Juanito. Upon seeing the gift, Juanito could not contain his gratefulness. "Oh, thank you *señor* Rip! Thank you so much! I have not had such a fine cigar in a long, long time! Thank you! Thank you!"

"Don't mention it, amigo," Rip said. Then he placed one in his mouth and handed one to Billy. "Say, Juanito, I'm sure you have a cutter here, don't you?"

"*Si, señor* Rip. I smoke many cigars, but not so fine as El Rey del Mundo Suprema. Here. You can cut your cigar with this." Juanito handed Rip his cigar cutter, and Rip snipped off the tip of his Suprema. He then handed it to Billy and instructed him to do the same. Rip then lit the cigar and held out his match for Billy. Billy puffed on the cigar until it was well lit, then handed the cutter back to Juanito, who readied one of his cigars.

The three men happily puffed the cigars as the cab made it's way through the dusk towards El Floridita. Billy had never smoked a cigar before and had imagined that it would be harsh and unpalatable. But he quickly realized that the smoke was mild and sweet with a very pleasant fragrance, nothing like the ten cent versions smoked by most Americans.

"Give us an hour and a half, Juanito," Rip said.

"I will be back *señor* Rip, don't worry." After taking a long puff he added, "Thank you again for the fine cigar."

Rip gave his usual tribute to the maître d' and the touts got a good table near a window. They feasted on a meal that began with mariquitas—fried plantains with a garlic sauce—and a delicious Cuban black bean soup. For the main course, Rip ordered Pernil Asado, a slow roasted pork dish, while Billy got Camarones al Ajillo, shrimp sauteed in garlic and olive oil. The two touts also ordered the house specialty drink—daiquiris. It was at El Floridita that daiquiris were developed some twenty five years earlier, and the bartenders there took great pride in preparing their signature cocktail. The old restaurant was quaint and charming, complete with ancient ceiling fans which slowly whirred overhead.

"This is another of Hemingway's haunts," Rip said. He pointed towards the bar and said, "He spends as much time here as he does at the Bodeguita, maybe more. Whenever you come to Havana, chances are you'll see him either here or there."

Billy paid the bill and the two touts walked outside the restaurant to wait for Juanito. Rip handed Billy a cigar and took one for himself. He bit hard on the end and spit a chunk of the cigar into the street. "No cutter. Gotta use your teeth," he said. Billy mimicked Rip's actions and within seconds the touts were contentedly puffing on an after-dinner smoke. As they stood silently enjoying their cigars, Rip stopped smoking and turned his head, as if straining to hear something.

"Hear that?" he said.

"No, what?" Billy asked.

"Shhhh! Listen. That's machine gun fire off in the distance. And return fire. There's a gun battle goin' on outside of the city. That must be the rebels Papa was talkin' about. Hey, fuck *this*. We're gettin' outta here as soon as Juanito gets back."

A few minutes later Juanito's cab pulled up in front of El Floridita and the anxious touts jumped in. Rip instructed him to get to the airport on the double, and Juanito complied. They boarded the plane and 45 minutes and three drinks later, they were back in Miami.

The opening day of the Tropical Park meeting was met with bright sunshine and a huge crowd of enthusiastic racing fans gathered outside the gates waiting for them to open.

As Billy and Rip entered the track, they could see a commotion occurring in front of the tip sheet stand. Three men stood there, arguing with each other, and their voices were loud and their speech filled with obscenities. Each of the men held a stack of tip sheets and, curiously, they were all the same color—red. As the two touts drew closer, they could hear some of what the men where shouting about.

"Fuck you two!" one of the men screamed. "I have proof this is my sheet! You two can go fuck yourselves!"

"Yeah? We'll see about that, asshole!" another said. "I bought this sheet months ago! I have a bill of sale!"

"I don't give a jolly shit what either of yous say!" the third man shouted. "Money talks and bullshit walks! And yous are the ones who's gonna walk!"

This three-way scream fest went on for several minutes before the admissions manager came out and broke it up. "Everybody be quiet!" he yelled. "I want to know what the hell's goin' on here!"

The three men all started talking simultaneously until the admissions man interrupted. "Okay, everybody shut up! I'll ask the questions from here on, and don't speak until I tell ya to!"

Billy and Rip took their positions in the tip sheet stand and waited for the gates to open. Jigger Higgins had gotten to the stand a bit early and had witnessed the whole debacle.

"Jigger, is this what I think it is?" Rip asked.

"Yup. That slimy fuck has done it again. It's a miracle he's not in jail."

"What?" Billy asked anxiously. "What happened?"

"There's a guy called 'the Roach' who pops up every once in a while at racetracks," Rip said. "He somehow gets to manage sheets from time to time because he's a fair handicapper and an expert printer. Anyway, a few years back the Roach is puttin' out a sheet at Hot Springs. Durin' the meet, he spreads the word that he's gonna sell the sheet at

124

the end of the meeting and he makes contact with a few guys who want to buy it. At the end of the meet he sells the sheet, not to one guy, or two, but *four*. Yup, four suckers put up the cash to buy the sheet. So when the next meet rolls around, four guys show up thinkin' they own the sheet. Now for the kicker: the crooked bastard never owned the sheet in the first place! He just took money from four assholes and when it was all over, none of them owned anything but a bleedin' ass compliments of a reamin' they got from the Roach."

"Is that what happened here?" Billy asked.

"No doubt," Jigger said. "The Roach worked that red sheet last year in Florida. I'm sure he pulled the same scam that he did years back in Hot Springs."

The admissions manager settled the dispute by refusing to allow any of the "new owners" to sell any sheets until he was able to ascertain who was in legal possession of the business. The melee subsided and shortly thereafter, the bell rang and the Tropical Park meeting was underway.

Opening day at Tropical was generally like those Billy had experienced elsewhere. Big crowds, good racing, and large receipts. After the day's selling was finished, a trip to the bar and an introduction to all of Rip's friends followed, as usual. Not only were the days becoming routine, but the race meets were becoming routine, also. The life of a racetrack tout in 1957 was leisurely and lucrative, and Billy was enjoying himself very much.

By the time racing in Florida had commenced, he had a handle on which of the other touts liked him, which ones didn't, and which ones were indifferent. He did what any person would do in his circumstance—he fraternized with those who were amicable and tried to make little contact with those who he considered hostile. His skirmishes with Curly were now fewer and farther between, mostly due to the fact that Billy ignored him whenever possible. He did the same with Cockeye Sol and, to a lesser degree, Crazy Tommy, the Alligator, and Bullet Bob. Nearly everyone, Billy included, tried to ignore Big Mike. It seemed that no good could ever come by interaction with him.

Toward the end of the Tropical meeting, Billy received a message that his father was trying to contact him. After giving it much thought, he declined to return the call. Billy was having quite a good time in Florida and he was sure that his father would try, in some way, to derail it. Besides, in a few months he would be back in New Jersey, and he could stop by to visit his parents. At any rate, he wanted it to be on his terms, not his father's, when he made contact.

Several weeks later, on Christmas Eve, Billy decided it was finally time to call his parents. Armed with several dollars in coins, he walked into a telephone booth outside of Tropical Park and dialed home. The phone rang and rang, but there was no answer. Billy couldn't understand it; his parents were always home the night before Christmas. Over the next couple of hours, he tried several more times with the same result. Billy called on Christmas day, too, to no avail. Finally, he reasoned that the most likely explanation was that his parents had gone to visit relatives for the holidays, and he figured he could contact them at a later time.

The racing action in Florida moved to Hialeah Park after New Year's Day, 1958. Billy thought that Hialeah was the most beautiful track he had seen so far—palm trees everywhere, pink flamingos in the infield, Italian marble and gold plated fixtures in the rest rooms, lush grass in the infield, a huge, ornate fountain at the entrance—everything seemed to be first rate and high class. The racetrack was owned by Eugene Mori, who also owned Garden State Park, and it was evident that he spared no expense in the pursuit of luxury.

Hialeah was the winter playground of the rich and famous. Over the course of the season, Billy saw such celebrities as Bob Hope, Mickey Rooney, Marilyn Monroe, and Bing Crosby.

One day shortly after the beginning of the meet, Billy and Rip were having a drink at the clubhouse bar when Billy mentioned the celebrities he had seen so far.

"Oh," Rip said, "I guess everybody who's anybody has been here at one time or another. Harry Truman used to come by once in a while. I saw Winston Churchill here once, too. Some of the old timers say that Al Jolson loved this place and so did George Raft. John Philip Sousa and Will Rogers were others they talked about."

Rip took a gulp of his drink, then continued, "Before they were elected, President Eisenhower had been here and so had his VP, Nixon. Another guy who used to go to the races is a senator named Kennedy. His father, Joe, made a fortune cozyin' up to politicians and was an investor in this joint at one time. I remember seein' his boys—Teddy, Bobby, and Jack—here gettin' drunk and pickin' up women. Jack—he's the senator—was the oldest and as I remember a pretty nice guy. He was single then. Bobby was the middle brother. He was a little on the quiet side. But the youngest one, Teddy —he was probably 14-15 years younger than Jack—was a mouthy, arrogant little turd."

Hialeah was also a proving ground for young racehorses. The track featured several important stakes for horses headed to the Kentucky Derby, including the Everglades Stakes and Flamingo Stakes. Many horses who later proved successful in the classic races had "cut their teeth" in those major races at Hialeah.

One day during the meet, Billy and Issy struck up a conversation about handicapping while Issy was preparing the sheets for the day.

"So," Issy asked, "have you been handicappin' much? Have ya been bettin'?"

"Well, I have been handicapping every day, but I don't bet very often. I'm still learning and I don't have the confidence to do much betting as of yet."

"That's a smart move," Issy said. "Most guys jump into bettin' before they know what they're doin'. They put the cart before the horse, so to speak. You ought to know about handicappin' before ya go plungin'."

"Well that's what I'm trying to do, Issy," Billy said. "I've been watching most of the races and taking notes, like you taught me. I'm getting to know a lot of the horses on the circuit."

"Any that you like in particular?" Issy asked.

"Yes," Billy said. "I've been following a horse named Tim Tam ever since I saw him race at the start of the meet. He's won a couple of races and I think he might become one of the best horses in the sport."

"I know the horse," Issy said. "I saw him race at Garden State right before I came down here. I agree with you, he looks like the real deal. He's been gettin' better and better with each race. It's a long time between now and the Kentucky Derby, but he's headed in that direction. It'll be interestin' to see if he can make it. He's a Calumet colt trained by Jimmy Jones. Calumet has raced some of the greatest horses ever; Whirlaway, Citation, and last year's Derby winner, Iron Liege, to name a few."

Billy took advantage of Issy's handicapping knowledge whenever possible and used this opportunity to ask questions.

"Issy, I was wondering about horses' times," Billy said. "I'm having trouble separating horses using their finish times."

"That's because time," Issy said, "is for guys in jail to worry about. In handicappin' it's not very important at all. Ya see, times can be misleadin'. Lottsa things affect the time a horse gets. How fast—or slow—the track surface is. How fast—or slow—the early fractions of a race are. How much head—or tail—wind there is. How hot—or cold—the temperature is. Lottsa things affect times. That's why often a horse can win a race in fast time, then next out he's nowhere in a slower race. Finish times are unreliable for comparin' horses."

Issy stopped setting type and looked directly at Billy. "Now class," he said, "is the single most important thing to consider. If a horse has been racin' against tougher company than he'll be meetin' today—droppin' in class—he should run better. The best bet you can make is on a horse who's shown he can beat the kind of horses he's racin' against today. Class is the most important thing to consider in handicappin', no doubt. Even jockeys and trainers are more important than time. A classy horse, ridden by a good jockey, conditioned by a capable trainer, is what I always look for when I make a bet. I never worry about time because it really isn't that important."

Over the course of the Hialeah meet, Billy's faith in Tim Tam paid dividends. The colt went on a winning streak, capturing both the Everglades Stakes and the Flamingo Stakes in impressive fashion. Each race brought his favorite horse closer to the Kentucky Derby, which was now less than three months away.

The final stop for the Florida winter racing circuit was Gulfstream Park. Although a very comfortable and utilitarian racetrack, Gulfstream could not compare with the beauty and elegance of Hialeah. The crowds, racing, and profits were very good there, however, and Billy was able to earn enough to maintain the lifestyle to which he—thanks in large part to Rip—had become accustomed.

Tim Tam continued his winning ways, taking both the Fountain of Youth Stakes and the Florida Derby at Gulfstream, thus providing Billy with sizable returns on bets he had placed on him. Those victories assured the colt of a berth in the coveted Kentucky Derby, and when the meet was over, the big race in Louisville was only a few weeks off.

Rip, if nothing else, was consistent. During the winter months in Florida, he drank regularly and kept company with a variety of accommodating women. Billy, however, spent a great deal of his time thinking about Kerra. He looked forward to the time when he would see her again, and resisted getting involved with any of the women who fraternized with the touts.

Despite the scare they had encountered on their first trip to Havana, the two touts made several more Sunday excursions to the tropical playland over the winter months. Rip introduced Billy to the Havana nightlife, which included trips to Cabaret Montmartre, San Souci casino, and the Tropicana, places they visited after a day of racing at Oriental Park. Billy dabbled with craps and roulette at the casinos in Havana, but found them basically boring compared to the thrill and satisfaction he felt from picking a winner at the racetrack.

The winter passed quickly and as it gave way to spring, there were yet more decisions to be made. Although it was inevitable that the two touts were going to return north, when—and how—that would occur was up in the air. The discussion emerged as they sat at the tavern one night toward the end of the Gulfstream meeting.

"Well, Billy boy, how did you enjoy the winter in sunny Florida?" Rip asked.

"It was great," Billy said. "I never realized how good it feels to be warm during the winter. And those trips to Havana were fabulous. I'm really glad that I made the decision to stay on with the sheets."

"From here we go to Hot Springs." Rip said. "It's a terrific town and they have a very short and lucrative meet."

"Where *is* Hot Springs?" Billy asked. "I've heard you guys talk about it but I never knew where it was."

"Arkansas." Rip said. "It's an old resort town. They have hot mineral springs there. People with arthritis and shit like that go there for therapy. They sit in the mineral baths and it makes 'em feel better. Personally, I think it's bullshit. They could probably do the same by sittin' in a bathtub of hot water with epsom salts in it. But long ago somebody sold people on the medicinal properties of the springs and they've been comin' ever since. The one good thing is that they have a racetrack there, and people come from all around for that, too. Texans, Georgians, Okies, you name it. And they spend. That's why we go there when that joint—Oaklawn Park—is open. They only race about 24 days a year."

"How far is that from here?" Billy asked.

"Oh, it's a good ride," Rip said. "It's a two day deal. About 550-600 miles each day. We'll go about halfway, then flop for the night. Next day we'll be there."

A week later, the Florida racing season was over and the two touts packed up and left for Arkansas.

CHAPTER 8 – Hot Springs

It was late afternoon when the touts drove into downtown Hot Springs. The day was unseasonably warm, and Rip had put the roof of the convertible down earlier in the afternoon. The sound of clapping and cheering echoed off the buildings along the street and they noticed a crowd gathering at a park up ahead. As they reached the park, Rip slowed down to see what the commotion was about. In the center of the park a man addressed the crowd through a microphone from a big wooden stand adorned with bunting. His voice was loud and his accent was heavily southern.

"If I'm elected, I promise to run every who-er, pimp, drunkard, and gambler outta Hot Springs fer once and fer all!"

His proclamation was met with cheers and thunderous applause.

"Oh, these assholes again." Rip said. "Every year the fuckin' politicians come out before Oaklawn opens and rally all the holy rollers. This is part of the bible belt, and most of those people don't think there should be any drinkin' or gamblin' here. What these fuck nuts don't realize is that even though the track is only open about one month a year, all the local businesses make a killin' in that short span. It's good for the economy, and it helps keep taxes down. If they had any brains, they'd all just go the fuck away for a month and not make such a big deal out of it. Truth is, once the track opens, half of these hypocrites will be right in there bettin' and drinkin' with everybody else."

Rip drove across town to a quiet street lined with huge willow oak trees. He pulled up in front of a quaint two-story home with a wrap-around porch and rose bushes in the front yard.

"This is our place for the meet," he said. "Nice old lady lives here and rents rooms to a couple of touts during the season. The rooms are small, but we aren't gonna be here for long, anyway. The track is only a few blocks away—walkin' distance. I like this place because it's nice and peaceful; none of the other hustlers are anywhere around here."

The two touts met the landlady—Mrs. Armitage—and unloaded their belongings. They immediately headed to one of Rip's favorite watering holes in all of Hot Springs—Maxine's. They entered the barroom and took seats at the long wooden bar. The decor was old and the room filled with trappings reminiscent of a century earlier. After ordering a couple of draft beers, Rip began to educate Billy on the history of the ancient building.

"This joint once was, and probably still is, a notorious whore house." Rip said. "The upstairs is a so-called 'gentlemen's club.' The madam of the place is Maxine Jones, and she's known around these parts as the 'brothel queen.' Some of the richest guys from Dallas, Atlanta, Chicago, places like that, come to this joint for some booze, entertainment, and women. I've also heard there are a couple of craps tables and roulette wheels up there, too."

The bartender delivered the cold beer and Rip wasted no time in guzzling half the glass straight down.

"They say that ol' Maxine is a shrewd businesswoman." Rip said. "When she first started out shortly after the war, the cops weren't adverse to takin' a little bribe now and then, and she wasn't adverse to givin' it to 'em. I've heard the payoffs came not only in the form of cash payments, but in the form of pussy, too. Hey, cops are like any other men. They enjoy gettin' a little on the side like any other guy, and Maxine made her girls available to 'em. So, by keepin' the law happy with money and tail, she ensured there would be no trouble from the coppers. For all I know, it's still goin' on. I come here all the time when I'm in town and I never see anybody gettin' hassled by the law, so, who knows?"

"Say," Billy said, "I was wondering. Now that we're here, what are we going to do? I mean, how are we going to sell sheets? Issy is on his way to Garden State and you don't have *Jack's*. Where does that leave us?"

Rip put his hand on Billy's shoulder and said,"Don't worry, my boy. I've got us covered. There's a guy who comes here from Chicago every year. He calls his sheet *The Golden Arm*. He says he was a big pitchin' prospect in the minor leagues when he fucked up his arm and had to call it quits. You'd never know it to look at him now—he's a fat fuck who waddles when he walks. I call him Dizzy; he thinks it's for Dizzy Dean but I call him that because he can be a bit of a loon. But, he's a damned good handicapper. He'll give us some sheets on consignment. Every sheet ya sell for him ya keep half. The great thing about that is his sheets sell for a buck, so we get a half a smash for each one."

After another gulp of his brew, Rip continued, "Say I just thought of somethin'. Up north you work for Issy, and down here you'll work for Dizzy. Pretty funny, huh?"

132

"Yeah, that is pretty funny I guess," Billy said, displaying an obvious apathy towards the quip.

"Ya know," Rip said, "There's only one thing worse than not carin' about somethin', and that's *makin' believe* you care about it. I'd have preferred if you just said 'I really don't see the humor, jackass'."

"I'm sorry," Billy said. "My mind is elsewhere. So, do they have booths in the track or what?"

"Well, that's the rub." Rip replied. "They have booths inside but they do things a little different down here. See, ya have a choice. Either ya can give the track your sheets, have them sell 'em at the booths inside and they keep half, or ya can sell your own outside the track and you keep everything. Ya can't do both. The thing is, if ya sell outside, you can't get into the crosswalk where all the people come into the track. Ya have to stay off to the side and call 'em over to ya. Some guys let the track sell the sheets. Some guys sell their own. The *Golden Arm* guy sells his own outside the joint, so that's where we come in."

"Well," Billy said, "why would anybody give sheets to us and pay us half when they could be sold inside at a booth and pay half to them?"

"Two reasons," Rip said. "First, a guy can have a couple of guys workin' for him outside, still work for himself in the best spot and keep *everything* he sells. Second, word is that the stiffs who sell the sheets for the track aren't exactly the most trustworthy guys in the world. Remember when we worked the clubhouse and we took all the undecideds for ourselves? Well, every person that comes up to the booths and asks 'who's the best' or 'who do ya recommend' gets one of the sheets owned by the guys that are payin' the sellers off. If you don't play that game, ya better be outside 'cause ya won't sell anything inside. Get it?"

"Yeah, I can see why some guys would want to sell their own," Billy said.

The two touts continued to drink and chat as nightfall descended upon the town. A bluegrass band assembled in the far corner of the room and began to play a variety of folk music. After a couple more drinks, Billy and Rip had finally had enough for the night and left for the rooming house.

They carefully crept past the parlor in order not to disturb Mrs. Armitage, who had fallen sound asleep in her rocking chair.

133

The next morning, the two touts set out to find Dizzy. They walked the three blocks to the racetrack where a horde of hustlers was mulling around, waiting for the crowds to materialize. In the middle of the throng stood a short, portly man sporting a big black durango hat with a huge feather tucked inside the band and sticking back from the side.

"That's him," Rip said. "The guy with the big feather in his hat is Dizzy."

Rip shoved his way past some of the hustlers and yelled, "Hey! Dizzy! Over here!"

"Rip!" Dizzy shouted. "I wasn't sure ya was gonna make it this year! I almost hired a couple of bustouts! C'mon over here and get some sheets!"

Rip pulled Billy through the mass of men standing around and finally got to where Dizzy was waiting.

"Dizzy," Rip said, "this is Billy Mulray. He's a damned good hustler. Okay if he works the far side of the track for ya?"

Dizzy looked Billy up and down, then turned to Rip. "Looks kinda young. Ya sure he can handle it here?"

"Yeah, he'll be alright," Rip said. "He's been battlin' it out against some pretty tough hustlers in Jersey and Florida. Give him a shot."

"Well, if you say so," Dizzy said. "Here. Take 100 sheets apiece. You know the deal. Lates start at quarter to two."

Rip and Billy took the sheets, then Rip instructed Billy on the "house rules" for selling sheets at Oaklawn Park. "First, your spot is down the end of the grandstand. Dizzy gets the left side of the entrance and I get the right. Whatever ya do, stay on the sidewalk. Don't go in the street and don't step off the sidewalk for any reason. Some of these cops are real pricks around here. They love to hassle the touts whenever possible. The thing that pisses 'em off the most is gettin' off the sidewalk. I've seen 'em take guys to jail for it."

The fans began to slowly trickle in as the touts took their positions on the outside of the racetrack. Unlike the other tracks where Billy had worked, Oaklawn was a veritable free-for-all. The hustlers—and there were plenty of them—had no set place to work from, other than the sidewalk. This made for many uncomfortable moments, especially when an aggressive hustler tried to prevent a sale and take it away for himself. Despite annoyances of this kind, Billy was holding his own, and had 60 sheets sold by 1 p.m.

Rip also had been selling well. He had more than half the sheets sold when a prospective customer stopped in the "free zone" between the sidewalks, which was off limits to hustlers. The man started yelling *"Golden Arm*! Who has the *Golden Arm*?"

Rip instinctively stepped off the sidewalk and onto the free zone. He walked up to the man, handed him a sheet and the man gave him a dollar. No sooner had he taken the money than the shrill sound of a police whistle filled the air.

A policeman who had been directing pedestrians in the crosswalk that led into the track raced over to where Rip was walking back toward the sidewalk.

"Now, I know for a fact that y'all know better than to step off the sidewalk!" he said to Rip in a deep southern accent. "You lucky I don't haul yo' ass off to jail right now!"

"Geez, I'm sorry officer," Rip said. "The man needed help. He didn't know which way to go."

"Now don't be givin' me none of yo' backtalk, boy! I told ya a thousand times to stay on the sidewalk! Now git over there where ya belong 'fore I lose my temper!"

Rip stopped in his tracks. "Boy? Is that what you think I am? A boy?"

"That's it! Yo' goin' to jail! Yo' goin' to jail!" the officer shouted.

The policeman took his handcuffs out, placed one around Rip's left wrist and walked him over to a chain link fence next to the entrance and placed the other cuff through it. During the procedure, Rip dropped the remaining sheets on the ground next to the fence.

Billy had heard the police whistle and had observed the incident from afar. Once he saw his friend was in trouble, he tucked his sheets inside his pants and ran over to where Rip was cuffed to the fence.

"What the hell happened here?" Billy asked.

"Oh, I stepped off the sidewalk for a second and a cop saw me." Rip said. "Never mind all that. Pick those sheets up and put them in my hand—the one cuffed to the fence here. Then, go inside and get me a beer. Be careful, though. You're not supposed to drink alcohol outside the racetrack."

Billy put the sheets in Rip's left hand and went inside to get him a beer. When he came out, he saw a sight that would remain in his memory forever. Securely cuffed to the fence, Rip was shouting, "Over here! *Golden Arm*, winners today, winners everyday! The sheet so good it's just been declared illegal!" and people were coming over and buying sheets from him! Rip would remove a sheet from his left hand, wave it and deliver the pitch, then have the customers place the dollar in his top pocket.

Billy wondered how Rip was going to drink beer and handle sheets with only one free arm. He handed Rip the beer and the answer became evident immediately; Rip drank the whole cup of beer down without taking a breath. He threw the cup on the ground, let out a loud belch, then resumed hustling the sheets.

"Better get back to your spot," Rip said. "Lates are comin' right up and you sure don't want to miss out on them."

Shortly before the first race went off, the police officer who had handcuffed Rip walked over to where he was standing. He removed the cuffs and said, "This ain't no good gettin' off on the wrong foot on openin' day. I'm gonna cut y'all a break; no jail for ya today. Just don't make me hafta take ya in anytime in the future. I know ya know the rules; ya'll been comin' down here long enough. I hafta admit, I admired the way yo' sold the sheets after bein' cuffed to the fence. I cuffed a lotta guys to this fence before, but nobody ever had the stones to do that. Most of 'em just stand there lookin' like a smacked ass 'til I let 'em go. Even had one guy cry like a baby. Anyway, better get in there before ya miss the first race."

Rip thanked the officer—grudgingly—and left for the races. Billy saw Rip being released and met him inside. From there, the two touts made their way through the huge crowd and into a crowded barroom. As they stood at the bar drinking beer, Rip began to explain the debacle to Billy.

"I spent an hour tellin' you not to step off the sidewalk, then I went and did it myself," Rip said. "At least now you know I wasn't bullshittin'. The cops here take that as some kinda challenge to their authority. At least that guy today didn't run me in like he could have. He knows me from comin' down here for years, and he knows I don't cause much trouble. Now if somebody like the Alligator did that, his ass would be in jail before he knew what hit him."

"Say, I did pretty good today," Billy said. "I sold more than sixty sheets early and about thirty late. Is it this good every day here?"

"Well, not quite *this* good," Rip said. "But good. This is a short meet so there are big crowds everyday. Don't worry. We'll make more than enough dough here to cover our expenses. This isn't the only way to make money here. You'll see tomorrow."

The next day, Rip woke Billy early. They got ready and walked a couple of blocks to where Dizzy was preparing the *Golden Arm* sheets for the day.

"Hiya, Dizzy," Rip said. "Me and the lad here want to get the early crowd. Got some sheets for us?"

"'Course!" Dizzy said. "I was wonderin' if you fellas were gonna give that a shot. But be careful. One of the hustlers got his ass whipped at the end of the meet last year."

"Yeah, I heard about that," Rip said. "That's kinda rare. All in all, it's worth the risk."

Billy was a bit concerned about "getting his ass whipped" by selling sheets and asked Rip what Dizzy's warning was all about.

"No big deal," Rip said. "Last year, some asshole said the wrong thing to the wrong guy. Don't get wise with the customers and everything will be okay."

Dizzy gave the touts 50 sheets apiece and Rip, with Billy walking beside him, headed in the direction of the track. But when they reached the end of the street, Rip turned away from the track and continued walking in the opposite direction. Billy was confused about the situation and asked him about it.

"Um, where are we going? The track is the other way."

"I know. We aren't goin' to the track. We're goin' there," Rip said, pointing to a long, two story, Best Western.

"A motel? Why would we be going to a motel?" Billy asked.

"'Cause that's where the customers are," Rip said. "The Texans and Okies stay here for days at a clip when the track is open. They buy sheets much better than the locals do. Now, I'll take the first floor, you take the second. Just start knockin' on doors. When somebody answers the door, you say 'Excuse me. Are you goin' to the track today? I have what ya need to win!' Hold out the sheet and see if they take it. That's all there is to it."

"I don't know, Rip," Billy protested. "This doesn't sound like such a good idea to me."

"Goddam it!" Rip said. "I've been doin' this for years! It *is* a good idea! We have a chance to make 30 clams apiece before any of the other hustlers get out of the gate! I have a special deal with Dizzy for this. We split the sales *three* ways, so let's not fuck this up!"

137

Billy wasn't convinced this little scheme would work, but he agreed to give it a try. The two touts entered the motel and, as planned, Rip took the first floor and Billy the second.

Billy walked up to the first door and knocked. He was about to leave when the door opened and a man, his hair disheveled and his eyes bloodshot, poked his head out.

"What?" the man said in an agitated tone.

Billy began his pitch, "Excuse me. Are you goin' to the track today? I have..."

The man, who was obviously nursing a terrible hangover, interrupted Billy and shouted "No!" before slamming the door in his face.

Billy shook his head and walked up to the second door. He knocked and was greeted not by a person, but by a woman's voice through the door.

"What do ya want?" the voice asked.

"Are you going to the track today? I have..."

"Don't bother me!" the voice replied.

Billy was really beginning to question the wisdom of this plan now. He decided that if the same thing would happen at door #3, he'd call it quits, no matter what Rip said.

Billy knocked on the third door and within a few seconds, the door opened wide. Standing in the doorway was what appeared to be a 6' 5" Texan, wearing a big cowboy hat and boots—and nothing else. The man had one other striking feature—a large erection—which was protruding through the door and seemingly into the hallway. Billy stood dumbfounded, unable to speak.

"Why howdy, pardner," the man said. "What can I do fer y'all?"

Billy didn't know exactly what to do at this point. He simply stood mute, with the tip sheets in hand.

"Oh, y'all got the sheets fer today!" the man said. "Yup! We'll take one! I need all the help I can git!" Then the big Texan grabbed the sheet from Billy's hand, turned and shouted into the room, "Hey darlin', would you git this here feller a dollar?"

The man thanked Billy and returned inside the room. In an instant his female companion, a young, beautiful brunette, appeared at the door. She was wearing a cowboy hat and boots—and nothing else. Her breasts were large, and her erect nipples indicated a high level of arousal. She smiled at Billy and said, "Here y'all go!" as she handed him a one dollar bill, then slowly closed the door.

Billy stood for a moment, not quite believing what had just transpired.

After collecting his composure, he resumed knocking on doors. He was soon averaging about one sale per three doors, and he sold the last of the sheets shortly before he reached the final door on the second floor.

Billy took the elevator to the lobby where Rip was waiting. He was anxious to tell Rip about the Texan and his girlfriend.

"Hey, Rip," Billy said excitedly, "you're never gonna believe what happened!"

"No? Well try me," Rip replied.

"When I first started knocking on doors," Billy said, "I got the first couple slammed in my face. Then, I knocked on the third one and a big guy wearing a cowboy hat and...."

Rip interrupted Billy in mid sentence. "Boots and a big hardon bought a sheet and his big titted girlfriend with hard nipples paid, am I right?"

"Yeah," Billy said. "How do you know that?"

"I've run into those two before. They're obviously a couple of exhibitionists. I gotta admit, though, I really enjoy gettin' a gander at those big, beautiful titties. Did you get a good look at 'em?"

"Well, no," Billy said. "I was a little taken back by it. I didn't want to stare or anything."

"Shit, boy," Rip said, "that's what they do it for! Next time just take a good, long look at them puppies and smile. They always buy a sheet, so they're givin' us what we want. It's only proper for us to give 'em what *they* want!"

Rip thought for a second, then chuckled. "Ya know, it's too bad Bernardo never comes here. I've never seen a man so crazy for big tits as that guy. Every single girlfriend he's ever had has owned a big pair of jugs. I'm sure he'd appreciate the set that cowgirl has."

The two touts walked back to where Dizzy was finishing up his printing job for the day. Rip had sold out, too, so there was $100 to split three ways, which they considered not bad for a little more than an hour of work. They divided the cash, then Dizzy gave the touts their sheets for the day. It was getting late and time the hustlers headed to the track.

The next day the touts walked to Dizzy's to get sheets for the early sales at the motel. As they left and walked in that direction, they chatted and finally the question came to the forefront.

"So," Rip said, "got any problem with goin' to that room again? You know, the one with the two Texans?"

"No," Billy said. "I won't be surprised this time. If they show up naked again, I'll take the dollar, say thanks, and leave."

"Okay," Rip said. "Because if ya do, I sure wouldn't mind another look at that babe. She's the hottest thing to come out of Texas since Tabasco sauce."

"I think Tabasco sauce comes from Louisiana," Billy said.

"Close enough," Rip replied.

"Well, don't worry. I can handle it myself," Billy said.

The men split up at the motel and Billy headed for the second floor and Rip the first. After rejections at the first two rooms, Billy found himself in front of door #3. He paused for a moment and took a deep breath. Then he knocked on the door and waited to see what would transpire this time around.

The door opened and, this time, the beautiful cowgirl answered. She was once again wearing nothing except her cowboy hat and boots and, as yesterday, her nipples were large and erect. Billy couldn't help but admire them this time, and took a long look as she stood in the doorway.

"Oh, ya came back today...good!" she said with a broad smile and a twinkle in her dark blue eyes. C'mon in. I'll git yer money."

"Um, I don't know," Billy said. "I think I'll just wait out here."

"Now don't be silly," the cowgirl said. "If'n your worried about Harlen, he's gone. It's just little ol' me in here now."

"Well, be that as it may," Billy said, "I'd rather wait outside."

The cowgirl went inside the room. As Billy stood outside waiting, he heard her voice from within. "I have yo' money in here," she said. "Come and git it!"

Billy peeked inside the room. The cowgirl had a dollar bill in her hand, and she was waving it back and forth. "C'mon now," she said. "Don't be shy. I won't bite ya!"

Billy could have left without payment, but he found himself intrigued by the situation. Finally, his curiosity and sense of adventure got the best of him, and he slowly entered the room. Once inside the doorway, he instinctively glanced around. The last thing Billy wanted was having to explain to a 6' 5" angry boyfriend why he was in a motel room with his naked girlfriend.

"Now that's mo' like it, shuga!" the cowgirl said. "Now, close the door!"

Billy closed the door and with that, she instantly began to move around the room, waving the bill and saying, "C'mon, handsome! See if y'all can catch me! Ya can't have the money unless ya catch me!"

The whole scenario was so inane to Billy that he burst out laughing. The cowgirl stopped on the opposite side of the room and began to wave the bill in front of her with both hands, like a matador waving his cape.

"Toro! Toro!" she shouted. "Come n' git it, bully, bully!"

The cowgirl obviously wanted to play, and Billy suddenly had an overwhelming urge to join the game. He dropped the tip sheets on a nearby table, then put his hands on the sides of his head, with his index fingers pointing out like horns. He began to snort and rub his feet on the floor as a bull would do prior to charging a matador.

"Oh, no!" the cowgirl shouted. "I think I done got the big, bad, bull mad at me! Lookout! Here he comes!"

Billy lowered his head and charged at the cowgirl. Just before reaching her, she stepped to the side and waved the bill behind her. Billy ran past her and stopped. He pulled off his shirt, exposing his bare chest, then took up his position again. He snorted and lowered his head with his fingers pointing at her. The cowgirl moved again and waved the bill in front of her. Billy charged—and missed—and this time he kicked off his shoes and removed his pants.

"Nice try, bully bully! But y'all gonna hafta do better 'an that!" she said. "Give it another go! Here, bully, bully!" The cowgirl moved again—this time with her back to the bed—and began to wave the bill. Billy charged her and as he neared his target, she threw herself onto the bed. Billy's momentum carried him right on top of her, and in an instant she had her tongue wrapped around his in a hot, sensuous kiss. Billy didn't even need to stop kissing the cowgirl in order to remove what remained of his clothes. The festivities had left him fully aroused, and as he easily guided his penis into the cowgirl it was apparent that she had been brought to that state, too. She wrapped her legs—still wearing her cowboy boots—around Billy and he began to pump wildly. He had been celibate for

141

months, ever since his encounter with Kerra, and although he knew that slow and steady would be a better way to go, he had an especially difficult time controlling himself. After a couple of minutes of that intensity, the cowgirl spoke up.

"Easy, cowboy," she said. "take yer time. We ain't in no rush here. Now lay over here and let me git on top."

Billy complied and in an instant the cowgirl had him straddled. She began to gyrate in a circular motion, and as she did, she began to shout. "Eeeeeeeeeeeeeee-ha! Ride 'em cowgirl!"

The cowgirl was still wearing her boots, and as she rode Billy she reached up with one hand and held her cowboy hat and with the other she made a circular motion, as if getting a lasso ready to toss. "Woo hoo!" she screamed. "Ride that wild bronco!"

After only a couple minutes, Billy could no longer contain himself and had an explosive orgasm.

The cowgirl hopped off Billy and with a puzzled look, said, "Damn, shuga. Things went kinda quick. This wasn't yer first time at the rodeo, was it?"

"Of course not," Billy said, sounding a bit indignant. "I guess you're so good at 'bronc bustin' that I couldn't help myself."

"Well I s'pose y'all got a point there," she giggled.

There was a knock on the door and Billy panicked. He was sure that the big Texan would be in the room within seconds and he'd be in a serious predicament. The cowgirl went to the door and looked through the peep hole into the hallway. She opened the door and asked, "What can I do fer y'all?"

The sound of Rip's voice echoed through the motel room. "I'm lookin' for a friend of mine. I last saw him on this floor. I've been knockin' on doors and askin'. He's a young, trim, good lookin' kid, around 20 years old. He was sellin' tip sheets around the motel here. Have ya seen him?"

Billy had never been so glad to hear Rip's voice. As he struggled to get his clothes on he yelled in the direction of the door, "Rip! I'll be right out! Wait for me!"

A moment later Billy was dressed and ready to leave, and the cowgirl stood by the door with a dollar bill in hand. Billy walked up to her, and when he saw the bill, he chuckled. "Forget it," he said. "By the way, my name is Billy. What's yours?"

"Becky," the cowgirl said. "Becky Lou."

"Well," Billy said, smiling, "it was great to meet you, Becky Lou. Are you staying in Hot Springs for long?"

"Unfortunately, not," she said. "I'm leavin' fer Texas this afternoon. I might be back in a couple of weeks and, then again, I might not. Anyway, handsome, it was nice to meet y'all, too."

Becky Lou gave Billy a peck on the cheek, and he left the motel room into the hallway where Rip stood waiting.

The two touts began to talk as they left the motel.

"This is too hard to take," Rip said. "Two of the hottest broads I've ever seen and you fucked 'em both? What are the odds of that?"

"Listen, Rip," Billy said, "it's not like I didn't have any chances; I did. I had some of the girls that hung with the touts in Florida come onto me. Then there were the *señoritas* in Havana. I had chances, I just didn't take them. Don't take it the wrong way, but I'm not the hound you are. I guess we're different in that way."

"Oh, I see," Rip said. "You go for quality and I go for quantity. Well, maybe you're right. I'll be sure to let Reenie know you said that."

"C'mon, Rip. You know that's not what I meant," Billy said. "Besides, to use Reenie as an example isn't fair. She's by far the best woman I've seen you with, and you know that's true."

Rip quickly changed the subject. "Well, one thing I know is true is that you're gonna have to come up with some cash to cover your little escapade today."

"What do you mean?" Billy asked.

"How many sheets did ya sell today?" Rip said. "'cause ya have to give Dizzy at least $20 for his cut of the sheets you didn't sell."

"What?" Billy said. "I'm not sure I follow you. I have to give him what?"

"Goddam it," Rip said. "you didn't sell a single fuckin' sheet today, did ya? Well what do ya think Dizzy is gonna say if ya come back to him and say that you got zipped? I'll tell ya what he's gonna say. He's gonna say, 'well I'm gonna hafta let somebody who knows how to sell sheets go to the motel.' To make things easy for ya to understand, he'll get rid of you if ya don't make him any money, so ya can't go back and say you didn't sell anything. Just pull a double sawbuck outta your wallet and forget about it. It was worth it, wasn't it?"

Billy simply mumbled something inaudible.

"I'll take that as a yes," Rip said. "Now keep those sheets—except for ten—and give him those ten returns and a $20 dollar bill. Everything will be settled then."

"What do I do with the other 39 sheets?"

"Keep 'em and sell 'em at the track today. Sell those before ya sell the ones he's gonna give us when we get back. This way ya get almost $40 right off the top. It means you'll sell less than you normally do at the track, but Dizzy won't fire ya for that. Sellin' at the motel is like shootin' fish in a barrel; ya should sell almost all of 'em every mornin'. Hustlin' at the track is a lot tougher, and easier to explain if ya don't do good. Ya can get away with this kinda shit every once in a while, just don't go makin' a habit out of it. This is a good little hustle we got goin' here and I don't want it to get fucked up."

Billy took ten sheets out of the stack and tucked the remaining thirty nine under his shirt. Later that day, he sold the sheets left over from the morning plus fifty more. Although the total he turned in to Dizzy was less than usual, Rip was right. Dizzy simply shrugged it off as a bad day.

Billy had dodged—if not a bullet—a bean ball from Dizzy's "golden arm."

The remainder of the Oaklawn meet was over quickly and it was time for the two touts to move on to the next stop. As they sat at the bar in Maxine's following the last day of the meeting, that discussion surfaced.

"Now it's on to Kentucky." Rip said. "We'll leave in a couple of days. We have a short meet at Keeneland then it's on to Churchill Downs. I know you've been anxious to see that horse run in the Derby. He'll probably get a couple of tighteners up there and that'll decide if he's goin'."

"I sure hope he makes it," Billy said. "I've been following Tim Tam all winter. I keep reading about that horse from California—Silky Sullivan—though. All of the papers seem to think he's going to be the horse to beat in the Derby because he runs late and will love a mile and a quarter."

"Yeah," Rip said, "Lots of people fall into that trap. They see a horse that runs late and think all he needs is a lot of ground and he'll run by everybody in the stretch. It doesn't always work out that way, though. If you really like Tim Tam, stay with him. Don't let the papers interfere with your handicappin'. If you're ever gonna be a handicapper, ya need to have confidence in your picks."

A couple of days later, the two touts left Hot Springs and set out for Lexington.

CHAPTER 9 – "While the gittin's good"

The red Corvette carrying Billy and Rip left in mid morning, made its way through Little Rock, and reached Memphis shortly before noon. As with most destinations, Rip had a favorite place to eat—and drink.

Rip drove through the busy streets of Memphis, finally pulling into the parking lot of a restaurant called "The Rendezvous." Billy thought it an odd name for a restaurant—it seemed more suitable for a clandestine night club—but he trusted Rip's opinion in such matters. The two stepped out of the car and, before they even reached the door, the pungent and delicious fragrance of barbecue overwhelmed them.

"Mmmmm. Smell that?" Rip asked. "That's the aroma of the best barbecue you're ever gonna eat! I stop here every year on my way from Hot Springs to Lexington. I wouldn't miss it for anything!"

Billy and Rip walked to the door, which led to a large basement outfitted as a restaurant. The room was already crowded and the waitress had to place the two touts in a booth in the far corner.

The waitress placed menus in front of the men, but Rip simply picked his up and handed it back to her. "No need to deliberate," he said. "I know the menu by heart and I know what I want. I'll take a full rack of barbecued ribs and a mug of Budweiser."

Billy handed the menu back to the waitress. "I'll have the same," he said.

"This joint started out as a sandwich shop right after the war," Rip said. "Then one day the guy who supplied the cold cuts gave the owner a case of ribs, you know, kinda like a reward for his business. Well the owner, who was Greek, rubbed a bunch of Greek spices on the meat and cooked it up. All the other barbecue joints at the time were loadin' up their ribs with thick sauces, so this was the first 'dry rub' ever used. It turned out to be a big hit and the business exploded. Wait 'til ya taste it. You're never gonna want to eat any other kinda barbecue."

The men feasted on the succulent ribs, and washed it all down with several cold beers. By the time they left the Rendezvous, they were quite full and happy.

"No time to waste here," Rip said. "We have a date for tonight."

"Date? What do you mean, date?" Billy asked.

"Oh, you'll see," Rip said. "Just a little surprise I have cooked up. But, there's one little thing I want to do before leavin' Memphis."

Rip drove across town and turned south. In a few minutes, the car pulled up in front of a mansion which was protected by a high, stone fence.

"Know what this place is?" Rip asked.

"Um, no," Billy said. "Should I?"

"I'd say so," Rip replied. "you're the fuckin' teenager, not me!"

"I'm not a teen anymore," Billy said. "I'm twenty. Soon to be twenty-one."

"Whatever," Rip said. "Anyway, that stone building with the big white pillars up on the hill is Graceland. That's where Elvis Presley lives. He bought it last year and had this big fence put up."

"Oh my god!" Billy shouted. "You mean Elvis.... Elvis Presley... lives right in that house?"

"Yup. And every once in a while, if he's home, he comes out of the house and you can see him. C'mon, let's walk up to the gate and see what's up."

The two touts left the Corvette and walked up to the stone and iron fence where several other fans were gathered, hoping to steal a glimpse of their idol.

As the men were about to leave, they heard a couple of the young female fans begin to scream. Shouts of "It's Elvis! Over here, Elvis! Please come by the fence, Elvis, we love you!" filled the air.

Billy and Rip turned back and saw a young man standing outside of the front door of Graceland. There was no doubt who the young man was. It was indeed Elvis Presley.

Presley stood staring in the direction of the two touts for a moment, then began to walk down the driveway and toward the front gate. The fans who had come hoping to see him crowded around, trying to get as close as they could. They pushed pads, cards, and photos through the gate in an effort to get autographs, and Elvis obliged. He seemed a genuinely humble person, and he constantly thanked everyone for their kind words and for stopping by.

Once the initial feeding frenzy had subsided, Elvis called out through the gate, "Gee, that's a mighty fine Corvette. That's the latest model, isn't it?"

"Yeah, it is," Rip said. "Got it right off the show room floor. It's loaded. Want to take it for a spin?"

"Wish I could," Presley said. "But these days I'm more or less a prisoner in my own home. I can't really go out in public so much; I have to be picked up by a limo whenever I leave. Thanks anyway. It sure was nice just gettin' a look at it."

With that, Presley turned and walked back up the driveway to Graceland. He left for the Army a few days later, and it was the last time either of the touts would ever see him in person again.

"Well now ya have a story to tell your grandchildren," Rip said.

"You can say that again," Billy replied. "But I should have gotten his autograph, damn it. Nobody will ever believe it."

"Yeah," Rip laughed. "You'd better start gettin' autographs or photos or somethin'. People are gonna think you're the biggest bullshit artist since the Alligator."

The two touts returned to the Corvette and resumed the journey. After a few more hours of driving, they reached the city limits of Nashville. Rip maneuvered through the city and made a turn onto 5th Avenue North, and within a few minutes they pulled up in front of a what appeared to be a big, brick church.

"This is it, my boy!" Rip said. "This is where they have the Grand Ol' Opry. I hope they aren't sold out. This joint is really popular."

"Grand Ol' Opry," Billy said, "what's that?"

Rip chuckled. "Don't say that too loud around here. This place is like the shrine for country music. Just about everybody who's anybody has played here. It's considered a great honor. You know, like your rock 'n' roll guys gettin' on Ed Sullivan or somethin'."

The touts trudged up the stone steps and entered the building. They walked up to the ticket office and were lucky enough to get two prime—albeit more expensive—seats for the show. The usher led the men to their seats, which were located only a few rows from the stage and in the center. The show had already begun, and on stage a female comedian wearing a long house dress and a flowered hat with a price tag hanging off it was doing a stand up routine.

"Know who that is?" Rip leaned toward Billy and whispered.

Billy softly chucked and said, "Um no. Should I know her?"

"Well you would if ya knew anything about country music or the Opry. That woman is named Minnie Pearl, and country fans love her. All the people in this joint are down-to-earth people and she is, too. That's why they love her and they love the Opry. No bullshit here. Regular people havin' a good time, that's all."

The crowd laughed through Pearl's monologue, including Rip and Billy. When it was over, she bellowed, "I love ya so much it hurts!" She then left the stage to thunderous applause, and a man walked out and took his place in front of a microphone.

The man, who was apparently the master of ceremonies said, "Ladies and gentlemen, Minnie's been a long time member of the Opry and one of our most popular performers. Much obliged, Minnie. Come back soon, ya hear?"

The applause slowly died down, then the man said, "Ladies, when you make those biscuits your family loves so much, remember: No flour compares to Martha White's. Those biscuits will always come out flaky and tender, and your family'll eat 'em right down and ask for more. Take it from me, T. Tommy Cutrer; Martha White flour. Good gracious, it's *good*!"

Billy softly giggled, then whispered to Rip, "Geez, Rip. What are they doing? Reading commercials to the fans in the auditorium?"

"Don't be a simpleton," Rip said. "Don't you see the sign that says "WSM" on the front of the mike? That's the local radio station. This show is being broadcast. The commercial was for the people listenin' at home."

The MC finished the commercial, then introduced the next performer. "Comin' right up I'd like to welcome a fellow Mississippian. You might have heard of him—his name is Mr. Johnny Cash."

The auditorium erupted with cheers and applause as the young man walked onto the stage and started to strum his guitar. Then he began to sing "I Walk The Line," a song that was well known to everyone in the building, including Billy.

Cash finished his number one hit to the raucous approval of the crowd, then departed the stage. Once again, the MC addressed the crowd, "Johnny's got a new album comin' out on the Sun label later this year - it's called 'Songs That Made Him Famous,' and that great song you just heard is on it, along with a whole bushel of other great tunes. But right now I want y'all to give our next duo a big country welcome. Let's hear it for the Everly Brothers!"

The two young men came on stage, but unlike the first two performers, they were met with only polite applause. Then the two broke out into "Wake Up Little Susie," a song that was well liked by Billy, but apparently only tolerated by most in the huge crowd.

After the song was over, once again the crowd delivered only polite applause. The brothers left the stage, and the show continued.

Billy leaned toward Rip and whispered, "Why didn't they get more applause? They're big stars. I even know of them."

"Well," Rip said, "there's a couple of reasons. First, you know these guys as rock 'n' roll artists. But, they started out singin' country songs with their parents. Some people think of country guys who sing rock 'n' roll as sell outs. Also, the song they sang is about a teenager and his girlfriend stayin' out late in a car. Most people don't think anything of it, but that doesn't sit well with a lot of these country Protestants."

The rest of the evening highlighted other stars of the country / western genre. Stonewall Jackson previewed his greatest hit song "Waterloo," Patsy Cline sang her first hit, "Walkin' After Midnight," and Little Jimmy Dickens treated the fans to a comical country song entitled, "Cornbread and Buttermilk." Finally the show came to an end and as the two touts left the auditorium, Rip had one more destination in mind.

"Let's take a walk around the corner. Things are just gettin' started there," he said.

Billy was amenable to the suggestion. He had thoroughly enjoyed the evening at the Ryman Auditorium and said, "You know, I didn't think that I'd like going to that show. But it really was terrific. Some of the guys I knew, and the ones I didn't were good, too. I have to admit it was a great experience."

"You know it," Rip said. "In case ya never get this way again, at least ya can say you've been to the Ryman."

The men chatted as Rip led the way. As soon as they turned the corner, music filled the air and there were people crowding the sidewalks, standing in front of taverns that were lit with bright neon signs.

"They call these bars 'honky tonks,' Rip said. "Some really good musicians play in 'em. In fact, some of the guys we just saw in the Ryman got their starts playin' in joints like these. Ever hear of Hank Williams?"

"Of course."

"He was only a boy when he started playin' in places like this," Rip said.

The touts had to squeeze by the people standing outside the honky tonks. "C'mon," Rip said. "Let's see if we can find one that ain't so crowded so we can get a beer and listen to some music."

Finally, they found a honky tonk with a couple of seats at a table inside. They ordered beer from the waitress and began to drink while a loud country band played and people danced both inside and outside on the sidewalk. Billy looked across the crowded room and as he glanced at the people at the bar, his eyes fell upon a young, pretty, petite blonde girl with pigtails held in place by red ribbons. She was wearing a red and white checkered dress that ended above the knee and displayed a pair of shapely legs. The young lady had her back to the bar and was staring directly at Billy, flashing a wide smile. On each side she was flanked by a huge young man wearing overalls and they were chatting back and forth behind the young woman's back.

Billy and the young woman were locked in eye contact when she left the bar and walked to where he was sitting.

"Howdy. My name's Sue Ann," she said. "What's yours?"

"My name's Billy."

"Oh my!" the young woman said. "A yankee! My brothers wouldn't like it if'n they knew I was talkin' to a yankee! Good thing I don't care what they think anyways. Do y'all mind if I sit down?"

"No," Billy said, "make yourself at..."

Before Billy could finish his sentence, Sue Ann hopped onto his lap and threw her arms around his neck. Her face was now inches from his, and he could see that her eyes were glazed and she reeked of alcohol.

Rip had witnessed the episode and mumbled to himself, "I have a feelin' this isn't gonna end well."

The young lady was in no mood for small talk. She closed her eyes and began to kiss an astounded Billy on the lips. Billy did not reciprocate and refused to close his eyes; he looked at Rip as if there were some way that he could offer assistance. The best Rip could muster was to softly chuckle as he slowly shook his head.

Across the room, the two hulks who had been aside of the young lady at the bar turned and saw her sitting on Billy's lap, locked in a long and—at least to her—passionate kiss. They immediately made their way across the room and in an instant stood next to the table where the trio were sitting.

"What the hell's you two guys doin' with our little sis?" one of the behemoths said.

"We don't like nobody foolin' with our kin," the other said.

"They wasn't doin' nothin'!" Sue Ann said as she jumped to her feet. "We was just talkin'! Ain't no harm in talkin'! Y'all two never want me to have any fun."

"Shut up, Sue Ann!" one of the brothers shouted. "Y'all get involved in somethin' like this ev'rytime we make the trip to Nashville! Now if'n y'all gonna keep this up, y'all ain't gonna be able to come with us no more! Y'all can stay at the farm and do chores!"

Then the other giant folded his arms, and looking at Billy and Rip said, "I think y'all oughta git outta here while the gittin's good."

"Well, haystacks," Rip said, "I think you oughta go fuck yourself."

Before either of the big men could react, Rip leaned forward and delivered a vicious karate chop behind the knee of the hulk nearest him. The big rube collapsed backwards, toppling his brother and starting a chain reaction in the crowded bar. Within seconds, several people lay on the floor, spilled beer was everywhere, and a huge bar fight had broken out.

Rip grabbed Billy by the arm and pulled him through the crowd and out the front door. They quickly worked their way through the people mingling on the sidewalks and back to the Corvette, which was still parked in front of the Ryman Auditorium. Rip started the car and they roared towards the highway that led to Lexington.

"Jesus Christ," Rip said. "I hope you're not gonna start this shit everyplace we go. I was lookin' forward to havin' a couple of beers and listenin' to some good country music. But no. You gotta go fuckin' with some local broad with crazy ass brothers. Ruined our whole night!"

"C'mon, Rip," Billy protested. "You saw the whole thing. I didn't ask her to come over, I didn't ask her to sit on my lap, and I certainly didn't ask her to kiss me. You heard one of her brothers. She pulls that kind of stuff every time they go somewhere. Can I help it if she picked me out of the crowd?"

"Well, I suppose not," Rip said. "Besides, one of these days the fact that women like you might just pay some dividends for me. You can't have 'em all. Just try not get entangled with chicks like that one, okay?"

"Okay," Billy said.

The two touts, now thoroughly exhausted after a long day, continued to drive through the night and crossed the Tennessee border into Kentucky. After a couple more miles, Rip pulled the Corvette off the highway and into a rest stop.

"We'll get a couple of hours shut eye here and get back on the road in the morning," Rip said.

Billy and Rip laid back in their seats and quickly fell fast asleep. The next thing that Billy knew, it was daylight and Rip was shaking him by the shoulder. "Time to get goin'," he said.

CHAPTER 10 – Kentucky

The Corvette pulled out of the rest area and back onto the highway to Lexington. The sun was rising in the morning sky and Billy got his first good look at the Kentucky countryside. On both sides of the highway, for as far as the eye could see, was open farmland. Some of the farms were planted in tobacco, others were populated by livestock—dairy cows, hogs, chickens, and the like. Still others—and they became more plentiful the nearer they got to Lexington—were populated by horses. Finally, every farm they could see had herds of horses grazing, walking, and galloping in huge open fields.

One feature of the big horse farms that excited Billy was the number of foals that were running freely. "Rip!" Billy shouted, "Look at those baby horses! Tons of them! They're all playing with each other and some of them are running in big groups! It's fantastic!"

Rip chuckled, then said, "I thought you'd like that. This is foalin' season in Bluegrass country. The breeders try to mate their stallions with mares so that the babies are born anytime from the middle of January to the end of April. Lottsa mares have already had their babies and some others still have a little way to go. This is a great time to pass by these farms. Ya get to see those cute babies runnin' around and raisin' hell. In a couple of years, most of 'em will be at the track gettin' ready for their first race."

They passed farm after farm, some of them covering many hundreds of acres. Most of the farms had fieldstone fences which seemed to go on for miles. They drove all morning, and passed farms around Lexington with names steeped in thoroughbred racing history—Claiborne, Nursery Stud, and Elmendorf. As the touts drove past the farms, Rip would provide commentary on the significance each one had to thoroughbred racing.

"This farm," Rip said as they slowly drove past the gates of Claiborne, "was the birthplace of some of racin's greatest horses. Gallant Fox, a Triple Crown winner and one of the sport's great sires, was foaled here in the late 20s. He's the only Triple Crown winner to sire a Triple Crown winner—Omaha. And last year, they put him in the Hall of Fame."

As the touts drove past Nursery Stud, Rip commented, "Now this place is special. The greatest horse in the history of horse racin'—Man O' War—was born here durin'

154

World War I. Matter of fact, he got his name because of that. This farm was owned by the banker August Belmont and later his son, August Belmont, Jr. Belmont Park is named for old man Belmont and so is the Belmont Stakes. Anyway, Belmont, Jr., who's 65 years old at the time, enlists in the Army and is assigned to get horses ready for World War I. Well, Belmont is preoccupied with the war and right before he leaves he decides to sell off all of his young stock at auction. One of the yearlin's he puts on the block is a chestnut colt his wife has named Man O' War in honor of her husband. He sells for five grand—a lot of money in those days—and goes on to be the greatest horse ever, winnin' 20 of 21 starts includin' lottsa stakes and settin' a mess of records. Nobody ever shed a tear for the Belmonts, though. Those people had so much money to begin with that they only raced for prestige, anyway."

After a short drive, Rip stopped the Corvette in front of a farm with a big sign that read "Elmendorf."

"This is one of the oldest farms in the country," Rip said. "The history of this joint goes back to shortly after the Revolutionary War, when this part of the country was bein' settled. It changed hands a few times and after the Civil War, they started to breed thoroughbreds here. Quite a few of the great horses of the late 1800s came from here. Some of the horses that passed through here were Preakness, Spendthrift, a couple of Derby winners, Ben Ali and Apollo, and a horse you should recognize—Salvator."

"Why should I recognize that horse?" Billy asked.

"Ya know the place where we drink in the Monmouth clubhouse? The place where Reenie works? Well that's called the Salvator Grill." Rip said. "It's named for the great 19th century racehorse, Salvator. Christ, boy! Who'd ya think it was named for, the guy who makes pizzas near the train station in Long Branch?"

"How do you know so much about this stuff?" Billy asked.

"I'm a bit of a historian, I guess," Rip replied. "I've always been interested in history, and with racin', there's a lot of it."

Once again, the touts drove away and headed to the next farm on Rip's "tour."

Rip directed the Corvette up a long driveway that was lined with tall oak trees and had fenced in paddocks on both sides of the roadway. Then he stopped the car outside of a big, white barn at the end of the driveway.

155

The men got out of the car and while they stood looking around, Rip said, "Any idea which farm we're at right now?"

"Well, no. Which farm is this?"

"Calumet!" Rip said. "Over the years, this joint has been more or less a factory for top notch horses. They've won nearly every important race there is, includin' six Derbys. Citation and Whirlaway were born and raised here. So was that horse you like so much, Tim Tam."

An old black man with white hair came out of the barn and slowly walked towards where the touts were standing. As the old man drew closer, Rip smiled and shouted, "Quarter Pole!"

The old man looked at him quizzically for a moment, then a smile came across his face. "Missah Rip!" he said. "I aint laid eyes on you since Moby Dick was a minnow! How y'all been? What brings y'all to de farm?"

"I been fine, Quarter Pole," Rip said. "I don't usually stop by the farms when I come to Lexington, but I wanted to show my friend, Billy here, breedin' country."

"Well, y'all come to de right place!," Quarter Pole said. "Dis here farm done turn't out some o' de bes' ho'ses ever looked through a bridle! An' we done got us a mess o' new ones runnin' around all over de place!'"

"You know it, Quarter Pole," Rip said. "Say. Why don't ya tell Billy here how ya got your nickname?"

"Sho' thing. Back in de days when I rubbed some o' de top ho'ses in de game, I used to tell de other grooms in de race: 'Y'all ain't got nothin' to worry 'bout. It'll all be over by de quarter pole.' And mo' offen den not, it was."

The three men shared a chuckle at the story, then Billy asked, "So, Tim Tam was born here? He's my favorite horse."

"Well," Quarter Pole said, "right now he eve'ybody's fav'rite ho'se 'round here! He goin' to de Derby, and missah Jones think he gotta good chance to win. We win las' year's Derby wit a ho'se named Iron Liege, so we gotta chance to make it two in a row! Jus' de other day I heared missah Jones tellin' missus Wright that he gonna give Tim Tam a couple o' tighteners 'fore de Derby. He say he gonna run him right over at Lexin'ton pretty soon.

"There ya go, Billy," Rip said. "Looks like you're gonna get to see him race here before the Derby."

"Man, that would be great," Billy said. "There's not much time between now and Derby, and I'd love to see him race again beforehand."

Quarter Pole gave the two an unofficial tour of the farm. He showed the touts where Citation and Whirlaway were born and the stall where Tim Tam was stabled after being weaned from his mother. They also got a look at the breeding shed, the place where many great stallions and mares had been mated over the years.

Billy and Rip thanked Quarter Pole for the tour and resumed their journey to Lexington. The warm spring sun was shining brightly and, with the roof of the convertible retracted, the men were able to take advantage of the beautiful weather. As they drove, Rip and Billy talked about their visit to the farm.

"Most people will never get the chance to visit a place like Calumet," Rip said. "Everybody knows their horses, but almost nobody sees where they came from. Sometimes it seems like people just think that horses show up at the racetrack one day and start racin'. It's a long process, and it all starts at farms like Calumet."

"Yeah, that was some experience," Billy said. "I was wondering. How long have you known Quarter Pole?"

"Many years," Rip said. "That old man probably knows more about horses than any livin' human being. When Quarter Pole was a young man he went to work for the Wrights, rich people who made their money in bakin' powder. They had a standardbred farm—that's trotters and pacers—in rural Illinois. But, old man Wright wanted a better place to breed his standardbreds and settled on Lexington. He bought the farm we were just on, renamed it Calumet after his bakin' powder brand, and when he moved here from Illinois, Quarter Pole came with him. Quarter Pole was originally a trotter groom, and from what I've heard, he was one of the best. A horse in his care actually won the Hambletonian—harness racin's biggest race—in the early 30s."

"I'm a little confused," Billy said. "If that farm was for trotters, how did it turn into a thoroughbred farm?"

"I'm gettin' to it," Rip said. "Anyway, right after winnin' the Hambletonian, old man Wright kicks the bucket and the farm is left to his son. Well, his son sees the writin' on the wall and figures the future is in thoroughbred racin'. He takes a gamble and converts

Calumet to thoroughbreds and imports top breedin' stock. Within a few years, he turns Calumet into one of racin's most successful enterprises. They breed—and race—a slew of top horses who win millions of dollars in purses. And this brings me back to Quarter Pole. Old Quarter Pole was here when Wright's son converted the farm and Quarter Pole made the leap into bein' a thoroughbred groom. Some things are the same no matter what the breed of horse. They get bandaged the same, poulticed the same, feet picked the same, and so on. Well, Quarter Pole knows so much about takin' care of horses that in no time he's the top thoroughbred groom for Calumet. One of the horses he cared for went on to win the Kentucky Derby, and it's my guess that no other groom has ever won both the Hambletonian *and* the Derby. What that old man doesn't know about horses isn't *worth* knowin'."

"Wow," Billy said, "that *is* impressive. So, how did he wind up staying at the farm?"

"Well," Rip said, "Groomin' isn't exactly an easy job and Quarter Pole, like anybody else, was gettin' on in years. At some point, it gets too hard to do seven days a week. So, he got moved from the racetrack to the farm. Ya see, people in racin' tend to take care of their own. An old timer like Quarter Pole is basically pensioned on the farm. He gets a room and a small salary to get by on. Right now, he's still helpin' out with the breedin' stock. Once he gets too old for that, they'll probably make him a night watchman. People like him spend a lifetime takin' care of the horses that make other people a lot of money. It only seems right that they should get to live out their years in peace and surrounded by the animals they love."

The two touts checked into their boarding house on the outskirts of Lexington and were ready for the Keeneland meeting which began a few days later.

Kentucky had very old racetracks, but Keeneland wasn't one of them. Unlike Churchill Downs or Ellis Park, which dated back to the 19th century, Keeneland was only a little more than twenty years old. The grandstand and clubhouse seemed quite modern, and everything was extremely clean and well maintained.

Billy and Rip were able to catch on with a local tip sheet and stayed with it for the short meeting. The atmosphere at Keeneland was a bit different than that of Hot Springs—the people in Lexington seemed much more refined and upscale. Rip referred to those who attended the Keeneland races as the "horsey set"—a term to describe the wealthy insiders who frequented the clubhouse there. Although the racetrack wasn't very old, the breeding industry in Kentucky—primarily around Lexington—was. As soon as it was built, Keeneland became the showcase for the many wealthy farm owners in the area who bred and raced their own stock. Keeneland was run in the old tradition of Kentucky racing, and did not have an announcer for the races. The horses were simply loaded in the gate, dispatched, and allowed to race without commentary, the only major track in the country to do so.

The highlight of the meeting for Billy was when Tim Tam raced in and won an allowance race, as Quarter Pole had predicted. The next stop for the horse, and the two touts, was Churchill Downs in Louisville, where the Kentucky Derby would be held, as per tradition, on the first Saturday in May.

Toward the end of the Keeneland meeting, Billy was in his room studying the *Racing Form* one evening when there was a knock on his door, followed by a voice. "It's me. Let me in. I have somethin' to ask ya."

Billy opened the door and Rip entered. He seemed distressed and began to talk immediately. "I have a favor to ask of ya," he said, nervously. "I'm in a bit of a jackpot. I need some cash right away. You have some stashed away, don't ya?"

"Yeah, sure," Billy said. "Say, what's the problem?"

"Well, I got into a high stakes card game with some trainers over at the horsemen's lounge at the racetrack. Seems I got overextended shootin' for a big pot and wound up losin' the Corvette. I need some cash to see if I can win it back."

"Oh my god!" Billy shouted. "You lost the car? Oh my god!"

"Yeah, I know," a dejected Rip whispered. "I can't just walk away without takin' a shot at gettin' it back. So, I need to borrow some money from ya and go back."

"How much do you need?" Billy asked.

"Twelve hundred oughta do it. I needed that much to call the guy who won the pot. I didn't have that much cash and had to put up the Corvette. I'm gonna go back and see if I can get him to play me straight up for the title."

"Hold on," Billy said. "Let's think this over for a minute."

"What's to think about?" Rip said. "Are ya tellin' me that you won't lend me the money or somethin'?"

"Of course I will!" Billy said. "But I think it might be a good idea to talk it over and not make such a hasty decision."

"Goddam it!" Rip shouted. "There's nothin' to decide! I'm goin' back there and try to get my car back!"

"Alright, alright," Billy said. "I only want to bring up one thing. I remember watching a bunch of the guys playing poker back in Jersey one night. Jigger's luck was running so strong that he wiped everyone out. Now, he doesn't usually have that much success when he's playing. But this one night he was on a streak. So, do you think it's a good idea to go right back and challenge that guy while he's in the middle of a lucky streak? Couldn't you wait until tomorrow night and go back then?"

Rip thought for a minute before answering. "You know, I hate to admit it, but you could have an idea there. For one thing, my luck was lousy all night, and that guy's was scary good. Maybe puttin' a little time between now and when I take him on wouldn't be a bad thing to do. It's hard to resist goin' back right away, especially considerin' who it was that took the Corvette from me. I can't stand that prick."

"Who is that guy?" Billy asked. "Is he a trainer or something?"

"Yeah, he's a trainer. His name is Whalebone Williams. Been trainin' horses in Kentucky for decades. He got the nickname 'Whalebone' from the good luck charm he wears around his neck. It's a gold chain with a horseshoe charm made of whalebone. Word is he won it in a card game years ago and it's been his lucky piece ever since."

"Okay," Billy said. "I'll get you the money and you can go back to that place and win the Corvette back tomorrow."

Billy took a box from underneath his bed and opened it. He removed $1,200 from it—almost all he had saved—and gave it to Rip. Rip thanked Billy and left for his room.

The next night, Rip got Billy, and the two touts took a bus to the racetrack and entered the horsemen's lounge. The air was thick with cigar smoke and the room reeked of stale brew. A group of men sat around a card table puffing on stogies and drinking beer while several other new players were mulling about waiting for a chance to get into the game. The men had just finished up a hand of poker when one of the players at the table saw the touts and spoke up. He was a stocky man in his late fifties. He wore a St. Louis Cardinals baseball cap which partially hid a full head of gray hair. Without saying, Billy knew that the man was Whalebone Williams.

160

"Well if it isn't MacKenzie. Hiya, MacKenzie! Back for more, I see. Apparently ya didn't have enough last night, huh?"

"The name's McKenna," Rip said sarcastically. "I figured you might be in for a little one-on-one, ya know, you and me."

"Let me guess," the man said. "You're here to try to get your 'vette back, aren't ya?"

"Good guess," Rip said. "I've got $1,200. I want to play one hand for the pink slip."

"Ha!" the man laughed. "I bet y'all do! That car is worth about four grand. How's about ya put up four grand if ya want to play for it!"

"That's bullshit!" Rip shouted. "I put up the car because I was outta cash! Now we both know that it only would've took $1,200 to call ya!"

Before Williams could reply, the other men in the room came to Rip's aid. A torrent of comments filled the air. "He's right, Whalebone! The fair thing is to play for $1,200! Hey, don't be a jizz, man! Give the guy a shot to get his car back!"

The grumbling continued until Williams shouted, "Okay, okay! But we play by my rules! It's one hand, winner take all. Five card draw and jokers wild. I deal."

"What?" Rip protested. "Jokers wild? What kinda rinky dink bullshit is that? What's wrong with five card straight draw?"

"Nothin' if it's *your* rules, but it's not. That's the deal. Take it or leave it."

Rip thought for a second and realized he was in no position to bargain. He reluctantly agreed to Whalebone's terms, with one caveat.

"Okay, Whalebone," Rip said. "But *I* want to deal."

"Jesus Christ, MacKenzie," Williams said with a smirk. "Sure. Anything to get this over with."

Williams added the two jokers to the deck then threw the cards to Rip.

"Gentlemen, can I ask y'all to clear the table for a couple of minutes while I give this here fella another boxin' lesson?" Whalebone said.

The men at the table got up and Rip sat across from his nemesis. Rip threw twelve crisp $100 bills into the pot and Williams took a folded up title from his shirt pocket and tossed it next to the cash.

Rip expertly shuffled the cards and, after allowing Williams to cut the deck, quickly dealt the hands. Billy watched the proceedings quietly from across the room. He said a silent prayer as the men studied the cards in their hands.

Whalebone maneuvered the cards several times before throwing a trio of them face down on the table in front of him. "Give me three," he said.

Rip dealt the cards to Williams, then discarded a single card of his own and said, "One for me."

The room was deadly silent for a moment as the players settled their hands before the big showdown. Williams took his right hand and rubbed his chest, feeling for his whalebone good luck charm through his shirt.

"Let's see 'em," Rip demanded.

Williams stopped rubbing his charm and began to smile as he laid his cards on the table. "Trip-nines. Two natural and a joker. Sorry 'bout that bud." Then he added mockingly, "Now if only jokers wasn't wild."

Rip glared at Williams and said, "Nothin' to be sorry about. I agreed to the terms so everything is on the square."

Rip took two cards—the three of clubs and the four of spades—and dropped them on the table with his left hand. Then with his right hand he dropped the six of diamonds and the seven of hearts. There were now four cards face up on the table in front of Rip, with a sizable gap separating the two on his left and the two on his right. Every eye in the room was glued on the remaining card.

Rip took the final card and dropped it on the table in the middle of his hand.

It was the remaining joker, giving him a straight. The room erupted in a howling chorus of disbelief.

"Damn," Rip said. "I guess I needed a joker more than you did. Pretty funny, huh? What's even funnier is that the joker was my draw card. If jokers aren't wild, you have a pair and I, most likely, have nothin'."

Williams' face was beet red within seconds. His eyes began to bulge as he tried, unsuccessfully, to hide his inner rage. He hurriedly scribbled his signature on the title and flung it onto the table.

Rip picked up the pink slip and tucked it in his top pocket. He left the $1,200 in the pot and, looking directly at Williams, said, "I've got an idea. How 'bout we play one more hand. I'll leave the twelve hundred in the pot and you put that whalebone charm up against it. We'll play by your rules—you know I kinda like that 'jokers wild' thing. You can deal, too, if ya want. How's that sound to ya?"

Williams jumped up from his seat and stormed toward the door. Before he could make his exit, Rip yelled in his direction, "Oh, I guess when push comes to shove, we see who the chicken shit is! By the way, not only are you chicken shit, but you couldn't train a dog to piss on a fire hydrant, either, you no-trainin' bag o' blubber!"

Everyone in the room was now laughing at Williams as he disappeared out the door of the lounge. He had very few friends in the crowd and was generally regarded as an arrogant bully who was, on those occasions that he lost, a sore loser. Most of the men in the lounge were actually happy to see Williams get a dose of the medicine that he too often had inflicted on others, and several of them actually congratulated Rip on his victory.

Billy was elated. He had been worried sick ever since Rip had told him about losing the Corvette, and now he was at ease. Without a car, Billy knew that any plans they had for the next couple of months would have been in serious jeopardy. Now that Rip had won the Corvette back, everything was back on track.

The two touts moved on to Louisville on the eve of the Kentucky Derby. As the Corvette approached the racetrack, Rip pulled it to the side of the road and stopped at a gate near the backstretch of the track. From their vantage point, they could see the form of Churchill Downs through the waning sunlight. Billy was a bit awestruck when he got his first look at the venerable grandstand with its twin spires stretching high into the early evening sky.

"This place," Rip said, "is to racin' what Yankee Stadium is to baseball or what Madison Square Garden is to boxin'. The Derby is the biggest, most prestigious race in the sport and they've been runnin' it here every year since 1875. Chances are—many years down the road—you'll remember this moment, when you first laid eyes on Churchill."

The touts sat silent for a few minutes, taking in the view. Then Rip drove the car to the freeway and into the countryside of Jefferson County before coming to a stop at a small motel about 12 miles from the racetrack.

"This is about as close as we can get the night before the Derby," Rip said. "Every joint closer to Louisville is taken, and the prices are at least triple what they normally are. We can flop here tonight and get to the track tomorrow to sell sheets. After tomorrow, things will calm down and we can move into a place right down the street from the track."

Rip, not surprisingly, had a favorite place in the area where the two were able to eat and drink. After a meal and several cocktails, the touts left for the room but not before Rip was able to secure a couple of six packs of cold beer. They drove to the motel, checked in and settled down for the evening.

Rip downed a couple of the beers and fell asleep on his bed while Billy, who had been able to buy a *Racing Form* where Rip had gotten the beer, put the television on and laid in his bed, handicapping the Derby day card. Billy could hear a gentle rain on the motel roof which seemed to steadily increase in intensity until the sound rivaled Rip's snoring.

Billy was nearly finished with his handicapping when there was a break in the programming on the Louisville TV station.

"We interrupt tonight's telecast to bring you important weather information," the announcer said in a stern and dramatic tone. "This just in from the National Weather Bureau. We have a confirmed touchdown of a tornado in this area of Jefferson County," the weatherman said. Then the man pointed to a section of the map that Billy recognized as the vicinity of their motel.

The hair stood up on Billy's neck as he shouted, "Oh my god! That's where we are! There's a tornado *right where we are!"*

The rain became thunderous at that point, and swiftly turned to hail which sounded as though it were going to cave the roof in. Despite the pummeling the motel was taking, Rip, still sound asleep in an alcohol induced stupor, remained unfazed.

Billy tried to remain calm and thought that perhaps he was overreacting. He told himself that he would be reassured if he called the front desk and talked to someone who was used to this kind of weather.

Billy collected himself, picked up the house phone and dialed the lobby. In an instant the desk clerk answered the phone and Billy said in his calmest voice, "I just heard on TV that there may be a tornado in the area. Do you know anything about it?"

Instead of a calm, rational, reassuring voice on the other side of the line, Billy got a panicked clerk who shouted, "Please, sir! Take cover at once! There's a tornado comin'!"

Now Billy, too, was panicked and shouted at the clerk, "What should I do? What should I do?"

"Get into the bathroom and lock the door!" the clerk screamed. "Do it now, sir! Please! Do it right now!"

Billy slammed the phone down and ran over to where Rip was still sound asleep and began to shake him. He had to scream to be heard above the roar of the hail smashing on the roof. "Get up, Rip! You have to get up right now!"

A woozy Rip jumped to his feet and began to look around, confused and disoriented. "What? What the fuck's goin' on here?" he said.

Billy grabbed his arm and shouted at him, "C'mon! We have to get into the bathroom and lock the door! C'mon we have to do it right now!"

Rip pulled his arm from Billy's grasp and said, "What? What the fuck are you talkin' about?"

"There's a tornado coming!" Billy shouted. "We have to get into the bathroom right now!"

Even Rip, who was groggy with sleep and booze, could understand the urgency of the situation now and the two touts made a hasty retreat toward the bathroom. But, just before Billy reached the doorway, he stopped dead in his tracks, and Rip ran into him.

"Never mind this bullshit," Billy said. "If I'm going to die tonight, I'm not going to do it like some rat, cringing in a shithouse. I'm going out on my own two feet."

Then, as the hail continued to threaten to break through the roof, Billy walked over to a small refrigerator where the beer was stored. He took two cans out and opened them. He handed one to Rip and kept the other for himself.

"It's been good to know ya," Billy said, raising his beer to Rip.

"Likewise, my boy," Rip said. The two touts raised the cans to their lips and took a long drink. They stood in their room and looked up at the ceiling as the hail pounded the little motel. They could hear a roar in the distance which slowly built until it sounded like a freight train rumbling down the street. The men held their breath for a few seconds, then, as quickly as it had started, it was over. The night air became deadly silent, and the touts let out a sigh of relief, having survived the episode.

Billy walked over to the window and couldn't believe what he saw. The ground outside the motel was covered in hail—several inches deep. The cars, the trees, the roofs, the ground—everything—was covered. Billy opened the door of the motel room and looked at the odd sight. It seemed like a winter wonderland, although it was the first week of May in Kentucky.

One by one, the other doors of the motel rooms opened and bewildered guests were shocked at what they witnessed. Apparently, most of those staying at the motel had no experience with the weather that spawns tornadoes, either, and many of them chatted with each other about the ordeal.

Rip and Billy walked through the ankle deep slush and examined the Corvette. By a great stroke of luck, Rip had put the canvas top up when they had gotten to the motel and it had held up to the onslaught of hail. They brushed as many of the ice balls off the roof of the car as they could and checked for other damage. Once again, luck was on their side; the car had been parked by a nearby tree and, except for a couple of nearly imperceptible indentations, the car had escaped unscathed.

The evening's excitement now over, the touts got a good night's sleep before leaving for Churchill Downs and the Kentucky Derby the next morning.

The touts were able to continue to work for the same local Kentucky tipsheet that they had been with at Keeneland. On the day of the Derby, sales were so brisk that both Billy and Rip ran out of sheets before the first race. This was fine with Billy, who wanted to spend the day as a fan, and not simply as a hustler. Rip, on the other hand, had seen several Derbys and was more interested in profits. He was annoyed that the tipsheet owner hadn't printed enough sheets for such a big day. However, once Rip made his way to his favorite Churchill bar, all was quickly forgotten as he immersed himself in one of his favorite pastimes—drinking alcohol.

After checking out, Billy stopped off at Rip's spot at the bar. He figured that once separated there was a very good chance they'd never reconnect, so Billy wanted Rip to know his whereabouts. Rip stood at the bar talking to a well-dressed middle aged, rotund man wearing a bowler hat when Billy approached.

"Say, Rip," Billy said, "I'm going to try to get a decent view of the racetrack. I really want to see the Derby."

"Well, that may be a little easier to do than you think," Rip said.

"How so?" Billy asked.

Rip put his hand on the man's shoulder and said, "This man is Colonel Shelby. He has an extra ticket for a seat in the grandstand. He's offered it to me, but if he doesn't mind, I'd like you to have it."

The man smiled and said, "Mind? Of course I don't mind! Any friend of yours is a friend of mine!"

Tickets for seats at the Derby had always been extremely hard to get and very expensive. Billy had resigned himself to being stuck among the hordes of people standing in front of the grandstand, straining to get a view of the track. Now, thanks to Rip and his friend Colonel Shelby, he would get an unobstructed view of the action.

It was a stroke of luck too good to be true.

Colonel Shelby handed the ticket to Billy and said, "There ya go, young fella. I get very good seats for the Derby—a little bit up the stretch from the finish line. My family has owned the rights to them for many decades. I make the big race every single year!"

Billy took the ticket from Colonel Shelby and offered to pay him for it.

"Absolutely not, young man. It's my pleasure to give it to you. Now if you gentlemen will excuse me, I have to be getting back to the box before my wife begins to worry about me."

Billy shook the Colonel's hand and thanked him for the ticket. Rip simply saluted him and nodded his head, and the Colonel left for the grandstand.

"Who is this fella Shelby, Rip? Was he a military guy or something?" Billy asked.

"Yes, he was," Rip said. He was a tank commander with Patton when they broke through to Bastogne in the Battle of the Bulge. His family has been in Kentucky for nearly 200 years, and lots of his ancestors were military, too. The Revolution, Civil War—you name it—his family served in it. Anyway, nowadays he's a tobacco farmer, and a pretty big one. He owns a huge farm outside of Lexington and from what I gather, he's pretty damned rich. Be that as it may, he's always been a down to earth guy, to me, anyway."

The atmosphere on Derby day was similar to the opening day he had experienced at Monmouth Park, only intensified many times over. Almost all the women in the crowd were clad in long, flowing gowns and wore very wide and colorful hats of all descriptions. Billy made his way through the raucous crowd and up the ancient wooden grandstand where he surrendered his ticket to an usher. The man placed a band around Billy's wrist and led him to the box where Colonel Shelby and his wife were seated.

"Right this way, young man!" Colonel Shelby said to Billy as he approached the box. "Billy, this is my wife, Lorene. Lorene, this young fella is Billy. He's a friend of Rip McKenna's. He will be joining us today"

"Well, it's very nice to make your acquaintance, Billy," Lorene said.

Mrs. Shelby was almost a female counterpart of her husband. She was short and rotund, and she wore a flowing blue party dress adorned with ruffles and a wide blue hat with a huge snow white bow.

Billy smiled and momentarily took Lorene's outstretched hand in his. "Same here, ma'am. And I'd like to thank you for inviting me to your box."

The box had four folding chairs inside of it, and Colonel Shelby and his wife occupied the two nearest the track. Billy took the seat directly behind the Colonel, reasoning that he'd get a better view looking past his bowler hat than he would behind Mrs. Shelby's.

Billy noticed that both the Colonel and his wife were drinking from tall glasses that had some kind of large stalk protruding from the top. Finally, his curiosity got the best of him, and he decided to ask about it.

"Excuse me," Billy said. "But do you mind if I ask what it is that you're drinking? And what is that vegetable hanging over the side? Is it celery?"

The Colonel and his wife looked at each other and chuckled. "My," the Colonel said, "don't you recognize these drinks? Why these are mint juleps, my boy! That 'vegetable' is a whole stalk of fresh Kentucky mint. What would a Kentucky Derby be without a couple of these? You *must* try one before the day is over!"

"I sure will," Billy replied. "If you don't mind, I will buy a round once you are finished with those."

The Colonel and his wife slowly sipped their juleps, and the first race was over before Billy was able to make good on his promise to buy a round of drinks. Once he had departed his seat to do so, he had to battle crowds of people until he found a vendor who had just emerged from below track level with a whole tray of mint juleps. Once the man stepped onto the floor, a line immediately formed and people bought the drinks as quickly as he could dispense them. Billy was fortunate to get three before the vendor's supply ran out. As luck would have it, there was a good deal of time between races, and Billy was able to get back to the box in plenty of time before the second race.

Billy distributed the drinks to his hosts, then sat down with one in his hand. He took the mint stalk and swirled it around the cracked ice in the drink, then raised it to his lips and took a sip. The drink was unlike any he had ever had; it was sweet, minty, and strong all at the same time.

"Well," Colonel Shelby said, "what do you think?"

"I like it," Billy said. "It seems strong, but it's very tasty. Actually a little sweet."

"That's the syrup," Mrs. Shelby said. "It's made with mint and sugar. Lots and lots of sugar! The sugar is boiled with some water for a few minutes, then crushed mint is added and it sits overnight so the mint flavor gets mixed with the sugar. The next day the crushed mint is removed. Then the syrup is added to the ice and bourbon gets poured on top. Then it's mixed, the mint stalk is added, and finally you have what we call 'the drink of the Kentucky Derby'! So, tell me, Billy. Did you hear the angels sing?"

Billy smiled at the question. "Um... hear the angels sing?" he asked.

"Why yes," Mrs. Shelby said. "They say that if a mint julep is made just right, you can hear the angels sing when you take that first sip!"

"Oh, were those angels I heard?" Billy said, still smiling. "Why yes, I did hear them! I guess I didn't recognize who was doing the singing!"

Billy and his hosts shared a good laugh at the quip. The Shelbys were very cordial and Billy was enjoying his day at the races very much.

The afternoon went on and Billy had picked four winners out of the first seven races. He had taken his time and carefully handicapped the races the night before in the motel, and his investment had delivered dividends as a couple of the winners returned double digit payoffs.

Before each race Colonel Shelby and Billy would compare their selections, and Billy's picks put him well ahead of the Colonel.

"My, you're having a fabulous day," the Colonel said after Billy had registered his fourth winner.

"Yes," Billy replied, "but I would trade all four of those to have the winner of the Derby. That's more important to me than anything."

"Yes, I suppose you would," the Colonel said. "By the way, who is your choice in the Derby?"

"I've been following Tim Tam ever since I saw him in Florida this winter," Billy said. "He's been my favorite horse, and I think he can win today. How about you, Colonel? Who is your pick?"

"I'm going to take a lot of heat for what I'm about to say," Shelby said, "but I have to give the edge to that big horse from California, Silky Sullivan. He's such a great stretch runner that I think he will relish the mile and a quarter distance. I almost always back a Kentucky bred horse, but I'm afraid this colt may just be too good to ignore."

"I'm certainly worried about him," Billy admitted. "But Rip brought up a good point a while back. He said that sometimes a horse who comes from far back doesn't really like a lot of distance, like you might think. I'm sure hoping that Rip's right about that because Silky Sullivan could fly past everyone in the stretch if he does."

Finally, the time for the Derby was at hand. As the horses entered the track the University of Louisville Marching Band struck up the familiar song, "My Old Kentucky Home," and thousands of fans—many of whom were proud, native Kentuckians—sang along. The horses continued onto the track in the post parade and as the field passed by the grandstand, the fans cheered the horses. None received a greater ovation than Silky Sullivan and, as could have been predicted, he was the favorite in the wagering.

Billy stood and prepared to make his bet. The Colonel turned to him and said, "Billy, are you going up to make a wager? Would you mind making a bet for me?"

Billy was grateful for all the Colonel had done for him that day and didn't mind at all placing a bet for him.

"Sure," Billy said. "I'm going up to the window right now so I can make it back before the start."

"Great," the Colonel said. He reached into his pocket and pulled out a wad of bills held together with a rubber band. "Here's two thousand," the Colonel said, handing the wad to Billy. "Bet it all to win."

Billy gulped. "Okay," he said. "Two thousand to win on Silky Sullivan."

"No," the Colonel said. "Two thousand to win on Tim Tam. I've been to a lot of Derbys and I've never seen anyone knock out winners like you have today. You're obviously a good handicapper and I won't go against you. Bet it all on Tim Tam to win."

"Will do," Billy said.

Billy fought his way to the $50 window and bet $2,200—two thousand for the Colonel and two hundred for himself—to win on Tim Tam. He made it back to the box just as the horses were going into the gate. He handed forty tickets to the Colonel and kept four for himself.

The crowd began to cheer as the horses were loaded into the starting gate. Billy and the Colonel toasted each other with a mint julep and wished each other luck as the bell rang and a thunderous roar rose from the crowd.

The horses were off, and a cavalry charge emerged—led by 45-1 longshot Lincoln Road. As the field reached the first turn several horses were in hot pursuit of the leader and mud, a remnant from the previous night's storm, was flying in all directions. Tim Tam was allowed to settle in behind the leaders and Silky Sullivan fell far back early, as expected.

The horses straightened out for the run down the backstretch and Billy's heart began to pound as he watched Tim Tam slowly edge closer to the leaders. He was beginning to think that his horse had a great chance to win now, as Tim Tam had run this way in many of his winning races during the year. However, Silky Sullivan hadn't begun to run yet, and there was still plenty of time for him to put in one of his patented stretch drives.

Lincoln Road, who had gotten the lead shortly after the start of the race, had shown no signs of quitting and still set the pace midway on the final turn. The pack of horses who had tried to keep up with the leader were now showing the ill effects of their efforts and, as a group, seemed to struggle as Tim Tam moved up behind them.

Billy felt that Tim Tam was in a favorable spot turning for home, but a quick glance at the back of the field revealed that Silky Sullivan had indeed finally kicked into high gear. The pride of California blew past the horse nearest him and appeared on his way to yet another miracle finish. But, as quickly as it had begun, Silky Sullivan's rally came to an end. The favorite began to struggle leaving the turn, and he was still very far back.

Silky Sullivan was finished.

In the stretch, Lincoln Road sprinted away from the field and took a clear lead with a little more than an eighth of a mile to go. The race was now his to win or lose.

Time was running out for Tim Tam. Billy's horse had closed well on the turn to reach contention, but had to wait for several precious seconds until his jockey, Ismael

Valenzuela, could find enough room to maneuver him around horses and get him clear for a run at the leader.

Colonel Shelby turned and shouted at Billy to be heard above the roar of the crowd, "I can't see Tim Tam! Where is he? Do you know?"

Billy had lost sight of his horse on the turn and didn't have an answer for the Colonel. Then, before he could say anything, he caught a glimpse of a horse forging through along the rail leaving the turn. "Yes!" Billy said excitedly. "He just got through on the inside! He's moving fast, too! He's going to make a run at the horse in front! C'MON TIM TAM!"

The Run for the Roses had come down to a two horse race—Lincoln Road and Tim Tam.

Valenzuela aimed Tim Tam at the leader, who was now more than three lengths ahead, and began to urge him on. The rider of Lincoln Road, Chris Rogers, took a quick look behind him and saw Tim Tam gaining with every stride. He furiously pumped Lincoln Road's neck in an attempt to help the valiant colt maintain his momentum as the finish line grew nearer and nearer.

Billy's heart felt like it would burst through his chest as he screamed words of encouragement to Tim Tam. "Come and get him, Tim Tam! Run at him, boy! You can do it!" Billy shouted as loud as he could.

Goose bumps began to raise on Billy's arms as Tim Tam caught Lincoln Road in the deep stretch.

The two horses were now stride for stride with less than a sixteenth of a mile to go, and it looked like either could emerge the winner. But Tim Tam dug down deep and, displaying the heart of a true champion, gradually edged to the front to win by a half-length over a courageous Lincoln Road.

Billy was overjoyed and continued to clap and cheer until Tim Tam pulled up after the race and returned to the winners' circle. He and the Colonel laughed and shook each other's hands while exchanging congratulations on having "won" the Derby.

Tim Tam was led to the circle where he was adorned with a huge blanket of red roses, emblematic of the Kentucky Derby champion. Billy stood and gazed at the sight from his place high in the grandstand, and a tear slowly trickled down his cheek as he was overcome with emotion. Although Billy had no real life connection to Tim Tam, he had come to love the horse, and his winning the Kentucky Derby triggered a spate of extreme pride in him.

Soon, the winners' circle festivities were over and it was time for the Colonel and Billy to collect their winnings. Sent postward as the second choice in the wagering, Tim Tam paid $6.20 for a winning two dollar ticket, giving Billy more than $400 in profit and ten times that amount—$4,200—was won by the Colonel. Billy thanked Colonel Shelby and his wife once again for their hospitality, then left the grandstand to look for Rip, finding him exactly where he had left him—at the bar.

The races were now over and as the touts were leaving the track, Rip gave Billy a hint as to what was in store for them that evening.

"There's a great place down at the end of Bardstown Road," Rip said. "It's called the Boot Hill Saloon, and it's across from a big graveyard."

"Sounds like some kind of place where rodeo people go to drink," Billy said.

"Yeah," Rip said, "I think they call it that because of the cemetery on the other side of the road. Don't worry, though. It's not some kind of wild west joint with gunslingers or anything. It's where lots of people who were at the races today will wind up."

The touts went into downtown Louisville where they enjoyed a Kentucky Hot Brown dinner and a few drinks before making their way to the Boot Hill Saloon. A huge two story building, the bar was already crowded and they were fortunate to find a parking spot behind the tavern. There was a line at the front door and, as Rip had predicted, many of the women waiting to get in were still wearing their wide hats from the Derby and a good deal of the men wore suits with flowers in their lapels.

Billy got out of the Corvette and began to walk toward the front of the tavern when Rip spoke up.

"Where are you goin'" he said.

"To get in line. Why?"

"Come with me," Rip commanded. "Only the greenhorns stand in line out front."

Rip guided Billy to the back door of the tavern where a large man stood guard. Rip reached into his pocket, peeled a $10 bill off his roll, and handed it to the man. The man opened the door and the two touts stepped inside the tavern.

"What was that about," Billy asked.

"Well," Rip said, "the cover charge here is a fin. If you're hip to the jive, you come to the back door, grease the guy there, and avoid the line out front. If you're a tourist, you stand in line and it costs ya the same. Now, which makes more sense to you?"

"Yeah, I guess," Billy said. "But there aren't many people coming in the back. Why not?"

"Jesus Christ," Rip said. "Don't be such a dumb ass! The guy at the back door is there to *prevent* people from gettin' in without payin'. Anything he gets on the sly is gravy for him. He ain't *supposed* to be takin' money."

"Oh, I get it," Billy said. "I should have realized if there was a way around something, you'd know what it is."

"Don't be a wiseguy," Rip smirked. "That's *my* job."

The touts walked down a long hallway and quickly found themselves in a crowded barroom where a country band was playing in the corner.

"This joint has four or five different bars," Rip said. "Each one has a different kind of music. This one has country and western. Another has bluegrass. Another one has a rock 'n' roll band. Another—I think it might be upstairs—has jazz. No matter what kind of music ya like, it's here somewhere."

Billy and Rip made their way through the crowd to the bar. After drinking a couple of beers, Billy asked the bartender where he might find a pay phone.

"There's one in the men's bathroom," the bartender said.

Billy, having never heard of a pay phone inside a bathroom, asked the man, "Did you say in the *bathroom*? The pay phone is in the men's *bathroom*?"

"Yup," the bartender said. "It's the only one on this floor."

Billy turned to Rip and said, "Okay. I have to go make a call. I'll be right back."

Billy had been thinking about his mother quite a bit of late, and he wanted to finally make contact with her. He worked his way to the men's room and, upon entering, was astonished at what he saw.

The men's room was crowded, and a line consisting of a half dozen men who wanted to use the pay phone had formed. Billy got in line and within a few minutes realized what had caused the backup. At the front of the line, leaning on the pay phone and chatting, stood a young man in his mid twenties. Billy could overhear the fellow's conversation, and it seemed like nothing more than idle chatter to him.

Billy tapped the shoulder of the man in front of him in line and asked, "Say, how long has that guy been on the phone, anyway?"

The man answered in a distraught tone, "I'm not exactly sure, but I think he's been on there at least fifteen or twenty minutes. He's not saying anything important, either. It sounds like he's only talking nonsense to his girlfriend. While he's been tying up the phone, this line has formed."

Every minute or so, one of the men in line would mutter some sort of protest under their breath. "C'mon, man." "Geez, this is ridiculous." "Wrap it up, man," were some of the comments.

Billy didn't want to risk any problems and stood quietly in line while the guy continued his chat. Minute after minute passed and, although the men became more impatient, nobody directly confronted the young man.

The door opened and Rip walked into the men's room. He looked at the line and the guy who stood against the wall, phone in hand, softly smiling and staring out into space. "What the fuck is goin' on here?" he asked Billy.

"The guy up there has tied up the phone for a half-hour, maybe forty five minutes or more," Billy said. "I think he's talking to his girlfriend or something. Whatever, it doesn't seem like it's important or anything."

Rip walked up to where the young man was leaning against the pay phone and listened in on his half of the conversation. "Yeah. Well maybe. I don't know. You know, it could be. Yeah, somethin' like that. I guess so. You know, who knows?"

Rip reached past the young man and depressed the connection of the pay phone with a "click." The guy glared at Rip incredulously. "You just hung up on me," he said.

"Yeah, you bet I did," Rip said. "What the fuck is wrong with you tyin' up the only phone in this joint with all that bullshit? Now you can get to the back of the line or get the fuck outta here!"

The young man stared at Rip for a moment, then quietly exited the men's room.

The man standing in front of Billy said to Rip, "Man, let me shake your hand! That was one of the greatest things I ever saw!"

Rip ignored the man's outstretched hand and shot back, "Oh yeah? Well how come none of you guys did it? Why did you let the prick tie the phone up for so long? Any of yous coulda done the same thing!" Then Rip added, prior to leaving the men's room,

"Make it a five minute maximum on the phone, fellas. Let's see if we can get everybody outta this joint so people can take a piss if they have to!"

None of the men in line used the phone for more than a couple of minutes and shortly it was Billy's turn. He dialed his home number and after a couple of rings, Billy's father answered the phone.

"Dad?" Billy said, "It's me, I..."

Before Billy could finish a sentence, his father hung up the phone. It was becoming apparent to Billy that if his father had anything to do with it he wouldn't be able to contact his mother until he got back home in a few weeks.

The touts made the rounds, taking in a smorgasbord of sound as they moved from one band to another. Finally, the crowd began to thin, and the two had had their fill for the evening. They left through the rear door and as they walked across the dimly lit parking lot towards the Corvette, a voice came out of the darkness.

"I've been waiting for you," the voice said.

Out of the gloom appeared the young man who had tied up the phone earlier. Rip turned and slowly began to walk in the fellow's direction. "I'm havin' a hard time hearin' ya," Rip said, still approaching the young man. "Must be all that loud music tonight. What did you say?"

Rip stood only a couple feet away from the young man now, and he repeated, "*I've been waiting for you.*"

No sooner had the words left the young man's lips than Rip threw a vicious punch to the fellow's jaw.

He never knew what hit him.

The young man left his feet from the force of Rip's punch and, falling backwards, back peddled until he landed in a garbage can against the tavern wall, where he sat semi-conscious.

"I hope it was worth the wait," Rip said.

The touts got into the Corvette and drove back to the motel. During the drive, they talked about the Derby and Rip made a comment that somewhat confused Billy.

"That horse of yours ran a dead game race today," Rip said. "Just one little problem."

"Problem?" Billy said.

"Yeah, problem," Rip said. "I was in a good enough position to see that he didn't change leads in the stretch."

"What do you mean 'change leads'?" Billy asked.

"Well," Rip said, "a horse runs at a four beat gait. For example, he should start out left rear, right rear, left front, right front. That would be the right lead. They do that on straightaways. Now, when they go into a turn, they change leads. Right rear, left rear, right front, left front. That's the left lead. When a horse straightens out in the stretch, he's supposed to change from his left lead to his right lead. Tim Tam didn't do that today."

"So, why is that a problem?" Billy asked.

"Because, changin' leads helps to keep a horse from gettin' too tired. If a horse stays on one lead too long, he naturally gets tired faster. The fact that your horse was able to win today without changin' leads means he had to be much the best. But, horses refuse to change leads for a reason. Usually it means the horse has something botherin' him somethin' physical."

The touts moved into a boarding house near Churchill Downs and continued to sell sheets until mid-May, when it was time to move on to Pimlico where the Preakness Stakes are held.

CHAPTER 11 – Two Down, One to Go

As with each other stop along the way, Rip had something lined up for the touts at Pimlico. Baltimore was the home base for *Jack's Little Green Card*, and the local manager always needed extra help on Preakness day. Rip used his connections and was able to secure a spot selling *Jack's* in front of the grandstand, while arranging for Billy to sell a local sheet next to him on the stand.

The day had gotten off to a good start. There was an early crowd and the sales were brisk. About a half-hour before first post, some type of motorcade, consisting of several black limousines, drove up the street and stopped in front of the tip sheet stand. In the middle of the line of cars, a door opened and a man dressed in a pin stripe suit got out. He left the door of the car ajar and walked up to the stand where the touts stood vending their sheets.

"Okay, guys, you know the drill," the man said. The man then walked along the line, and each of the touts handed him a copy of their sheet.

Billy had no idea who the man was or why he should be giving him a copy of his card, but did so anyway because all the other hustlers did.

Once the man had collected the sheets he started back towards the car but stopped after a couple of steps, turned back and said, "I hope you guys realize that my boss is going to put you all out of business some day. He's watching you all!" Then the man got back into the limo and the motorcade continued in the direction of the Pimlico clubhouse.

"Who was that guy and why did I have to give him a sheet?" Billy asked.

Rip shook his head disgustedly. "That guy is a nobody, an aide," Rip said. "But did you catch a glimpse of the old prick sittin' in the limo? Know who that was?"

"I saw him but I don't recognize him," Billy said.

"That guy was J. Edgar Hoover," Rip said. "He's a horse racin' nut. Ya can see him at most any big track in the country at one time or another. Del Mar, Saratoga, Belmont. But D.C. isn't that far from here, so he goes to the Maryland tracks the most. Whenever ya see that motorcade comin', get a sheet ready. He always wants copies."

"What does he want the sheets for?" Billy asked.

"Whaddya think?" Rip said. "You don't think he just comes to the track to watch, do ya? He wants 'em so he can decide who to bet, like anybody else. Oh, he says he's monitorin' them for fraud or some bullshit, but he's really usin' the picks. He won't touch the sheets himself, though. He makes an aide, like the guy who he sent to pick up the sheets, handle 'em. I know a guy who was near his box once and heard Hoover say to an aide, "What fraud has *Jack's Green Card* perpetrated on the public in the *fifth* race?"

"So the director of the FBI uses tip sheets to play the horses?" Billy asked.

"Yup. Oh, and I also heard through the grapevine that Hoover's got a cozy little deal with the mob," Rip said. "I was told that they give him info on fixed races and in return, he turns a blind eye to the stuff they do. Imagine that. The top lawman in the country is in on the rig."

The races had begun and the touts stayed on the stand long enough to pick up a good amount of lates. Then, as customary, Rip went to his favorite bar and Billy left to find a decent place to watch the Preakness Stakes.

The Preakness Stakes turned out to be anti-climactic, and was nearly a replay of the Kentucky Derby two weeks earlier. As he had done at Churchill, Lincoln Road took the lead early, Tim Tam stalked until making a move in the stretch, and Silky Sullivan's rally stalled and he finished out of the money.

Tim Tam closed stoutly throughout the stretch and finished first by two lengths as the even-money favorite. Lincoln Road held well again and secured the runner-up spot.

In order to win racing's Triple Crown, and a piece of immortality, Tim Tam had to capture the Kentucky Derby, the Preakness Stakes, and the Belmont.

Two down, one to go.

CHAPTER 12 – Back Where We Started

The touts had only spent a couple of days at Baltimore and left for New Jersey as soon as the Preakness was over. Long Branch was a three hour drive from Pimlico, so Rip and Billy had plenty of time to talk as the Corvette roared up Interstate 95 towards their destination. Before long, the conversation turned to the Preakness Stakes.

"That wasn't much of a race today," Billy said. "I mean, don't get me wrong, I'm really glad Tim Tam won, but it just looked to me like a repeat of the Derby, minus the excitement."

"Yeah," Rip said, "it was kinda like watchin' a rerun of some TV show that you just saw a couple of weeks ago, right on down to the way your horse ran his race. Do you know what I'm talkin' about?"

"I think so," Billy said. "Are you talking about 'leads'? Didn't he change leads again?"

"Nope," Rip said. "Not only didn't he change leads, but I didn't like the way he pulled up. He looked sore to me. I hope he holds up for the Belmont, but that's only three weeks from now. If he's hurtin' as much as I think he is, I doubt he'll be good for that race."

The time went by quickly and the red Corvette pulled up in front of the old Victorian house shortly before dark. Rip had a key and the touts opened the heavy front door and brought their bags in.

"Well, here we are, Billy boy," Rip said, "back where we started!"

Billy looked around the empty house and asked, "Where are the other guys?"

Rip turned to Billy and said, "Well, the others go to Garden State for their spring meet. Issy, Bernardo, Mike all of 'em. That meet doesn't end until next week so we'll have this joint to ourselves for the time bein'. The people who own this place have things figured out to a tee. Durin' the summer, we get to rent it. Once we leave for Atlantic City, they rent it out to some group of college kids. They stay until May, then school is over and they leave. It's only vacant a week or two at a time because once they're out, we're in, and vice versa."

Rip put his hand on Billy's shoulder and continued, "This time, things are gonna be different, my boy. You're gonna get a real room. I'm sorry we couldn't expel that damned stooper last year and you had to stay in the attic. Tell ya what. You pick any room ya want, except for Mike's room—or mine—of course. Anybody puts up a beef I'll tell 'em to get the fuck out if they don't like it."

Billy thanked Rip, then chose his room and came back downstairs where Rip was checking the condition of the living room. "I have to get going, Rip," Billy said. "There are some things I want to do right away."

"I get your drift," Rip replied. "It's been a long time since you saw your folks. Why don't you take the car? I'm not goin' anywhere right now. Say, bring back a couple o' six packs, will ya?"

Rip tossed the keys to Billy, and as he drove to his parents' house he began to think, to formulate in his mind how this encounter would go. Billy had a good idea how he would be received by his father, but he also felt sure that his mother would be glad to see him. He had always had a special bond with his mother, and it caused him great pain that his father had refused to let him talk to her when he had called home earlier in the year.

Billy parked the Corvette in front of his parents' house and slowly ambled up the walkway towards the front door. As he walked, he noticed that the front lawn, which had always been meticulously kept by his father, appeared that it hadn't been tended to at all. Patches of grass grew wildly in places and weeds—which Billy had never seen in the lawn in his life —were taking hold in various spots.

Billy stepped onto the porch and rang the door bell, and as he stood waiting he silently hoped that his mother would answer the door.

Finally, the door slowly opened and Billy's father stood on the other side of the screen. His appearance was disheveled and scruffy, and it appeared to Billy that he had lost a considerable amount of weight.

"Hello, dad," Billy said.

"What do you want?" Billy's father snapped.

Billy looked his father in the eye and said, "Well, one thing I want is to talk to my mother. You can hang up on the phone all you want, but I'm here now and I want to see her. Don't make this any worse than it has to be, Dad. Now, if you don't want me in the house, alright, but I want you to bring her out here right now so I can see her!"

"I can't," Billy's father said, "Because she's DEAD!"

Billy was dumbfounded. "Dead? What are you talking about?"

"You're the smart one. I'm sure you know what 'dead' means. Do you recall getting a message I tried to send you at the end of last year? You know, the one you never bothered to answer? Your mother became despondent once she realized you were going to stay with your tipster pals, and she took ill just after Thanksgiving. She thought that maybe she would never see you again and, ironically, she was right. Anyway, she went downhill fast and passed away on New Year's day. She kept asking to see you, but I guess you were too busy drinking and gambling with your buddies to worry about your mother."

Billy was in shock and couldn't muster a reply. He simply stood with his hand covering his face as his father continued his diatribe.

"No doubt about it, boy," his father said, "you killed her. Just as sure as you're standing there, you killed her. You and all that tip sheet nonsense."

Billy's father slammed the door shut, but not before he blurted out, "Don't ever come around here again. You're dead to me now, too."

Billy had never experienced anything like the sorrow that swept through his soul that day. He turned, sat on the front steps and with his head in his hands, wept uncontrollably. Within his suffering, he couldn't help but remember the many times he had sat on that very step with his mother while growing up. Times when she had comforted him, times when she had advised him, times when they had exalted together, times when they had cried together.

Now Billy sat on the step and, for the first time in his young life, cried alone.

CHAPTER 13 - The Last Man Standing

The racetrack-bound bus turned the corner of Oceanport Avenue and made its way toward the final pickup for opening day of the 1998 racing season at Monmouth Park.

Waiting alone at the stop stood Bill Mulray. A cool spring breeze ruffled his gray hair and prompted the smoke from his cigar to waft into oblivion. The bus stopped in front of him and, after tossing the half-smoked Di Nobili to the curb, he ascended the steps and handed his fare to the driver. Mulray moved toward the back of the bus, as was his custom, and as he made his way down the aisle he passed the few passengers that were scattered among the many empty seats.

The riders were all old men, and most carried either a racing paper, a brown bag lunch, or both. One man, who breathed with the aid of a tank that forced oxygen into his nostrils through a plastic tube, looked up plaintively at Mulray as he passed by. Another clutched a crumpled racing paper in his hands and mumbled to himself as he stared directly into the back of the seat in front of him. A pair of octogenarians sitting together haggled over which one was going to use a free grandstand pass, thereby saving the two dollar admission fee. The faces of the men were time worn and sullen, and a silent air of futility the kind that accompanies the acceptance of inevitable defeat permeated the vehicle.

Mulray peered out the window as the bus crept down the avenue, and his thoughts turned to the many opening days he had experienced over the preceding four decades. He remembered the colorful cohorts he had been associated with—Onion Joe, Jigger Higgins, Cockeye Sol, the Alligator, Rip McKenna, Wingy, and Issy. Although widely regarded by those who knew him as a grumpy, insensitive man, Mulray's face softened with a nostalgic smile as he fondly revisited some of the times he had shared with those former contemporaries. Apparently, even a curmudgeon such as he enjoyed reminiscing about "the good old days."

Now there were only two left Mulray and Big Mike; the others were all gone. Mulray had been the youngest of the bunch and Mike was only a couple years his senior. They had survived the others simply by virtue of being born later.

The bus came to a halt across from the racetrack and the bang of the doors flying open brought Mulray out of his sentimental trance. He stood, then trailed the small group of seniors as they trudged down the aisle and stepped off the bus. Mulray wanted to get to the tip sheet stand before Big Mike, so he angled around the doddering old men and briskly walked past them, crossed the street and headed for the employee gate with his tip sheets securely tucked under his arm.

Mulray paused at the gate. The guard, who had manned that station for nearly twenty-five years, would normally have a few words of pleasantry for him on opening day. But this time, he just nodded as Mulray passed. Mulray thought it odd, but dismissed it. He pushed his way through the turnstile and plodded up the brick stairway that led to the clubhouse. He rounded the corner at the top of the stairs and entered the stand where the tip sheets were sold. Farther down the counter, the *Racing Form* vendor, John Blair, was counting his papers.

"Guess I beat him here again this year!" Mulray barked in John's direction.

Blair looked up briefly from his papers. "Yeah, I guess you did," Blair softly replied, trying to manage a smile.

Things did not seem normal to Mulray. He started to fold the tip sheets, but an uneasy feeling was now settling in the pit of his stomach.

At that moment, Monmouth's admissions director, Dave Ronek, appeared around the corner. He stopped in front of Mulray and placed an old bottle of wine and corkscrew on the counter.

"I'm sorry, Bill," Ronek said.

"When?" Mulray asked.

"February. I would have gotten ahold of you to let you know, but I didn't know how to contact you."

"How?"

"After the end of the meet last year, he started coughing up blood. He went to the hospital, but by then it was too late. He lasted 'til just around Ground Hog Day."

Ronek lowered his head and slowly walked away.

Mulray sat in stunned silence for a moment, staring at the bottle on the counter before him. He then leaned toward Blair, tossed his tip sheets onto the counter in front of him and exited the stand, bottle and corkscrew in hand.

Mulray walked outside and sat on one of the benches facing the track. He looked down at the bottle, inspecting its faded brown label. Using the corkscrew to carefully dislodge the ancient cork, he waved the bottle under his nose to get a whiff, then raised it to his lips and took a mouthful. He swished it around momentarily, then swallowed it as he stared into space.

Mulray repeated the ritual several times. He intended to finish the bottle. He had a right, indeed perhaps even a duty, to do so. After all, he was the last man standing.

Inside at the *Racing Form* stand, John Blair was joined by his old friend, Jay Wiley. Wiley was a writer for the *Form*, and he was always on the lookout for an interesting story on opening day. After exchanging tales of their off-season adventures, Wiley asked, "So, hear anything interesting that I might be able to use in the paper?"

Blair thought for a few seconds, then said, "Ya know, the old guy who was here a few minutes ago would make a good column. He sold tip sheets for more than forty years here, and just found out he's the last one left. I remember some of the characters that hustled the cards. What a bunch. They really had a party here in the old days."

"Where is he now?"

"He went out front," Blair said. "He's probably just sittin' out there. Ya can't miss him. Gray-haired guy. Sixty, maybe sixty-five. Had a bottle of wine in his hand. Name is Mulray."

Wiley nodded and headed out toward the track. He passed through the doorway and immediately saw Mulray, who was sitting alone among hundreds of empty seats and staring at the bottle of wine.

"Mr. Mulray?"

"Who wants to know?" he snapped.

"I'm Jay Wiley. I write for the *Racing Form*. I was wondering if I could interview you about the tip sheet business."

"What the hell for?" Mulray scowled. "It's over. What is there to tell?"

Wiley bristled from the gruffness of the reply.

"Well, John Blair told me that you sold tip sheets here for a long time, and that you had some interesting stories."

Mulray took a swig from the bottle and sat back. He paused for a moment, then motioned for Wiley to take a seat on the bench.

Mulray stared into space, as if straining to recreate the past in his mind's eye. The faint glimmer of a smile grew across his wrinkled face.

"This may take a while," he whispered.

Wiley listened and took copious notes as Mulray recounted his first year as a racetrack tout. The old hustler recited all of the stories about the touts, the racing venues, Tim Tam, the tip sheets, Cuba, and the tumultuous relationship with his parents which culminated in the death of his mother.

Mulray took another swig from the bottle and sat silent for a moment before Wiley spoke up.

"My god," Wiley said. "I'm sorry to hear what happened to your mother. That's so very sad."

"Yes," Mulray replied. "News of my mother's death hit me very hard. For a couple of years, I was very depressed and drank an awful lot. I blamed my father for what happened to her, and he blamed me."

"What happened to your father, if you don't mind my asking," Wiley said. "Did you ever reconcile with him?"

"Surprisin'ly, I did," Mulray said. "It took a long time, though. Despite what he told me that day, I tried to contact him a couple of times over the years, with no success. Then, I got wind one day that he was in the hospital. I went there and saw him. He was pretty old and beat up, and we weren't sure he was gonna make it. Anyway, the stubborn ol' bastard pulled out of it, thanks to some heart surgery and a pacemaker. So, we started communicatin' and we gradually grew closer. He even went so far as to admit that he played a part in what happened to my mother and that it wasn't all my fault. I'm not sure it was *any* of my fault but, what the hell, I was willin' to share the blame if it made the old man feel better. He died about fifteen years ago and I was glad we were back on good terms."

"So, what happened between that first year and now?" Wiley asked. "You're the last one left. What happened to the business? What happened to all the others?"

"Well," Mulray said, "there's been a lotta water under the bridge since then. For a couple of years, everything was status quo. The crowds were terrific, and we all made a lot of money sellin' the sheets. The seasons just kept goin' round and we kept makin' the circuits. The 50s turned into the 60s and racin' never seemed more popular. Ya could go

186

into nearly any bar or barber shop and find a bookie to take bets on the horses. Even the factories had guys bookin'. And everybody seemed to go to the track from time to time. Truth is, things were goin' so good, we thought it would never end. But, what's the old sayin'? 'No good thing lasts forever' or somethin' like that? Well, that sayin' turned out to be true for us, 'cause our racket sure didn't last forever."

"What happened?" Wiley asked.

"It started out kinda slow," Mulray said. "In the 60s, the crowds started slippin'. There are a lot of theories about why. One of 'em is that a lot of the people who fought in the war and were spendin' money like crazy when it was over, had gotten married. They had kids, mortgages and expenses. Gamblin' money was kinda low on their list of priorities. Another thing was television. TV wasn't nearly so sophisticated in the late 40s and 50s as it was becomin' in the 60s. Lots more sports on the air by then, and almost everybody could watch their teams on the tube. Don't forget, racin' has to compete with other types of entertainment– other, *cheaper* forms of entertainment. TV, even movies or bowlin', won't cost ya what a day at the races can wind up settin' ya back. I think people started optin' for cheaper ways to entertain themselves. Another thing is, there wasn't a whole lot of racin' around these parts before the war–in fact it was illegal in some places. But the state realized they could pull in some extra dough by legalizin' it and taxin' it, so they did. It was quite a novelty for a while, but after fifteen or twenty years, it started to wear off."

Mulray took a short swig of the wine and continued. "There's somethin' else that people rarely mention," he said, "and that's takeout. The percentage the tracks charged for makin' a bet gradually crept up over the years. When this joint opened in the 40s the bite was only 10%. But, no, they couldn't leave well enough alone makin' a fortune. They—and I mean the state as much as the tracks—had to test the waters. 11%, 12%, 13%, and up and up it went. One thing they never realized was that raisin' the takeout to such high rates would kill the goose that laid the golden egg. Ya see, most bettors don't know how the takeout affects them and that's what the tracks counted on. Management figured the bettors wouldn't squawk because they didn't understand it. They were right about that, but they were wrong—or didn't predict what the bettors *would* do. They started to give up on racin'. Why? Because a guy may not know what the takeout at the track is, but he does know when he goes home with no money. And every time the takeout goes up, the track gets more and the bettors get less. So, more and more bettors were goin' home broke more and more often. After a while, people get disgusted and stop comin'. I don't think any of the stuffed shirts counted on that happenin'. So what do the geniuses do? Do they drop the takeout back to where it was when they were doin' good? NO! They come up with new bets that have an even *higher* takeout! They come up with exactas—you have to pick the winner *and* the second place finisher—and trifectas—a bet that demands ya have the first three in order. Well, those bets go for a takeout of 20% to 25% or so. What the swindlers hoped is that the bigger payoffs would muddy up the fact that they're glommin' such a big amount of the bettin' pools. And it worked—for a while. But then, the bettors go home broke more and more often and faster than ever. Attendances and bettin' handles drop. And drop. And drop. When I started in the game, Garden State used to get 40,000 people on a Saturday. Now they're lucky to get *4,000.*"

Mulray went on with his diatribe. "Then, around the early 70s, lotteries started comin' out. The states wanted in on the gamblin' dollar themselves. Ya see, when some guy used to take the numbers on a street corner, that was shady and illegal. But when the state does it, it becomes very above board and respectable. That took some of the money and attendance from the track. Instead of havin' to find a guy who would book it, people could go into any candy or liquor store and buy 'em. But the real crusher was the casinos. In the mid 70s, the politicians got together and got that law passed for Atlantic City. In no time, half of the people who used to go to the track were goin' to the casinos. Every racetrack within 200 miles was affected. Things have gotten so bad that some tracks are on the verge of closin'. I think you can guess who got the worst of it—Atlantic City Racecourse. The guy who runs that joint just announced that this is the last year of racin' for that great place."

Mulray paused and took a Di Nobili from his top pocket and lit it. He took a long drag and slowly blew the smoke toward the afternoon sky. "Sorry about the cigar," he said. "It's a habit I picked up from my days in Havana."

"Where was I?" Mulray said. "Oh yeah. The politicians have gotten their hands into just about everything. First they took control of the numbers racket. Then they got their fingers into the casinos in Atlantic City. They even took over racin' in this state. Around the mid 1970s the government built a racetrack up north at the Meadowlands as part of the Sports Authority. They filled it with relatives of politicians, connected people, that sort of thing. Well, because politicians love places where they can warehouse their imbecile brothers and nephews, they start eyein' up this joint. But the Sports Authority doesn't have the right under their charter to buy the place, so they have to cook up a scheme. So they fall back on the oldest political scam in the book. They pick somethin' they know the people will go for—in this case Major League baseball—and they put the right to buy racetracks into the bill with some small type addendum on the bottom, you know, like an afterthought. Now, they're aware that New Jersey can never get a big league team—the Yankees, Mets, and Phillies all have veto power over that—but they know the suckers will support the bill anyway. So at the bottom of the bill they put 'The Sports Authority shall have the right to purchase a racetrack anywhere in the state to generate revenue,' blah, blah, blah. Well the boys in Trenton pass the so-called 'baseball bill' and get what they *really* want—Monmouth Park. Did New Jersey ever get a major league baseball team? Of course not. But that wasn't the objective, anyway. It's funny. I can still remember that gap-tooth governor—Kean—on TV, smilin' and wearing a baseball cap that said 'NJ' on the front. He was probably smilin' 'cause he pulled off the con without a hitch. So they get to work right away buyin' this place and puttin' their hacks in here to run things. The first guy they put in charge—Hal Handel—came here by way of the Racin' Commission. Before that, I think he was with the Motor Vehicle Department or Fish and Wildlife, or some shit. At any rate, he's a lifelong political leech. What he knows about racin' could be written on the head of a pin, but not knowin' what you're doin' really doesn't matter in politics. This asshole—Handel—boasts one day that he doesn't know how to read a *Racin' Form*. Imagine that. Proud of the fact that he has no idea how his product works. Ya know, one of the dirty little secrets in this game is that most of the management types consider their customers suckers. Pricks like Handel don't even know how to bet and think that anybody who does is some kind of sick degenerate. In their minds, what they do is similar to dope dealers who supply addicts with their daily fix. Another thing. Just to show ya what kind of people the state brought in, one of Handel's protégés—the son of a politician—was overhead askin', 'what's the eighth pole.' Not where, *what*. He didn't even know that the eighth pole was the marker an eighth of a mile from the finish. To top it off, that idiot wound up the general manager of a couple of racetracks. And people wonder how racin' could have gotten to this point."

"So, what happened to the other guys you worked with," Wiley asked.

"Let's see," Mulray said. "Issy, believe it or not, worked right up until about five years ago. He was in his nineties when he finally called it quits and moved back to Baltimore to live with his nephews. Ya know, Issy put those boys through school. He sent money to his sister for years to help out. I guess they must have been grateful 'cause they did take him in at the end of his life. Anyway, hearin' that Issy passed away was hard to take. He was one of the best people I, or anyone, ever met. I never saw anybody who was more universally liked than he was. I owe him a lot. He taught me almost everything I know about racin', especially handicappin'. He always steered me right. Oh, another thing. Do ya remember that Issy was a great pool shooter when he was young? Well, the guy he used to beat like a rented mule—New York Fats—changed his name to *Minnesota Fats* after they made a movie about a pool hustler by that name. Issy thought that was hilarious. I mean, somebody who couldn't carry his cue stick became famous and Issy wound up an unknown sellin' tip sheets. Goes to show ya how life is sometimes."

Mulray paused for an instant, then added, "I really miss the old son of a bitch."

He took a drink of wine and continued, "But the first of the crowd to go was Bernardo. He wound up workin' for the *Racin' Form* and was managin' things here at Monmouth. About a dozen years ago, he came down with lung cancer. He went to Florida that winter and never came back. We got word that he died down there. Damned shame. He was a great guy. I was really sorry to hear that he withered away like he did."

Mulray puffed on the cigar. "Then, Jigger checked out. He was a lifelong grab ass, and one night at simulcastin' here, he grabbed the wrong one. Seems he had a load on and rubbed the ass of one of the female security guards. She put up a major beef, and Handel told Jigger to hit the road. So he goes to Florida, and last we heard *he* got cancer and died. Only he didn't get lung cancer; it started in his ear and spread. That was really weird. I've heard of cancer in lots of different places, but in the ear? Never heard of that before or since. Anyway, Jigger was another one that I got along with real good. He was one of the happiest guys around. Drunk most of the time, but happy. He just couldn't resist puttin' his hands on women's asses. It got him into trouble a few times over the years and finally did him in for good. Too bad. He loved this joint and I hated to see him thrown out the way he was."

Wiley intently wrote down Mulray's comments in shorthand. He found Mulray's story riveting and was sure that it would make good copy.

190

"Next," Mulray said, "Curly kicked the bucket. Ya see, in recent years most of the touts wound up livin' close by the track here and stayin' all year round. Things elsewhere were in decline too, so there wasn't much sense in the guys runnin' all around the country, especially since they were gettin' older. Most of the touts were bachelors and kept rooms in boardin' houses nearby. Anyway, Curly actually was married and his wife and him had a house in Long Branch. For years, Curly used to manage a card called *Longshot Riley*, but when the owner packed it in in the early 90s, Curly just bounced around. First he put out the *New York Handicap* for a coupla years until the owner of that sheet came in and ran it himself. After that, he hung around, fillin' in when a guy needed a day off, or jumpin' in for lates after somebody left for the day. Durin' the off season one year, he dropped dead; I heard it was a heart attack. They tell me that they buried him with a *Racin' Form* and wearin' a Monmouth Park cap. I can still remember what Rip told me in that graveyard years ago, though. 'When a guy who's been a a motherfucker all his life dies, he doesn't suddenly become a good guy. He just becomes a dead motherfucker.' Well, maybe I wouldn't exactly say Curly was a motherfucker, but I would say he was an arrogant, ornery, argumentative prick. I never liked the guy and never got along with him, even after workin' together for all those years. I was indifferent towards him while he was alive, and that's what I was when I found out he died—indifferent."

Mulray pointed to the far side of the racetrack. "Over there, on the railroad tracks that cut through the backstretch, is where Bullet Bob met his end," he said. "Seems Bob came down with some form of terminal liver failure, cirrhosis, I guess. He hung around here while his health steadily went south. Finally, his gut swelled up and he turned yellow from jaundice. Well, one night Bob took a bottle of Hennessey and sat on the tracks, waitin' for the 9:15 southbound. Best as anyone can piece together, he just laid down on the tracks and let the train cut him in half. I felt really bad about that. He could be an absolute goofball sometimes, but he really wasn't a bad guy."

Mulray swirled the wine at the bottom of the bottle and said, "Let's see. Oh yeah. Wingy and Sol were two of the guys who didn't stay around here all year. Durin' the winter, Wingy went home to someplace in New York and Sol used to go to a boardin' house in Hot Springs. Wingy was pretty damned old the last time I saw him, which was around the same time Issy left for good. Towards that time Monmouth was down to only four or five sheets after havin' a dozen when things were good. So, guys like Wingy and

Sol didn't have much to do around here anyway. Those two guys disappeared from the scene one year and were never seen around these parts again. Funny thing. Each of the old touts knew somebody who would eventually stop by Monmouth and fill us in on their condition. I used to call those people 'death messengers' or 'death watchers.' Well, sure enough, we got word about Wingy, then Sol. I forget what got them, but it could just have been old age with those guys. Wingy was a sorry soul, always flappin' the wing at ya. Unfortunately, things got so lean around here that there wasn't enough business to support keepin' guys like him around. Oh, one thing, though. Wingy did win that bet with Bullet Bob. Like Wingy predicted, both the Dodgers *and* Giants left New York for the West Coast after the 1957 season. Ya know, for years and years, people blamed Walter O'Malley for movin' the Dodgers. Truth is, it was that scumbag Moses who forced 'em to move. That old bastard had a 'vision' for New York, and baseball wasn't part of it. O'Malley wanted to build a first class joint, with a dome and everything. He even had a spot picked out, an empty lot less than a mile from Ebbets. Moses said, 'No way,' and that was the end of Dem Bums in Brooklyn. Here's the kicker: that lot has been sittin' there for more than fifty years and is still vacant today. The Dodgers are long gone but the fuckin' lot is still there. How's that for irony? The only reason the Mets were ever able to get to play in New York was because they were willin' to settle miles away in Queens, where Moses wanted to stick the Dodgers. Moses. A class 'A' motherfucker if you ever saw one. I lost my team because of that piece o' shit. Anyway, back to the bet. Watchin' Bob fork over that thousand dollars to Wingy the next season was a classic. I never saw Wingy so happy or Bob so sour."

Mulray ran his hand across his face, then said, "Now Sol, he's a different story. Issy had him nailed when he called him 'one of the cheapest bastards you'll come across.' In all the years I was around him, I never saw the skinflint spend a penny. Word is he saved nearly everything he ever made, so when it came time to get out, he had a nest egg. I heard he moved down to Hot Springs and stayed in some retirement home that catered to Jews. Can't say that I ever missed him and his cockeye. Dropped dead down there one year. Another rat, in my book."

Mulray sat back and chuckled. "The Alligator was a trip. He used to try every scam and boondoggle known to man to try to make a buck at the track. I saw him do 'em all. Around 1990 or so he leaves hustlin' and goes to Florida to train greyhounds. Now mind ya, he ain't never trained anything in his life, but he bullshits some guy who owns dogs that he knows what he's doin'. Anyway, him and his assistant trainer, Crazy Tommy—another guy who doesn't know which end of the dog to put a muzzle on—get to racin' dogs near Miami. By some miracle, they do good and win a lot of races. Well, I suppose that those two fuck nuts pulled one of their stunts on the wrong guy, 'cause they went missin' and have never been found. My guess is they got a one-way trip to the Everglades from somebody who didn't appreciate their bullshit. I've always assumed they're both dead 'cause I'm pretty sure they'd have shown up at some track somewhere along the line, and they haven't. Damned shame. They were assholes but good assholes, if ya know what I mean. They were harmless—to other touts, anyway—and ya could always count on 'em for a good laugh."

Wiley looked up from his pad and asked, "What about Rip? And yourself? You never said what happened to you two."

"I'm gettin' to it," Mulray said. "We still have a couple of guys to go. Onion Joe was another that drifted away in the 80s. He actually went back to his onion farm in New York. His wife had run things since he left all those years ago and turned the business into a real money maker. Word is, she never took another man and actually let him come back home; my feelin' is that she felt sorry for him. His kids were grown by then, had families of their own, and weren't quite so forgivin'. They say that his kids would never come around when he was there. Even if his wife could find it in her to forgive Joe, they couldn't. It serves him right, if ya ask me. The fuckin' kook abandoned his family. I don't think it gets much worse than that. He's lucky his wife had it in her to pick up the ball and go on without him. He wound up gettin' pneumonia and passin' away on the farm."

The horses for the first race were walking up the track towards the paddock for saddling. Mulray stopped his monologue long enough to look at them as they passed by the clubhouse fence.

"Can you tell me what happened to Rip?," Wiley asked.

"Rip. Good old Rip," Mulray said, with nostalgia in his voice and eye. "We were about as close as friends could be for years and years. Right from the start he took me under his wing and showed me the ropes. He introduced me to everybody he knew. Told me who was okay and who to avoid. Took me to some of the best places anybody's ever been. Take Havana for example. We went there quite a bit until Castro overran the island

and put a stop to all gamblin', includin' horse racin'. Did ya know that Castro turned Oriental Park into a junk yard? Anyway, I'll never forget meetin' Ernest Hemingway. It must have been a stroke of luck to meet him the first time I went there, because we never ran into him again in Cuba."

"So, what happened to Rip?" Wiley asked again.

"Well, Rip and I hung together from the time I came to the track until right before he died, which was only about two years ago. As you already know, Rip was, well, a drunk, and not only didn't it decrease as he got older, for a few years before he died it actually got worse. His temperament went south, too he even got surly with me half the time. Anyway, Rip lived over in Long Branch in the same boardin' place as Big Mike, and I live about twenty miles from the track. I only come around the track during live racin' in the summer. Once the Monmouth meet ended, I wouldn't even see Rip until the track opened again the next spring. So, durin' the winter a couple of years back, Rip is hangin' out at simulcastin' here one night and he's got a pint of Jim Beam hidden in his coat pocket. He polishes most of it off before the last race and starts walkin' home. It's dark and a lot of the sidewalks around here are uneven because of the roots of old trees that push them up in every direction. So, he's staggerin' home with the bottle in his hand and he stumbles on a bad section of sidewalk. Down he goes head first and when he puts his hands out to break his fall the bottle shatters and slices his hand and wrist wide open. Well, the old bastard picks himself up off the sidewalk, holds his hand against his coat to keep the blood in and walks about two miles to the hospital. He's lost a lot of blood by then so they give him a transfusion and stitch everything up. They want him to stay a couple of days to keep an eye on him, but what does the stubborn fuck do? He walks out of the place and goes home. The next mornin' he wakes up with blood everywhere and walks back to the hospital. They patch him up but this time they call somebody in from the state and the next thing ya know they have him in some kind of nursin' home. Poor son of a bitch got stuck in there for a couple of weeks and wound up dyin' there. I was told that they got social workers from the state involved and everything, ya know, like he was some kind of nut or indigent bum or somethin'. The worst part of the whole thing is that I didn't know anything about it until Monmouth opened a few months later. Big Mike knew but never called me to let me in on it. Turns out they didn't release him to go home 'cause the old ladies that ran the roomin' house didn't want him to come back. Mike would never admit it, but I'm sure he had somethin' to do with that. Mike could be a sneaky bastard and I'll bet my bottom dollar that he told the old ladies not to let him come back, that he was too much of a drunk or somethin'. Mike could have called me, but I'm sure he knew that I'd have gotten him out of there and back to his room. I just hope that Rip wasn't askin' for me and Mike told him I wouldn't come. Of all the nasty, underhanded, treacherous bullshit Mike had pulled over the years, that was the worst, and I never forgave him for it."

The wine was nearly gone now, and Mulray took a short sip in order to conserve it. "Mike I think you already know about," he said. "Most of the guys smoked, but he was the worst of 'em all. In his prime he'd go through three packs a day. Anyhow, I guess it finally caught up to him. Just today I found out when I came in that he had been coughin' up blood and croaked durin' the off season. Mike had some good qualities I suppose, but he had plenty of bad ones, too. Say, I have a funny story about Big Mike. You remember that I told you what a good dancer he was when he was young? Well, he once told me, 'If I can get a woman to dance with me, I can get her to want me.' I have to admit, Mike did seem to hook up with a lot of the girls he danced with. The thing I could never figure out was, did they fuck him because he seduced them with his dancin', or did they fuck him because they were whores who also happened to like dancin'?"

Wiley stopped writing and asked, "What about Reenie? She and Rip seemed like a pretty good item. What happened with them?"

"Oh, Reenie." Mulray said. "She turned out to be a sad story. Ya see, she was madly in love with Rip. She never dated any other guys, even though Rip was away for eight or nine months a year. Every summer they would hook up, then Rip would leave. This went on for years and years. Finally, Reenie reached her forties, and she realized that Rip was never gonna feel the way about her that she felt about him. Rip was just the kinda guy who didn't want to be tied down. Anyway, Reenie quit workin' at the track one year and got a job at some tavern a couple of towns over. I used to stop by to see her every now and then to see how she was doin'. She tried to hide it, but it was easy to see that she was broken-hearted. I heard not that long ago that she never married and lives in a little apartment in Eatontown all by herself. I always felt so sorry for her. She was a great woman, she just fell in love with the wrong guy."

"I'm curious about one other thing," Wiley said. "I'm sure you realize that a lot of your stories won't make it into the paper, including the one about the cowgirl, Becky Lou. But I was wondering, off the record of course, did you ever meet up with her again?"

Mulray chuckled. "No, that was the one and only time I connected with her. Man, that was insane. I made it to Hot Springs for a couple more years before I stopped goin' south, but I never saw her again. I figure that was a good thing, though. She was gorgeous but she seemed wild and reckless, and I'm pretty sure that anybody who spent any amount of time with her would be askin' for trouble. Maybe I was lucky to meet her that one time and move on."

Mulray puffed his cigar, then said, "I suppose you want to know about me, too, huh? Alright. Well, to tell ya the truth, I've had a hell of a run. The first day I walked into this place all those years ago I could never have guessed how it would affect my whole life. I thought I would just be workin' a summer or two and finish up college. Obviously, it didn't work out that way. Once I got a taste of this life, it was impossible for me to leave. Ya know, the money was fabulous, the work was easy, and there was an adventure around every corner. I worked for Issy for the first few years. Then, in the early 60s, I bought a sheet called *Collier's* and went out on my own. I had become a pretty damned good handicapper by then and I guess it was just a natural progression for me. I loved Issy and made a lot of money with him, but I couldn't shake the itch to work for myself. Anyway, the first couple of years was pretty rough. The sheet wasn't a very good seller when I bought it, and it took a lot of hard work to get the sales up. Even though I was technically in competition with Issy, he helped me as much as he could. He sold my sheets along with his own on the train gate and made sure I got a fair shake. Back when I went on my own, the big tracks had a lot of different sheets. This joint had twelve or thirteen at that time. The competition was fierce. All of the hustlers were in their prime and nearly every day there were a couple of sheets that had a big day. But, by the 70s, as the crowds got smaller, some of the sheets began to drop out. Some of the hustlers were startin' to get a little long in the tooth, too. *The Owl*, *Ad-Tab*, *Dan Carter*, *the Wizard*, *Domino*, and a couple of others were gone by the mid 80s. After that, the 90s saw *Turfmaster*, *New York Handicap*, and *Longshot Riley* bite the dust. By then, sales were nothin' like they had been durin' the boom days. One of the reasons was that the racetracks had started to print a different kind of program in the early 90s that had past performances and, of most importance to us, handicapped selections with comments. Even though our picks were certainly better, the ones in the program were *free*, and that's impossible to compete against. The management of the tracks had fucked up again, of course. The treacherous scumbags, led by Handel, figured they could destroy two industries with one swoop. They expected to cripple the *Racin' Form* and decimate the tip sheets by puttin' out that expanded program. That jerkoff Handel proudly bragged one mornin', 'We've declared war on the *Racing Form*!' Imagine that. *The Daily Racin' Form*—the publication that helped to make horse racin' playable by the average guy—was being openly attacked by this weasel. Well, with regards to tip sheets, what they did accomplish was the contraction of information that bettors used to base their wagers on. When there were several tip sheets and they were all sellin' good, there was a diversity of opinion that tended to spread the bettin' out among a number of horses. With everyone usin' the same info from the new programs, most of the money wound up on one or two horses, which lowered the payoffs. It doesn't take a rocket scientist to figure out that bettin' pools can be more favorable when the money isn't concentrated in one place. Whatever. Just another way this game has been mismanaged almost into oblivion. At the end, there was only me with *Collier's*, and *Lawton*, which Big Mike had 'inherited' when Issy left. We've been real lucky to break even the past few years."

"You say that there hasn't been much money in recent years. Are you broke? Were you able to save any of the money you made during the good years?" Wiley asked.

"Well, I suppose the answer to that question is yes—and no. I mean, in the early years, I pretty much went through most of my money. I would occasionally save some but, I hung with Rip, and I blew quite a bit of dough durin' the period. Drinkin'. Gamblin'. Eatin' at expensive restaurants. Takin' trips to Havana. Ya know, we made good money, but we pissed it away as fast as we got it because we knew tomorrow there would always be more. But after a couple of years of that, I wound up gettin' married and once I did, I stopped goin' to Florida in the winter and just worked the New Jersey circuit. I got a little more responsible and started to save a lot of the money I made. We bought a house and have been livin' a mostly normal life for the past 35 years or so. My wife had a good job, so we've always been able to get by, even when things started to drop off."

A woman approached the two men as they sat chatting. She was a distinguished, tall brunette and she wore a pair of designer sunglasses. She stopped in front of Mulray and, without acknowledging Wiley, began to speak. "I just heard about Mike, hon. Are you alright?"

"Yeah, sure. Thanks for askin'." Mulray said. "It was a bit of a shock at first, but I'm over it now. One of us had to go first, and considerin' the alternative, I can deal with it."

Mulray turned to Wiley and said, "I'm sorry, Jay. This is my wife, Kerra. Kerra, this is Mr. Jay Wiley from the *Racin' Form*. He wanted to know about the tip sheet business."

"Hello, Mr. Wiley, it's nice to meet you." Kerra said. "I guess if you want to know about any of that, Bill is your man."

Wiley nodded to Kerra and said, "Nice to meet you, too, Kerra. And yes, Bill has told me some terrific stories about the sheets. He actually mentioned you a couple of times. I was going to ask him about you."

"I looked for Kerra as soon as I got back from Florida in '58," Mulray said. "I had thought about her all that winter. Luckily, she wanted to see me, too. We dated for a couple of years, then when I came back from Florida in the spring of '60, we were married. After that, I never left Jersey to hustle sheets again."

Mulray looked at the track where the horses for the first race were entering after being saddled. The announcer introduced the field as they circled in front of the grandstand in the post parade.

"That reminds me. Remember my favorite horse, Tim Tam?" Mulray asked. "In case you didn't know what happened to him, well, he won the first two legs of the Triple Crown, then just when it looked like he was gonna take the Belmont, he broke down nearin' the wire. Poor boy hobbled across the finish line in second place and never raced again. Broken sesamoid bone. I'm not sure if Rip was right about him bein' sore, but I have to admit it was all pretty coincidental if he wasn't. Anyway, Tim Tam was one of the greatest horses ever, but nobody ever talks about him anymore. Why? Because he didn't win the Triple Crown. If he holds up for a few more seconds in the Belmont, he takes his place alongside the all-time greats."

"So, now that you're the last of the touts, what are your plans? Are you going to continue to sell your sheets?" Wiley asked.

"No," Mulray said. "I don't see the point of hangin' around here by myself. It just wouldn't be the same. I suppose the only reason I hung on the past coupla years is because somebody else was doin' it, too. It's kinda sad, but it's over now. The crowds.

The money. The camaraderie. The great times we had. It's all gone and it's never comin' back."

Mulray looked in turn at the track, the odds board, the flowers suspended from boxes on the upper levels of the clubhouse, and the benches on the ground level. "Ya know, I'm really gonna miss this old girl," he said. "After all, I've had summer love affairs with her for more than forty years."

As Mulray sat contemplating his departure, a solitary tear ran down his cheek. He brushed it away with the back of his hand and, his voice cracking with emotion, said, "Sayin' goodbye is a lot harder than I thought it would be."

Mulray took a moment to regain his composure, then stood and said, "Well, that's about it. There's nothin' left to tell, and there's nothin' left for me here." He took the last swig of wine, then threw the empty bottle into a nearby trash can. After thanking Wiley and saying his goodbyes, he locked arms with Kerra and the couple slowly strolled through the clubhouse, down the old red brick stairs and into the parking lot. The first race went off and, when Mulray heard the announcer, he instinctively stopped in his tracks. He resisted the urge to turn around, though, and after a few seconds he resumed walking.

Mulray and his wife got into their car and drove away.

He never entered a racetrack again.

Manufactured by Amazon.ca
Bolton, ON

10369186R00109